The Age of Enlightenment

A volume
in
THE DOCUMENTARY HISTORY
of
WESTERN CIVILIZATION

THE AGE OF ENLIGHTENMENT

edited by
LESTER G. CROCKER

WALKER AND COMPANY
New York

THE AGE OF ENLIGHTENMENT
Introduction, editorial notes, translations by the editor, and
compilation Copyright © 1969 by Lester G. Crocker.

Library of Congress Catalog Card Number: 69-15561.

Printed in the United States of America.

Published in the United States of America in
1969 by Walker and Company, a division of the
Walker Publishing Company, Inc.

Published simultaneously in Canada by
The Ryerson Press, Toronto.

Volumes in this series are published in association
with Harper & Row, Publishers, Inc., from
whom paperback editions are available in Harper
Torchbooks.

Contents

Introduction

THE FIRST, fundamental, and thorniest question is simply this: What was the Enlightenment? As with other catchwords the danger lies in attributing to it an absolute historical quality, which in practice turns out to be some rational scheme that appeals to a given writer. Thus the Enlightenment, it has been said, was characterized by unlimited confidence in man and his future, the Renaissance was the overthrow of medievalism by the rediscovery of the ancient world, and Romanticism was the revolt of the individual against rule and limit. Now there is truth in all these statements; yet each falsifies the historical reality by a process of simplification that abstracts from a complex, contradictory fabric of interactions of all kinds. The act of giving a simplified coherence to historical realities that escape our powers of conceptualization, of neatly categorizing and labeling them, has an almost irresistible appeal to the mind. We must beware of this betrayal of history.

To speak of the Enlightenment, then, is to speak at once of a historical fact and an ideal reconstruction. It is fact inasmuch as a group of writers, working self-consciously for over a hundred years, sought to enlighten men, using critical reason to free minds from prejudices and unexamined authority, and—somewhat later within that period—using the same weapon to explore the ills of society and to devise remedies. It is an ideal reconstruction inasmuch as the ideas of the period were a vortex of conflicting theories and proposals, at once a continuation of the past and a foreshadowing of the future. From this vortex historians, who inevitably make an *a priori* choice of the facts worth looking for and arrange them according to patterns of thought they find congenial, have often abstracted those that might be formed into a coherent movement; it is usually one characterized by optimism, liberalism, the teaching of morals, and other appealing tendencies. The idea of the Enlightenment is valid (like that of the Renaissance, Romanticism, or other labels imposed on history by a later time) only if we open our minds to the fullness of reality. We must realize that the Enlightenment did not exist in any such pure form as we should like to give it; that it was imbedded in the total matrix of the eighteenth century; that this matrix fashioned it from all sides, creating a complex of dynamic, dialectical tensions. The matrix included, among other elements, class interests, political and ecclesiastical authority, religious convictions, the progress of science, the challenge to values, changing views of history, new economic theories, competing views of man, political dissatisfaction. The tensions generated involved the role of nature and culture, the claims of individuals and society, freedom and order, traditionalism and revolt.

⟋ What we call the Enlightenment gradually took shape in individual minds, over several generations, before it became conscious of itself as a movement during the late 1740's. The principal galvanizing forces were Voltaire's ceaseless efforts in propagandizing and in whipping up "party" spirit,[1] and the prolonged battle over the *Encyclopédie*, which served to unite many of the *philosophes*, as we call the writers who were engaged in furthering the goals of the Enlightenment.[2] The *philosophes* were more often than not at odds among themselves on the answers they proposed to various questions or problems. Their solidarity lay in their awareness of a common foe—the *status quo*, and those who supported it, particularly Christianity and the Church. It lay also in their agreement on what the questions and problems were. The *philosophes* held certain ideas and aims in common. Among these were religious tolerance (belief in toleration of all ideas as well as personal tolerance was not universal among the *philosophes*); the conviction that human life can be improved through the improvement of society, since men are (more or less) shaped by laws and government; the idea that the enlightened group should influence those

[1] On this subject see John Pappas, *Voltaire and d'Alembert* (Bloomington, Ind.: Indiana University Press, 1962).

[2] The word *philosophes* is also vague and elastic. Rousseau was an enemy of the *philosophes*, but the label is often applied to him because of his early association with them and his opposition to the Old Régime. The author of the article "Philosophe" in the *Encyclopédie* defined a *philosophe* as one who "trampling on prejudice, tradition, universal consent, authority, in a word all that enslaves most minds, dares to think for himself, to go back and search for the clearest general principles, to admit nothing except on the testimony of his experience and his reason." The *philosophes* were the priests, soldiers, and propagandists of the new spirit of reason, tolerance, and progress.

who govern, both directly and through public opinion. Their
stance rested on a base of secularism and humanism. Regardless of
their varying religious beliefs, all the *philosophes* held that the
proper business (if there was any) of organized churches was the
salvation of souls. Science, government, economic policy, even
(many thought) moral values and personal morality had to be
freed from the dead hand of Christian authority. The Enlightenment was for unfettered critical reason, for social experience to
indicate what course men should take in meeting the challenges
involved in ameliorating human affairs. God, if he existed, had no
influence on these—Bayle had demonstrated that, before the end of
the seventeenth century. To the *philosophes*, churches were what
we would now call "power groups" and, like all such groups,
interested primarily in themselves. Revealed religions were fantasies
or downright frauds. Christianity, especially, was hostile to the
demands of human nature and pretended (the critics claimed) to
direct men away from their self-interest in this life to a mythical
paradise in a nonexistent life beyond. Reaction against the Christian
world view and religious control of thought had been the very
origin of the freethinking (*libertin*) movement in the seventeenth
century. The *philosophes* were united by the conviction, above all
else, that man must control his own destiny for the sole purpose of
a better life on earth and that he must do everything possible to
enlarge that control./

This program and state of mind had been formed gradually out
of many influences. Like any other period, the eighteenth century
was a confluence of earlier events and intellectual developments,
which it shaped by its own historic character into what appears to
us as a relatively stable system of dynamic tensions. The stability
was imperfect, or at least temporary, and the French Revolution
wrote an end to it. But part of the Enlightenment flowed as a
legacy (called good by some, evil by others) into the new systems
which were its successors in the history of Western culture.

Christianity was a world view with metaphysical and moral
dimensions, a value hierarchy, and a political institution, particularly in a Catholic country like France. For a millennium and a half
the most significant factor in European culture, it fashioned the
individual psyche and suffused the social fabric. Since the rejection
of Christianity and the substitution of a secular philosophy were at
the core of the new outlook (even though more conservative

reformers held onto a vague Christianity as a moral safeguard, a
social stabilizer, or even a personal faith), the eighteenth century
inevitably turned back to classical antiquity. In art and in literature
the influence of Greece and Rome remained strong. Even the
Quarrel of the Ancients and the Moderns (see p. 14) and the
campaign against Homer, which formed one bridge between the
seventeenth and the eighteenth centuries, worked in this direction.
In the realm of ideas, the ancient philosophers were thoroughly
read by the *philosophes*. The atomism of Democritus and Lucretius, the moral works of Plutarch, Cicero, and Seneca, the politics
of Plato and Aristotle permeated eighteenth-century thought.

The Renaissance—as we vaguely denominate a period that spans
four centuries—had few philosophers of the stature of the Ancients; but its intellectual stirrings were the real headwaters of the
Enlightenment. A combination of critical rationalism and recrudes-
cent naturalism, especially in the Mediterranean countries, had led
to the questioning of traditional beliefs and values. The works of
Machiavelli (1469–1527) and Fernando de Rojas's *La Celestina*
(1499), for instance, are no longer the joyous diversions of the
medieval *fabliaux* or Boccaccio's *Decameron*, but give a view,
impregnated with moral nihilism, of politics and human relations,
of men and their lives. The Copernican revolution, as it slowly
made its way into the European mind, had profound effects. As the
closed world gave way to an infinite universe, cosmic anguish was
born (Pascal's *"le silence éternel de ces espaces infinis m'effraie"*);
the security of a hierarchical Creation in which everything, especially man, had a proper place and a meaning, faded into cosmic
disorder and the specter of meaninglessness (John Donne's "Tenth
Anniversary"). The loftiest minds, Shakespeare, Cervantes, and
others, were perplexed by the human situation as they now saw it.
Intellectual developments such as these undermined the hold of the
Church, which was already weakened by internal abuses and dis-
sensions. Erasmus, remaining within Christianity, propagated a
rationalistic humanism. But the Protestant Reformation, an out-
come of economic and cultural changes as well as of the inward
decay of Catholicism, destroyed the monolithic power of the
Church of Rome. Luther's affirmation of the evil nature of men
and the need for a despotic state was essentially similar to that
which Thomas Hobbes was to develop in *Leviathan* (1651), although Hobbes was nonreligious and close to Machiavelli in his

realism. In sixteenth-century France, Montaigne's pungent essays had also applied a skeptical reason to all human activities. In *"Apologie de Raimond Sebond,"* whatever his motives may have been, Montaigne showed that man was not essentially a rational being, that his reason was untrustworthy, and that, despite his having been created with an immortal soul and in God's image, he was close to the animals—indeed, inferior to them. Thus the traditional idea of the world, of the state, and of man was in each instance challenged.

The seventeenth-century atmosphere was dominated by the Catholic Counter Reformation, which followed the Council of Trent (1545–63). In France, the absolute monarchy of Louis XIV allied itself with an all-powerful Church to repress internal opposition. But this period of reaction had unexpected results: the reduction of the nobility to political futility weakened the feudal basis of the régime. However, the rising middle class of merchants, bankers, tax farmers, and lawyers did not yet challenge the predominance and privileges of the decaying aristocracy, but rather sought to assert its own importance and to rise into the *noblesse de robe*. The Church overreached itself with the revocation (1685) of the Edict of Nantes which, since 1598, had brought religious peace to a strife-torn land. The ensuing intolerance and persecution of the Protestants not only outraged many Frenchmen as a cruel and senseless remnant of a bygone age but also weakened France economically, as the harassed Huguenots sought haven in England, Germany, the Low Countries, and the American colonies, taking their skills and industry with them. Respect for the Church was further undermined by its own intestine quarrels. The authoritarian Bossuet crushed the mystical and sentimental religious movement known as Quietism and broke the free-spirited Fénelon, a bishop who supported it. Far more serious was the quarrel between the worldly, practical, often morally compromising Jesuits and the Jansenists, whose moral rigor covered a fundamentalist, puritanical reaction against the worldliness and moral weaknesses of Church and society. The central Jansenist tenets of predestination and salvation of the elect were close to the Calvinist heresy; their impact on the minds of many Frenchmen was to emphasize God's incomprehensibility in human terms and to abolish his absolute goodness. The dispute, waged fanatically on both sides, was to last a century, despite papal condemnation and Louis XIV's burning of

Port-Royal, the Jansenist center (1712); it lasted, in fact, until the expulsion of the Jesuits from France in 1762. Its disputations, sometimes written with great skill (Pascal's *Lettres provinciales*, 1656–57), made the public into judges of the quarrel to the discredit of both parties, while its political extensions, in the eighteenth century, pitted the Jansenist courts (*parlements*), which represented the upper-middle classes, against the king (Louis XV).[3]

Beneath the splendor and pomp of Versailles, decay was beginning to set in, and the forces of resistance were far from extinguished. The aristocracy, humiliated by royal power, lived a ritualized social existence that covered its growing sense of futility and its moral weakness.[4] Louis XIV's megalomania led France through a series of unprofitable wars which, combined with his extravagance, undid the constructive economic policies of Colbert and bled the nation white. Misery spread throughout the countryside. Between 1695 and 1715 the population fell from twenty to seventeen million. Towns declined and were overrun with beggars. The increasing accumulation of wealth in the hands of the Church exacerbated a bad situation. Under such conditions, people began to grumble, and some began to think. Toward the close of the seventeenth century, a few voices dared to express themselves in protest. La Bruyère's *Caractères* (1688–96) contained a coruscating satire of France's decadence. Fénelon's popular *Les Aventures de Télémaque* (1699) was an outspoken object lesson in the proper conduct of kings. Five years earlier he had written a remarkable, anonymous letter to Louis XIV, painting the desperate condition of France and placing the blame on the king's love of war. "The whole of France," he wrote, "is nothing but a huge poorhouse, desolated and without resources." Even before these open protests, La Fontaine, in his *Fables* (1660–94), had here and there drawn a similar picture and attributed the peasants' misery to soldiers, taxes, creditors, and forced labor.

Meanwhile, intellectual divergence from the established ideology continued to flourish in a way that seemed quite independent of the social factors. The profoundest influence was exercised by the

---

[3] On Jansenism, see Robert Shackleton, "Jansenism and the Enlightenment," *Studies on Voltaire and the Eighteenth Century* (Geneva: Institut et Musée Voltaire, Les Délices), LVII, 1387–97.
[4] See F. Gaiffe, *L'Envers du grand siècle* (Paris: A. Michel, 1924).

philosophy of Descartes.[5] While Descartes's metaphysics and scientific hypotheses were to be rejected and ridiculed in the eighteenth century, his basic assumptions and his method—rationalistic deduction from "clear ideas" and the critical examination by reason of all notions—were to leave an indelible imprint on the French intellect. In the fields of scientific and cosmological speculation, Descartes represents a turning point between the medieval and the modern. Rejecting the authority of an entrenched medieval system of thought, he made the individual mind the criterion of certitude. Separating science and philosophy from religion, he proceeded as if the latter did not exist and deduced a system of the world on purely rational grounds. His great assumption was that sensory experience could and had to be reduced to mechanics and then to mathematics (for him, geometry), that is, to measurables. The world was a machine, indirectly created by God, but operating by itself on mechanical principles. Animals are machines, or automata, of a complex kind; and so are men, at least their bodies, though they are distinguished from the beasts by the presence of a soul. There is no essential difference, wrote Descartes, between a living man's body and a watch or other automaton; the body of a dead man is like that of a broken watch.

Descartes's great rival, Pierre Gassendi (1592–1655), also contributed to the rise of scientific materialism, although his method and principles were quite different. Combining the atomist theories of Epicurus and Lucretius (which he tried to reconcile with Christianity) with Renaissance advances in physics, he saw the task of science as the investigation of a world of material particles, possessing inertia and moving in a vacuum. This view contrasted with Descartes's definition of matter as extension and his description of the universe as a plenum. For Gassendi, too, God had only provided the initial impulse, after which all movements and combinations of particles were determined by the laws of mechanics. Although Gassendi had in mind a finalistic role for God and so was less radical than Descartes, he nonetheless made explicit the implications of the new science. At the same time, he also introduced a theory of hylopathism into his physics and his biology. Fore-

[5] *Discours de la méthode* (1637), *Méditations métaphysiques* (1641), *Principes de la philosophie* (1644), *Traité des passions de l'âme* (1650). See Aram Vartanian, *Diderot and Descartes* (Princeton, N.J.: Princeton University Press, 1953).

shadowing Diderot, he explained physical and biological phenomena by a notion of latent sensitivity, whose source is a certain
organization of atoms.

Another important undercurrent, less scientific in character, was
represented by a group called the *libertins*. The *libertin* attitude
had its roots in the naturalistic thought of antiquity and the
Renaissance. It formed a kind of underground resistance throughout the seventeenth century, which flowed into the larger pool of
influences that fashioned the eighteenth-century climate. The principal writers of this group (among whom Gassendi is also sometimes classified) were Théophile de Viau and Cyrano de Bergerac,
and, in more disguised fashion, La Fontaine, Molière, and La Roche-
foucauld; also the poets Chaulieu and La Fare, and the *littérateur*,
Saint-Evremond. These men were united (except Gassendi) by an
anti-Christian attitude. They doubted the immortality of the soul.
The purpose of life, they believed, was to find happiness here and
now. Human motivation could be reduced to two impulses: the
seeking of pleasure and the avoidance of pain. While some of the
libertins were also libertines, many believed in wise moderation in
the pursuit of pleasure.[6] As the new century began, their gathering
places, such as the salon of Ninon de Lenclos and the Société du
Temple (which the young Voltaire frequented), became the
centers of intellectual life. Later other salons sprang up around the
philosophes, and were headed by fashionable ladies with an intellectual bent (Mme. Geoffrin, Mme. du Deffand, Mlle. de Lespinasse,
Mme. de Lambert, Mme. Necker, and others).

Another stream of *libertin* thought, more radical in character,
expressed itself in a flow of clandestine manuscripts, some of which
were printed in the eighteenth century. These underground writings were quite influential, especially in the first half of the century. They were consistently antireligious, frequently argued for
determinism and against free will, and demanded a secular morality
related to man's need for happiness. More infrequently, they verged
on moral anarchism.[7] One of the most important was the *Testa-
ment* of Jean Meslier, a priest who had become an atheist, a politi-

---

[6] See J. S. Spink, *French Free-Thought from Gassendi to Voltaire* (London:
The Athlone Press, 1960).
[7] I. O. Wade, *The Clandestine Organization and Diffusion of Philosophic
Ideas in France from 1700 to 1750* (Princeton, N.J.: Princeton University
Press, 1938).

cal anarchist, and a proponent of the rights of the individual, which he carried virtually to the point of moral nihilism.

The two overtowering figures who bridge the seventeenth and the eighteenth centuries in France are Fontenelle and Bayle. Various writers in the period of French classicism had applied Cartesian rational analysis to the study of human nature. Fontenelle and Bayle turned this analysis, more broadly, upon the significant intellectual problems of the day.

Fontenelle (1657–1757) wrote for the elegant public of the salons. Wit and clarity distinguish his style, while skepticism characterizes his intellect. In his *Histoire des oracles* (1687), Fontenelle holds up to ridicule the pagan belief in oracles. His criticism is so general and yet so pointed that it implies an attack on credulity as such and subtly involves the Christian religion. The most popular of Fontenelle's books was his *Entretiens sur la pluralité des mondes* (1686), which responded to a growing interest in the sciences. In simple, almost fictional style, he explains the Copernican system, urges observation and experimentation instead of metaphysics, and promotes the antiprovidentialist view that the world was not made for man. Fontenelle's *Dialogues des morts* (1683) is a wider ranging work that delves into the foibles of human nature and insists on the all-pervasiveness of self-interest as motivation and of the desire for recognition and fame. An anonymous work also attributed to Fontenelle, *Traité de la liberté* (circulated in manuscript, not printed until 1743), attacks the doctrine of free will.

Pierre Bayle (1647–1706) was a Protestant who spent most of his life in exile. Little wonder he was one of the first and most powerful proponents of religious tolerance, which was to become a major theme of the *philosophes* and a focal point of their attacks on Christiantity and the Catholic Church. His *Pensées diverses sur la comète* (first edition 1682) was also an attack against superstition and credulity. Two of the paradoxes it contained—Bayle often sought to shock his readers' complacency by paradoxes—were to remain live issues. It had been taken for granted that religion and a belief in God were necessary to the social order. Not so, declared Bayle. Look at men's behavior, he argued. Christians are often more wicked than atheists. The springs of conduct are the same in all, and they are not the speculative opinions men may hold, but their passions. Men are naturally inclined to evil; although they are rational beings, aware of moral law, their judgments are corrupted and their reason enslaved by their passions or self-interest. What better proof of this than Christianity itself, supposedly a religion of peace and brotherly love, with its history of violence, persecutions, wars, and cruelty? No, social order depends on fear of punishment and the desire for approval and esteem. All men, atheists or Christians, follow the social norms and judge others according to them when their own passions are not involved. If anything, atheists will be better than Christians, since the latter are encouraged to cruel intolerance by beliefs that arouse their aggressive passions. Furthermore, Bayle goes on, a really Christian society could not subsist, with its disinterest in worldly things and its passivity in a world governed by force.

Bayle's major work was his *Dictionnaire historique et critique* (first edition 1697), which was widely read in the eighteenth century.[8] In this great work Bayle added an incomparable erudition to his already subtle logic. Applying Cartesian doubt to a new field, history, he sought factual truth, emphasizing rigorous documentation and historical methodology. With devastating lucidity, he destroyed Christian mythology and confounded theologians who imagined that they possessed rational proofs for their doctrines. His attacks on paganism and polytheism were really directed against Catholicism. The argument still rages whether Bayle was really a skeptic or rather a fideist who, by revealing reason's powerlessness, wished to turn men to blind faith. The controversy is futile. Bayle *was* a skeptic, since he shows the contradictions, incoherences, and absurdities that ruin every philosophical position. If indeed he went beyond rational skepticism to faith (and the evidence is not really convincing), that was a personal commitment which does not nullify his skepticism. This is evidenced by the fact that his own faith passed unnoticed and had no effect on the influence of his skepticism. In one sense the two positions, skepticism and fideism, were identical: both maintained that we cannot look to reason for answers to basic questions. (In this regard, Bayle, and not the English empiricists, is the true predecessor of Hume.) Whether or not Bayle intended to turn his readers to faith, his influence was entirely in the opposite direction. While

[8] Many of his ideas were expounded more systematically in various polemical works—Bayle loved controversy and delighted in confounding his opponents. These were brought together after his death in his *Oeuvres diverses* (1727-31).

Descartes begins with doubt, Bayle remains in doubt, intellectually at least. As we shall see later, on no question did he so agitate the consciences of his time and of the eighteenth century as that of the problem of evil and suffering in a world supposedly created by God.

One of the targets of Bayle's logic was the philosophy of Spinoza. Erroneously considered a materialist, atheist, and immoralist by a period in which few were prepared to understand him, Spinoza exerted a considerable influence in those same directions. His *Ethics* (1677) was pillaged for the passages which, taken out of context on a naturalistic basis, do seem to argue forcefully in favor of a naturalistic or materialistic philosophy. His *Tractatus Theologico-Politicus* (1670) was a storehouse of political ideas, diversely interpreted as propounding individual rights and liberties, or their surrender to the state; it also contained an erudite and vigorous criticism of biblical incoherences and miracles—a task which Bayle was to carry even further and the eighteenth century to take up with renewed relish.[9]

The great German philosopher Leibniz was also poorly understood and often mocked for his obscure metaphysical ideas, such as "pre-established harmony" and the "principle of sufficient reason." He was mostly known through Wolff's unfaithful simplification of his philosophy. Leibniz's *Théodicée* (1710) was an exculpation of God for the existence of evil. In *Candide* (1759) Voltaire mocked his doctrine that this is "the best of all possible worlds." Nevertheless, Leibniz's influence was far greater than eighteenth-century writers were willing to admit. In his *Monadologie* (1714), he transformed the ancient atomistic tradition. For Leibniz each ultimate unit of being (the monad) is a kind of spiritual atom, independent of all others, yet mirroring the universe; it is also a center of force, striving to persist in its being and containing within itself the principle of its changes, or its individuation. All monads are interrelated in the pre-established harmony of the universe. In this way Leibniz brought into eighteenth-century philosophy the concept of a dynamic, pluralistic universe, continuous but changing. With this theory went a new idea of organism. Whether it be the monad or the universe, an organism, Leibniz held, is more than

[9] See P. Vernière, *Spinoza et la pensée française avant la Révolution* (Paris: Presses Universitaires de France, 1954).

the sum of its parts—this "more" being the inner relations and reciprocities of the parts.

We have not mentioned England thus far, but the influence of English thought was about to make itself felt. Cosmopolitanism and an interest in alien cultures were characteristic of the eighteenth-century spirit of inquiry and of the universality of its minds. England did not have an Enlightenment in the same sense as France. It was not necessary, for that country was already relatively "enlightened" in the sense we give to that word. Economic and political freedom had been won for the bourgeoisie and the intellectuals in the glorious Revolution of 1688. There were no major grievances against the authorities or the social structure. In a less rigid and less authoritarian society, where there was no union between an absolute monarch and an exclusive Catholic Church, where the middle class was stronger, basic questions had been continuously and publicly examined with little fuss. Consequently there was no core group with a self-conscious mission to revise society and liberate the mind. Still another consequence was the absence of extremists and rebels, of radical reformers and utopians. There was also a greater adherence to the empirical, to what *was*, than to abstract rationalism. In fact, there was considerable opposition to the ideas of the French Enlightenment in England; an opposition which—contrary to the situation in France—engaged the talents of some of the best writers, including Swift, Dr. Johnson, and later, Blake and Burke. As in Germany, the Enlightenment was moderate and not anti-Christian in its stance.

England's greatest impact on the thought of the period was in science. Like Descartes, but in an entirely different way, Francis Bacon (1561–1626) stands at the turning point between medieval and modern science. In his *Novum Organum* (1620) he sought to set forth the foundations of science: the collection of facts, experimentation, and common sense freed of all rationalistic systems such as the Aristotelian. Sounding a new note that was to be heard far and wide, he demanded that science prepare men for the mastery of nature and the creation of a better world. Useful as his methodology was, he was not really able to formulate the modern scientific method. This was the work of Galileo (1564–1642).[10]

---

[10] Galileo's chief works are the *Dialogue Concerning the Two Chief Systems of the World* (1632) and the *Discourses on Two New Sciences* (1638).

Galileo not only founded the science of dynamics, but formulated and illustrated the scientific method as a combination of experiment and induction with the deduction of mathematically formulated laws. Hypotheses are to be formulated by induction from observations and then tested. The essence of the revolution was the substitution of quantitative methods for qualitative, particularly (in that period) in regard to the motion of bodies and celestial mechanics, a step that for the first time made space and time essential elements of physics and revealed the physical universe to be material and mechanical, governed by invariable laws.

Galileo's method found its most rapid acceptance in England. There the struggle that had to be waged against theological authoritarianism and pseudoscience could be carried on in favorable circumstances. In 1662 the Royal Society was founded (following a suggestion by Bacon in the *New Atlantis*), with an announced Baconian emphasis on utility that it soon abandoned. (The French Académie Royale des Sciences was established in 1667.)

Scientific activity was intense and productive during this period. The greatest name was that of Isaac Newton, whose theory of universal gravitation (*Principia Mathematica*, 1687) was to have a vast impact on the eighteenth century. In France, after a period of opposition from the Cartesians, Newton became the object of adulation, and the French often quoted Pope's famous lines:

> Nature and nature's laws lay hid in night;
> God said, "Let Newton be," and all was light.

What struck the minds of eighteenth-century men was that Newton had demonstrated that the universe is a machine which operates on the basis of a single law, a rational law that can be easily formulated and understood. They longed to extend this method to social and political problems, for nature and human nature, they reasoned, must be equally uniform and subject to laws.

From the progress of science and technology, which was observable in navigation, hydraulics, and optics, in such inventions as the thermometer, the barometer, and the microscope, arose the important idea of progress. While the interaction of science with economic, technological, and social factors was perhaps not realized, it was understood that the progress of science depends essentially on transformations of intellectual attitudes, such as the dissolution of the traditional notion of a cosmos, the geometrization of space, and

the invention of higher mathematics. In the Quarrel of the Ancients and the Moderns,[11] the "moderns" utilized the advance of
science as one of their main arguments. Progress was to become the
"faith of the Enlightenment." But it must be emphasized that most
eighteenth-century thinkers believed only in a more or less limited
progress—some even in cycles, or a necessary equilibrium of happiness and unhappiness—and that progress concerned science and technology, government and laws, economic and social structure, and
education. Moreover, the *philosophes* were often opposed to
"overcivilization"; they believed that technical progress should halt
at some *moyen terme* at which men would be happiest. They
believed human nature to be immutable, so that the ultimate
problem was one of managing people—the solution to which
certainly required enlightenment as one factor. The idea of inevitable and unlimited progress was expressed by Turgot and
especially by Condorcet at the end of the century, but it became
widely held only in the nineteenth century, particularly after
Darwin, and then lasted until the shattering experience of World
War I.

There were other important English influences. Hobbes had
described a state of nature in which all men were at war with each
other and force was the sole natural law. Only by complete surrender to the absolute power of the state, wielded by a monarch,
could peace and order be maintained. Locke's democratic *Two
Treatises on Civil Government* (1690) had little influence in
France. On the other hand, his *Essay Concerning Human Understanding* (1690) placed him alongside Newton as one of the two
idols and tutelary gods of the Enlightenment. Locke demolished
the Cartesian psychology of innate ideas. He reduced the origin of
all ideas to sensations inscribing their messages on a blank slate.
From Locke's *Essay*, his successors deduced the "universal law" of
human nature that paralleled the Newtonian law of gravitation.
Men are actuated by two motives only: the desire for pleasure and
the aversion to pain. Taken together, sensationism (or sensualism,
as it is commonly called) and the pleasure principle led to the

[11] The Quarrel of the Ancients and Moderns designates the long controversy
which took place in France, and also in England, in the late seventeenth and
early eighteenth centuries over the relative merits of ancient and contemporary thinkers, writers, and artists. The discussion took on broad implications
and the impact of scientific progress became an important factor.

important conclusion of various eighteenth-century French writers
that men's conduct could be controlled.

Mandeville and Shaftesbury proposed two opposite viewpoints
on the moral life. The former's *Fable of the Bees*[12] expressed a
shocking paradox: men's vices are necessary to the prosperity of
society and to happiness. Are they really vices then? Shaftesbury,
on the other hand, was an optimist who thought man endowed
with a "moral sense," the satisfaction of which brought him happiness.[13] The universe, he declared, is a harmony of the true, the
good, and the beautiful, and men are happy when their enthusiasm
for this trinity re-creates an aesthetic harmony in their lives.
Nothing in the universe is really evil. Defining "nature" (like other
writers of the age) in a way that suited his own predilections and
ideology, Shaftesbury affirmed that men have self-affections that
are benign, an aggressive selfishness, which he calls "unnatural
affections," and a love of the good of all, which he terms "natural
affections."

Shaftesbury belongs to a group of deists who were well known
in France. Alexander Pope's widely read *Essay on Man* (1734)
propagated an optimistic, rationalistic deism that for a while seduced Voltaire, until the reality of evil darkened his outlook. More
combative were Anthony Collins, who argued effectively against
free will (*A Philosophical Enquiry Concerning Human Liberty*,
1717), Tindal, Chubb, and Toland, all of whom attacked Christianity. These British writers had to some extent been inspired by
the French skeptical tradition. Their diffusion in France became, in
turn, a strong reinforcement of the growing popularity of deism,
naturalism, and a secular morality.

While clandestine manuscripts circulated in abundance and many
minor books promoted a secular morality, the first masterpiece of
the new spirit was published by Montesquieu. The *Lettres persanes*
(1721) is a coruscating and spicy criticism of French institutions
and a plea for reason, justice, and tolerance. In 1734 Voltaire,
already famous as a poet and dramatist, published his *Lettres
philosophiques*, the product of his exile in England. In it, he described and praised the English social and political conditions,

---

[12] Published in 1705 under the title *The Grumbling Hive;* in 1714 it first
appeared under the title by which we know it: *The Fable of the Bees: or,
Private Vices, Publick Benefits.*
[13] *Characteristics of Men, Manners, Opinions, Times* (1711).

extolled that country's liberty and tolerance, its respect for commerce and the middle classes. He also expounded the philosophy of Bacon, Locke, and Newton and introduced the French to contemporary English literature. The *Lettres philosophiques* was condemned and Voltaire forced to flee to escape arrest, but the influence of his book was considerable.

The Age of Enlightenment may be roughly divided into three periods. The great changes in attitude, the crystallization of the new outlook, and the first skirmishes with authority took place, at an increasing tempo, between 1680 and 1745. Between 1746 and 1770, when most of the great works of the century were published and thought became more radical in many quarters, the battle reached and passed its climax. The next two decades witnessed a greater diffusion of the new thought and a general fermentation.

The "philosophic" group was to achieve self-consciousness and make important strides during the 1740's. A new turn in the development of scientific thought proved to be one important factor. Physics and astronomy had laid the foundations for a philosophy of materialism. Now French thinkers were turning away from physics and mathematics, and biology came to the forefront. The problem of life and of generation seemed to be the crux of philosophical interpretation in various areas. If man could explain how the living came from the nonliving, an answer to important metaphysical questions might be forthcoming.

To many minds life seemed to escape mechanism, to be radically different from the nonliving, in a word, to be a transcendental mystery not capable of scientific analysis. But, as we have seen, efforts were being made to bring the science of life into the naturalistic world view reached earlier by the physical sciences. Do organic matter and organic processes originate only in living systems, or do they derive from complex structures of matter which are explicable in terms of the known laws of the physical sciences? These questions are still debated today. Some noted biologists still maintain that the purposefulness of organisms, the adaptation of structure to function, and other properties of life are totally incomprehensible in chemical terms. In the main, however, advanced biological speculation in the eighteenth century pointed the way to the later developments of biology: living organisms are dynamic and changing systems, and their phenomena are amenable to the methods of physical analysis.

many theories

While the many theories that were debated are too complex to be analyzed here,[14] one dramatic development was the discovery by Abraham Trembley of the regenerative powers of the freshwater polyp. Trembley's work influenced La Mettrie, whose *L'Homme machine* (1747) was the first systematic treatise on materialism. The polyp showed that purposive motion, or a "built-in finalism," was a property of matter in its highly complex organization in living bodies. "The man-machine," writes one scholar, "was automatic in a manner that no man-made machine, requiring direction from without, could duplicate."[15] Thought, it followed, may be a result of organized matter. There is no such thing as freedom of the will or moral responsibility. Even more scandalous were La Mettrie's *Anti-Sénèque, ou Discours sur le bonheur* (1748) and his "Discours préliminaire." In these works he presented the first system of moral nihilism, deduced from his materialism. Moral limitations are neither rationally nor naturally justifiable, and everyone has the right to pursue his egoistic pleasure and self-aggrandizement. On the other hand, society has an equal right to protect itself by repressing those who hurt it. La Mettrie was excoriated throughout the century by the *philosophes* as well as by the pious. Some *philosophes* shared his views but condemned his publicizing them at the risk of fomenting immorality and social disorder. Nevertheless, La Mettrie remains one of the most original, consistent, and daring thinkers of the eighteenth century.

Maupertuis, like La Mettrie, was opposed to all systems not in accord with observed facts and to particular final causes.[16] In *Vénus physique* (1745), he approached the problem of heredity in a way that foreshadows modern genetics; but his ideas on this subject were largely ignored in his own time, which was committed to organismic rather than particulate biology. Maupertuis also tackled the problem of generation, both in that work and in the *Système de la nature* (1751), rejecting theories of the simultaneous creation of all germ cells by God (preformation, encase-

---

[14] See Jacques Roger, *Les Sciences de la vie dans la pensée française du XVIIIe siècle* (Paris: A. Colin, 1963).

[15] Aram Vartanian (ed.), in La Mettrie, *L'Homme machine*, (Princeton, N.J.: Princeton University Press, 1960), p. 19.

[16] On the most general level, Maupertuis's "law of least action" was a proof of God's existence and providence.

ment) in favor of epigenesis. Like chemical substances, he suggested, parts of the developing germ are attracted to each other by irresistible affinities to form the most complex organs. From this hypothesis he concluded that the ultimate particles, though physical, possess such qualities as desire, aversion, and memory, in elementary forms. Heredity depends on there being two germ cells. Variations are therefore possible, and all species may have come "from two single individuals" as a result of accidental changes in "the arrangement" of the "elementary particles." In his *Essai de cosmologie* (published in 1750, written earlier), Maupertuis pictures a universe of change and suggests a non-Darwinian idea of natural selection based on inner viability. Maupertuis thus carried further the thinking of Leibniz and that of La Mettrie. His conception of a dynamic universe in process of change, his incipient transformism, and his thinking on the problems of life and generation created a ferment that excited the imagination of Buffon, Diderot, and other writers.

The younger intellectuals like Diderot and Rousseau, who were still scarcely known, were to find 1748 an exciting year. Toussaint's *Les Moeurs*, a minor deistic work advocating a prudent secular morality, aroused the ire of the ever vigilant repressors, and the unlucky author was forced to seek safety in exile. In the same year, Montesquieu published one of the enduring masterpieces of the century, *De l'Esprit des lois*. Montesquieu's purpose was to conduct an empirical investigation leading to the formulation of the natural laws that determine political societies, in general and in the several historical forms into which they can be classified. He also sought to formulate laws for the major phases of their activities, such as legislation, religion, economics, population, and so forth. He laid great emphasis on the interrelationships of the social and political phenomena he examined. For these reasons, Montesquieu may be considered a founder of political science and sociology. In his work, however, he was not sufficiently empirical; despite his efforts, his mode of thinking remains basically Cartesian, or deductive. One feels that he had his generalities, or "clear ideas," well in mind and that he selected the data and interpreted it to prove them. Nevertheless, Montesquieu was to be attacked by later utopians, such as Morelly, Rousseau, and Mably, for being *too* empirical, for respecting the "is" more than the "ought." In fact, Montesquieu was a realist as well as a reformer. Unlike the utopians, he recognized the forces and the values of history and tradition and never thought it possible to start over from scratch in remaking men or their societies. He has affinities with Burke, while the utopians belong to a lineage that includes Plato and Marx.

The year 1749 was made exciting by two important publications. Diderot's first significant work, *Lettre sur les aveugles*, was the more dramatic of the two. Its picture of the universe is evolutionary, but not in the modern biological sense; it pictures matter, governed by necessary laws and by chance, disentangling itself from chaos and combining to produce by a process of trial and error all the inert and the living forms. God is excluded as a fruitless hypothesis—indeed, as an unacceptable notion in a blind, purposeless universe filled with ephemeral monstrosities. Even more significant is the ethical import: in such a world, man's moral notions are without any metaphysical basis or justification. Morality, like man, is an anomaly in the universe; it is made by man, and depends on his physiological and psychological make-up. Therefore, one might conclude (and this is Diderot's intention), the moral structure should reflect human nature and human needs; it should take into account that man is both an individual and a social being and not express absolutes based on fictitious supernatural revelation.

The other work was the beginning of one of the great monuments of eighteenth-century intellectual endeavor: the first three volumes of Buffon's *Histoire naturelle*, the fifteenth and final volume of which appeared in 1767. Aside from his contribution to the concepts of a developing physical and biological world, and to the questions of life and generation (he proposed the theory of a *"molécule vivante"*), Buffon helped to liberate science from the dilemma of choosing between Cartesian certitude (of which it was in any event incapable) and skepticism; that is, from the choice between an order beyond human knowledge and the acceptance of disorder. Nature, he contends, is a knowable order of phenomena, susceptible of formulation into laws independent of God and metaphysics. Science is man's strength to understand and to master nature. The idea of progress is built into such a concept.

The next auspicious year was 1751. It began with the publication of Rousseau's first work, the prize-winning *Discours sur les sciences et les arts*. This was the first stage in his radical critique of existing societies. Specifically it was an attack on intellectual and scientific progress and on luxury; Rousseau denounces these as instruments of social oppression and as causes of moral deterioration. Man is seen as an egocentric individual who has been unable to become a social being. Rousseau's friends did not realize that his essay contained the seeds of a philosophy utterly opposed to their own.

Not long after the *Discours* came the prolegomena to the great collaborative enterprise of the century—the *Encyclopédie*. This was the magnificent *Discours preliminaire* written by d'Alembert, who with Diderot was co-editor of the work. D'Alembert's essay expressed the Lockean philosophy of the age, with its emphasis on an empirical theory of knowledge and an experimental methodology. It also gave voice to the Enlightenment's hope for progress through knowledge and scientific discovery, whose social function is stressed. The *Discours préliminaire* is the exact counterpart of Rousseau's *Discours*. The first volume of the *Encyclopédie* followed later in 1751.

We cannot trace here the stormy course of that work.[17] The supporters of the Old Régime recognized it for what it was—the greatest weapon of the "subversives." The *Encyclopédie* was intended to be more than a compendium. Although one of its purposes was to make knowledge more accessible to the public, it expressed, sometimes openly, sometimes insidiously, rational criticisms of religions, of economic, and even of social and political institutions. The idea of progress through moderate change filled its pages. It gave an important place to manufacturing and the crafts and bespoke a new *bourgeois* society based on the spirit of liberalism. Tactically, it brought together a large number of writers who were conscious of their purpose. Attacks and persecution intensified as each volume appeared; indeed, the ultimate influence of the *Encyclopédie* may be ascribed less to its four thousand subscribers than to the interest aroused by opposition and persecution. In 1758, the scandal caused by Helvétius's *De l'Esprit* provoked a full-scale attack that led to the suppression of the work following publication of the seventh volume. Diderot, who had taken evasive measures against previous restrictions, rallied most of his collaborators and continued the work in secret. Early in 1766

[17] See P. Grosclaude, *Un audacieux message. L'Encyclopédie* (Paris: Nouvelles Editions Latines, 1951), and Jacques Proust, *Diderot et l'Encyclopédie* (Paris: A. Colin, 1962).

the remaining ten volumes were distributed. Persecution of the new ideas diminished; it seemed that the success of the *Encyclopédie* and the expulsion of the Jesuits (1762) had broken the back of oppression. Michelet picturesquely but correctly called the *Encyclopédie* the Trojan Horse of the Old Régime.

Other books left their mark on the 1750's. Condillac's *Traité des sensations* (1754) carried the Lockean psychology of the *tabula rasa* to its ultimate conclusions, opening the way for Helvétius's *De l'Esprit* and Rousseau's plan of behavioral control. These two systems are predicated on the belief that men can be shaped into a desired mold by controlling their habits, emotions, and thoughts through a conditioning process called "education." To these ideas Rousseau added fomentation of patriotic passions and censorship of public and private life. After he had carried his critique of a competitive, individual-centered society to extreme lengths in the "Préface de Narcisse" (1752) and the *Discours sur l'origine de l'inégalité* (1755), Rousseau developed his ideas on social organization and behavioral control in his article in the *Encyclopédie*, "Economie politique" (1755), in *La Nouvelle Héloïse* (1761), *Emile* (1762), the *Contrat social* (1762), and subsequent writings. Their true intent was not generally understood until the close of the century and later years. His use of words like "liberty," his concepts of popular sovereignty and suffrage were stimuli to those who believed in liberal democracy; but his ideal society was really a collectivist totalitarianism, and its later influence on Engels, Marx, and others was considerable. Another totalitarian system, that of Morelly (*Code de la nature*, 1755), had little impact.

Voltaire, throughout this period, had been ceaselessly active. His moderate deism and secular morality were expressed in the *Poème sur la loi naturelle* (1752–56). Increasing cynicism about human affairs and increasing pessimism about the human condition dominate some of his most enduring writings: *Zadig* (1747), *Micromégas* (1752), the *Essai sur les moeurs* (1753–56), which renewed the concepts of historiography, the *Poème sur le Désastre de Lisbonne* (1756), and *Candide* (1759). But Voltaire never lost his melioristic philosophy or his deep humanism. More and more he turned to social action, the spirit of which pervades his campaign against the Church, his *Traité sur la tolérance* (1763), and his essay on Beccaria (*Commentaire sur les délits et les peines*, 1766), as well as his campaigns to help those who were the victims of fanati-

cism and persecution (Calas, Sirven, La Barre). Voltaire's *Dictionnaire philosophique* (1764) was the summation of his philosophy,
and it remains one of his most living works. Voltaire was important
in other ways. Although he disagreed with Diderot's more radical
group on atheism, politics, and above all on the best strategy for
progress,[18] he remained by his mastery of propaganda the leader
of the *philosophes*, their most respected adherent, and the very
symbol of the new spirit.

Another group of some consequence was known as the Physiocrats. Its principal members were Quesnay, Le Mercier de la Ri-
vière, Dupont de Nemours, the Marquis de Mirabeau, and Le Trosne.
They were economists whose economic theories were part of
a metaphysical, political, and moral philosophy which postulated
a uniform natural order. If men only followed this order, they
would be happy and their societies prosperous. The Physiocrats
believed that natural law works through private good to the
general welfare; the conflicts of self-interest flow into a natural
social harmony. This belief led them to the theory of laissez faire.
However, as if to be sure that the natural order did work out, they
also favored enlightened despotism, or "legal despotism" (despotism within a framework of law) in their political theories, with the
proviso that the monarch would not interfere with the property
rights and the economic freedom of individuals.

From the seventies on, more radical theories of all sorts were
expressed with increasing boldness. D'Holbach's *Système de la
nature* (1770) created a sensation by its uncompromising atheism
and materialism. When others saw in this work a justification of
moral nihilism (as perhaps d'Holbach and Diderot also did in
private, and on intellectual grounds), the author went on in other
writings to propose plans for a moral and harmonious society. The
abbé Raynal's *Histoire philosophique et politique des établisse-
ments et du commerce des européens dans les deux Indes*, which
appeared in the same year, was only mildly critical of the régime.
In two later editions (1774, 1784), however, it was expanded by
Diderot and others into a powerful *machine de guerre*, second only
to the *Encyclopédie* in its effectiveness and far more radical. The
later editions emphasize tolerance, a "new" morality, and liberal
democratic ideas.

In the 1780's, as the battle for intellectual freedom seemed won

[18] See J. N. Pappas, *Voltaire and d'Alembert* (Bloomington, Ind.: Indiana
University Press, 1962).

and its heroes disappeared from the scene, the "philosophic" movement loses coherence. A new generation comes to the fore, sometimes given to extreme ideas, often more impatient to effectuate reforms. Perhaps they sensed the decline and fall of the old society, but the *esprit de réforme* did not become an *esprit révolutionnaire* until the series of governmental crises that began in 1787.[19] While writers such as Chastellux (*De la félicité publique*, 1772) and Condorcet (*Esquisse d'un tableau historique des progrès de l'esprit humain*, 1794) indulged in unlimited optimism about the future, and Mably, Mercier, Volney, and Restif de la Bretonne composed nonprimitivist utopias, other writers were extremely pessimistic about human beings and human affairs. The latter group included reactionaries like Linguet, Sabatier de Castres, and Rivarol, novelists like Choderlos de Laclos, Restif de la Bretonne (in another mood), and Sade. In these novelists, and especially in the works of the marquis de Sade, one finds the apogee of moral nihilism in theory and a picture of unleashed instincts for domination, power, evil, and the desire to find pleasure in hurting others. Some of the early writings of Saint-Just and the posthumous maxims of Chamfort (1796) must also be classified in this group.

At the same time Kant, who had been deeply influenced by the Enlightenment, began to react against it, against the social utilitarianism which dominated the Enlightenment's attempt to reconstruct ethics and also against the metaphysics of Hume (which was not typical of the Enlightenment). A new movement of "Ideology," headed by Destutt de Tracy and Cabanis, carried the psychology of the Enlightenment into the nineteenth century. These latter-day *philosophes* initiated a school of positivism which was to influence Stendhal, even as an eighteenth-century undercurrent of mystical, antirational illuminism, headed by Saint-Martin, Willermoz, and the Freemasons, was to exert a profound influence on the Romantic generation.

The turning point was, of course, the French Revolution (1789). The maintenance of adaptive fitness is as essential for the survival of institutions as it is for the survival of living things. In this the Old Régime, rigid and fearful, had utterly failed. Although the French Revolution was suffused with the idealistic philosophy

[19] See Leo Gershoy, *From Despotism to Revolution, 1763–1789* (New York: Harper, 1944); Daniel Mornet, *Les origines intellectuelles de la Révolution française* (Paris: A. Colin, 1933); Georges Lefèbvre, *The Coming of the French Revolution* (Princeton, N.J.: Princeton University Press, 1947).

of some of the writers we have mentioned, and although it ushered
in a new bourgeois society in which many of the goals of the
philosophes were to be realized, the Enlightenment has been un-
justly blamed for the excesses of that revolution, usually by reactionaries who forget that revolution has its own dynamics and who
also ignore the fact that "ideological conflicts have their origin in
economic and social pressures and that revolutions are never more
than partly due to intellectual causes."[20]

Looking back over the whole development of ideas, one may
summarize the intellectual enterprise which we call the Enlightenment as the commitment on the part of a group of writers (some of
whom were drawn into a loose organization, for a time, around
the *Encyclopédie*) to a dual task—liberation and reconstruction.
The intellectual inheritance we sketched at the outset came to a
focus between 1685 and 1730 in what Paul Hazard called *"la crise
de la conscience européenne."* It was necessary to free men's minds
for untrammeled speculative and scientific enquiry; and to accomplish this, certain social changes were requisite. The grip of authority, especially of institutionalized theology, had to be loosened.
Eventually it became clear that all the repressive forces of the
"establishment" were inseparable in defense of the *status quo*, despite their own bitter rivalries and enmities. It was not possible to
destroy the power of the Church without weakening that of the
throne, or to discard some privileges without endangering all privilege. It was not possible to bring some sacred and fundamental ideas
before the tribunal of reason and yet protect other ideas from
reason's searching challenge. The two great skeptics of the Enlightenment, Bayle and Hume, had made this evident. But radical
skepticism had little place in a movement of ideas that was oriented
to problem solving.[21] Only in the 1770's did these facts become
dramatically apparent, when Frederick the Great, a friend and
protector of the Enlightenment, realized its potentialities and

[20] R. Niklaus, "The Age of the Enlightenment," in *The Age of the Enlightenment. Studies presented to Theodore Besterman* (St. Andrews Fife: St.
Andrew's University Press, 1967), p. 403. In general, one may say that the
influence of Montesquieu was strongest on the first phase of the Revolution;
that of Rousseau on Robespierre, Marat, and Saint-Just, that is, on its most
extreme phase. The ideas of the *Encyclopédie* dominated among the
Girondins and triumphed under the Directory.
[21] See R. H. Popkin, "Scepticism in the Enlightenment," *Studies on Voltaire
and the eighteenth century* (Geneva: Institut et Musée Voltaire, 1963),
XXVI, 1321–45.

abandoned it in fright, even engaging in a debate with d'Holbach and Diderot. Others, such as Sabatier de Castres, were to follow his example and turn to extreme conservatism as the only hope of imposing order on the anarchic impulses the *philosophes* had uncovered in men and which a few writers justified.

If the task of liberation was politically the more dangerous, that of reconstruction was intellectually the more difficult. We refer here not to such areas as science, whose progress was carried forward by an internal dynamic, nor to aesthetics and historiography, which were relatively anodyne, but especially to morals and politics.

The deepest intellectual crisis of the eighteenth century concerned moral values. The rejection of their authoritarian, supernatural basis made necessary a new validation of restrictions on the egoistic propensities of the individual. The profound study of human nature, which the seventeenth century had begun and the eighteenth century carried forward, increasingly laid bare the potential for evil in human nature. While some writers recognized altruistic motives in men, other philosophers and novelists—even a dramatist like Gresset (*Le Méchant*)—were preoccupied by the aggressive drives centered on the desire to enhance the self through domination, power, prestige, and superiority to others. The trials of virtue and the triumphs of evil form a continuing theme, perhaps the most important single theme, of the novel. When evil is finally defeated it is either through a fortuitous concatenation of circumstances *cum* moralizing that announces the melodrama in sentimental literature; or else, as in the more powerful works of Restif and Laclos, because evil is revealed as ultimately self-destructive. But even moralists, beginning with Marivaux and Richardson, understood and communicated a certain delectation in immoralism and evil-doing. The satanic works of Sade were the frenetic culmination of a long development.

For the *philosophes*, the problem was most difficult. Pleasure and happiness were seen as the ineradicable motivation of all behavior. Nature imposed this motivation, and nature, it was held, was right. At the same time society, or culture, had its legitimate demands, summarized in the word "virtue," which meant the control of egoism for the benefit of all. All too often, the pleasure and happiness of people were derived from actions contrary to these demands; some individuals, indeed, could find happiness in no other way—the philosophy of determinism made this indisputable. It was necessary, then, to justify the social or cultural imperatives which we call morality.

The thinkers of the eighteenth century struggled incessantly with these problems. Intimations of moral nihilism (even when rejected) are to be found early in the century, especially in Bayle; but it is in the middle period that writers such as Meslier, Dulaurens, d'Argens, and above all Hume bring out the impossibility of a purely rational demonstration of moral values or of convincing the individual by reason that he should be virtuous. Rousseau described existing societies as essentially immoral beneath a mask of hypocritical "seeming." Other writers, such as Diderot, realized the impossibility of justifying moral values with rational certitude and even "experimented" in secret writings with moral nihilism. Aware of the challenge, the *philosophes*—as well as British moralists such as Shaftesbury, Price, Hutcheson, and Adam Smith—sought new foundations for ethical theory. The theory that there was a special "moral sense" was popular in England. The French preferred enlightened self-interest and a theory that made virtue and happiness equivalents: only the virtuous man, they argued (half believing it), is happy, and the evil man is necessarily unhappy. Were that not true, virtue, they sometimes admitted, would be invalid, since the quest for happiness was nature's imperative and man's highest value. More and more in both countries, philosophers turned to social utilitarianism, which placed the locus of moral value not in the individual's motives or conscience, but in the social consequences of his acts. Utilitarianism was to culminate in the work of Bentham (who was greatly influenced by Helvétius) and Mill. That the eighteenth-century moralists did not succeed in solving an unsolvable problem is evidenced by the upsurge of moral nihilism at the end of the period, by Kant's critique of the ethics of the Enlightenment, by Diderot's own admission of failure in theoretical ethics, and by the persistence of the same problems into the nineteenth and twentieth centuries.[22]

We may say, in schematic fashion, that the eighteenth century began with a revolt against Christian morality in the name of nature. There followed a retreat in favor of order, whose principal

---

[22] Confining ourselves to literature, one thinks immediately of such writers as Stendhal, Baudelaire, Lautréamont, Dostoevski, and the decadents in the nineteenth century; and of the literature of the absurd, from Jarry through Céline down to the post–World War II writers—as well as of the increase of violence and sadism.

and lasting product was utilitarianism. But in many minds the rationalistic defenses against immoralism were inadequate. In the latter part of the period, some went beyond rationalism to altruism and humanitarianism. Others rebelled against rationalism, against the indirect return to the anti-egoistic position of Christianity, demanding or at least describing an end to false compromises, to the illusion or "hypocrisy" of enlightened self-interest and the virtue-happiness equivalence (according to which a sacrifice is not a sacrifice). To the illusion of calling for renunciation in the name of "natural" laws they preferred a return to nature's law of the strong.[23] Kant, as we have said, was to react in a still different way, basing a categorical moral imperative on a definition of man as a creature with an autonomous will who prescribes rational law unto himself.

The other great challenge of the eighteenth century was that of politics and government. It was inextricably involved with the moral problem since it was generally held, following the psychology of Locke and Condillac, developed in its political dimensions by Helvétius and Rousseau, that men could be shaped by government, law, and education. From the dilemmas in which ethical theory found itself, two views followed. Either one could urge that social demands be made identical with natural demands (and this was particularly favored by "radicals" in regard to sexual mores), or else one could argue that society should mold behavior to coincide—more or less completely, according to the theorist—with its own demands. Indeed, the "optimism" of the Enlightenment concerned not men themselves but (in addition to faith in scientific and technological progress) the belief that a good society would make men good. It became clear that the relation of the individual to society was the core of the political as well as of the moral problem, and the two often fused. Eighteenth-century writers showed great inventiveness in their political constructions, which were ultimately determined by a given writer's view of human nature.[24]

There was a current of primitivism, especially in the first part of

[23] Ehrard, Mauzi, and Crocker, in the works listed in the bibliography on p. 325, agree in pointing out the deceptive or self-deceptive postulates in Enlightenment ethics.
[24] This relationship, as well as the conflicts and complexities of eighteenth-century thought, is apparent in any of the major questions that were debated throughout the period, such as luxury, the values of truth and falsehood, and slavery. Thus slavery was attacked by most of the *philosophes*,

the century, and writers who had read stories about good savages dreamed of simple societies with little or no government in which man's natural goodness led to happiness. At the other extreme, especially in the second half of the century, writers such as Morelly, Rousseau, Linguet, and Restif devised collectivist systems in which men, irremediably evil in competitive societies, were subjected to complete regimentation, thought control, and reshaping in the desired social image. Mably favored a communistic collectivism.[25] The main body of writers differed from these two groups in two basic ways. They rejected utopianism; and they believed that reform was possible, while a new beginning according to abstract, rationalistic constructions was impossible or undesirable. Whereas the collectivist group influenced Marxism and various types of totalitarian thought, this third group, which included Montesquieu, Voltaire, Diderot, the Encyclopedists, and Condorcet, laid the foundations of modern liberal societies. There were, to be sure, drastic differences among these latter writers. Moreover, modern labels are not only anachronistic but to some extent become meaningless, since there was no perception of the future or of what to us seem clear tendencies. Elements of what now appear as thinking of a liberal and a totalitarian type often occur in the same writer. Thus Rousseau, who designed a society that is a model of totalitarian collectivism, had a strong influence on liberal democ-

---

but strongly defended by those who spoke for commercial interests. De Brosses, who was attached to the philosophic movement, defends exploitation of primitive peoples in a passage that reveals the infiltration of amoralism and the limits of optimism: "I admit that since men are no better today than in the past, and since past events are moreover guaranties of those to come, the preceptors I would send them might not accompany their good instructions with equally good procedures. . . . The remedy would doubtless exterminate a large number; those who might escape would be the better for it. . . . I consider myself a philosopher on a large scale, who, far from confining himself in a circle of small inconveniences, goes as far as sacrificing men to mankind. . . . As a political thinker, I am becoming a Hobbist, and I consider men as being naturally in a state of war; as a merchant, my heart is tender only for my own interests. Are you just in asking me to be good, when either one of these titles is enough to justify my not being so? . . . Men are all wicked, and savages seem to me the worst of all. . . ." (Quoted, in J.-J. Rousseau, *Correspondence complète*, ed. R. A. Leigh (Geneva: Institut et Musée Voltaire, 1967), IV, 242–43.
[25] See André Lichtenberger, *Le Socialisme au XVIIIᵉ siècle* (Paris: Alcan, 1895); and Kingsley Martin, *French Liberal Thought in the Eighteenth Century* (3rd edn.; New York: Harper, 1963).

racy, because of his attack on feudal institutions, his demand for universal suffrage and popular sovereignty, and his frequent use of the word "liberty." In reality, he never dreamed of allowing the people "self-rule" except under conditions of careful control, surveillance, and guidance. Liberty had quite a different meaning for him than for us.

Eighteenth-century political speculation presents a varied picture, then, of primitivism, anarchism, collectivism, enlightened despotism, representative government, and even (Linguet) naked dictatorship. But if we are to take the *Encyclopédie* as most representative (though not most daring or original), we find that its contributors, most of whom were comfortable professional men, landowners, or investors in business and industry, were concerned with practical reforms that would advance commerce and industry, with an enlargement of what we would now call civil liberties, and with the correction of social inequities—the thinking of the rising middle class which after the French Revolution was to inherit the world.

The bourgeoisie was in an ambivalent position. On the one hand, they supported the moderate group of *philosophes* in order to obtain political and economic rights. On the other hand, they endeavored as an integral part of the feudal régime, which may be characterized as exploitative, to enhance their own interests. According to Marxist scholars, the fundamental antagonism was not between the privileged classes and the bourgeoisie, but between the feudal régime (including the bourgeoisie) and the exploited masses.[26] This would account for certain contradictions. The *philosophes* often defended the monarchy despite republican sympathies and hatred of despotism. They wished to loose the shackles of the feudal system, but without changing the status of the laboring force. Only a few "radicals," such as Meslier, Rousseau, Mably, Morelly, Dom Deschamps, and Restif, actually spoke for the people. The bourgeoisie was content to side with the king (*"la thèse royale"*) in order to eliminate the enemy class of aristocrats (*"la thèse nobiliaire"*), which they could not penetrate and capture. To be a "republican" was to substitute the bourgeoisie for the

[26] A non-Marxist, Marcel Bouchard, supports the view that this, rather than the three Estates, was the true division of society. See *De l'humanisme à l'Encyclopédie; l'esprit public en Bourgogne sous l'ancien régime* (Paris: Hachette, 1930).

privileged classes in the framework of a limited or parliamentary monarchy. After the Revolution, when the bourgeoisie won control of economic and political power, they defended their exploitative position by turning against the philosophy of the Enlightenment and by allying themselves with the Church and religion.[27]

Much more work has been done on the origins of the Enlightenment than on its influence upon the future. But history is a continuum; and if we cannot understand the Enlightenment without knowing how it came to be, neither can we understand fully the nineteenth and twentieth centuries without taking into account the legacy of the Enlightenment. We agree with Michelet that in writing the history of the dead, we must not stop thinking of the living. The problems—we might even say the anguish—of our own time have some of their roots in man's metaphysical, moral, and political dilemmas which the Enlightenment brought into critical focus. It was the Enlightenment that opened the consciousness of modern man—though the discovery had already been made—to the fact that he is lost among the stars, with no meaning to his existence except the meaning he creates; that he must therefore be his own guide, his happiness and well-being on earth his only lodestar. The attempts to meet this problem in its manifold aspects were varied and contradictory and pointed to many possible routes. From the Enlightenment we derive our faith in the conquest of nature and the rational ordering of society, as well as in political and civil rights and the right of the individual to self-realization. However, the Enlightenment also knew the labyrinth of evil and disorder in man and envisaged the means of controlling him and socializing him, assuming, as some did, that for his own happiness he had to be made an orderly part of a rational social order. But, whatever road was pointed to, it is clear that the Enlightenment was above all, if not always, the triumph of humanism.

---

[27] S. Stelling-Michaud, "Lumières et politique," *Studies on Voltaire and the eighteenth century* (Geneva: Institut et Musée Voltaire, 1963), XXVI, 1519–43.

I

The Human Situation

WHAT IS the quality of human nature? What kind of life is man destined
to live? What is his place in the "creation"? The writers of the Enlightenment often addressed themselves to questions such as these, and
this section offers some of the typical answers.

Taking them in approximately chronological order, we find Bayle
(Document 1) assessing human nature and life as predominantly evil,
and consistently so—a view which buttresses his semiserious support of
the Manichean heresy, according to which two coequal principles, one
of good, the other of evil, rule the world.

Mandeville's *Fable of the Bees* (1714) asserted the paradox that
civilization and prosperity are dependent on what are (from the
rigorous moral viewpoint) vices; from the social viewpoint, vices are
virtues. In one of his notes to the poem, Mandeville shows the harmony
between his paradox and human nature. His assessment was to be coun-
tered by Hume's and Adam Smith's doctrine of sympathy. (See Part
IV, Morals.)

La Mettrie (*L'Homme machine*, 1747) continues a tradition of
humbling man's pride in relation to animals. His purpose is not that of
Montaigne or Pascal, to disparage reason, but rather to advance the
cause of materialism by bringing man back into a common nature: he
does not have the exclusive privilege of "natural law"—an idea La Mettrie effectively deprives of moral content.

The selections from Rousseau's *Discours sur l'origine de l'inégalité*
(1755) express two ideas basic to his sociopolitical system. He rejects
reason as man's distinctive quality; this he finds, instead, in freedom
from the fixity of instinctual responses and in the capacity for progress
which is its consequence. Rousseau does not realize that the latter are
possible only because of certain powers of human reason (objectifying,
abstracting and comparing, symbol- and toolmaking). The second
passage gives us Rousseau's estimate of human nature in society and of
the quality of social life. Unless we keep this estimate in mind, it is
impossible to understand Rousseau's reliance on behavioral control in
his vision of a society in which men are made to be *necessarily* virtuous
and happy.

Helvétius (*De l'Homme*, published in 1772 but written earlier) tries to explain why Rousseau's picture of an innocent "original man" is wrong, why man was necessarily what we call evil. Helvétius's purpose is to make us understand the importance and power of "education"— the determination of behavior by developing habits—through a process of association with pain and pleasure.

Voltaire in *Candide* (1759) cast a sorrowful and almost despairing eye over the spectacle of human life. In his later *Dictionnaire philosophique* (1765), the article "Wicked" reveals a more mellowed judgment. In fact, Voltaire never gave up his commitment to melioristic social action.

In *Le Neveu de Rameau* (1762, published in the nineteenth century), Diderot conducts one of his "moral experiments," pitting two antagonists against each other. "*Moi*" ("I") defends the moralistic view, and man's love of virtue. "*Lui*" ("He") is the immoralist, who sees social life, beneath the masks of hypocrisy, following nature's law of the jungle. Diderot's *La Réfutation d'Helvétius* (1773, published 1875) reveals a strong humanistic reaction against some of the excessive conclusions of eighteenth-century materialism, in favor of man's distinctiveness and the reality of the moral domain in which he exists.

D'Holbach in *La Morale universelle* (1776) expounds the typical viewpoint of French materialism: what we call compassion or pity is only a disguised form, or a protective reaction, of self-love, the universal motive. Although d'Holbach does not refer to Hume or Adam Smith, his argument may be taken as a refutation of their theories.

All the currents of the most extreme materialism flow into the work of Sade. In *La Philosophie dans le boudoir* (1795), he not only reduces man to the undifferentiated status of animal, but applies the same laws of nature to the evaluation of his behavior. By a process of specious reasoning, he justifies murder as a legitimate act—no moral considerations being valid or applicable.

1.   Bayle, *Answer to the Questions of a Provincial*

THE HEAVENS and all the rest of the universe preach the glories, the power, the unity of God. Man alone, this masterpiece of his creator among all visible things, man alone, I say, furnishes strong objections against the unity of God. This is why:

Man is wicked and unhappy. Each one of us knows this by what goes on within himself and by the commerce he is obliged to have

SOURCE: Translated by the editor. The text is taken from La Haye, *Oeuvres diverses*, 1737.

with his fellows. It suffices to live five or six years to be completely convinced of these two statements; those who live long and who are deeply involved in affairs know it even more clearly. Travels are constant lessons on this subject. They show us everywhere the monuments of the unhappiness and wickedness of man: everywhere prisons and poorhouses; everywhere gibbets and beggars. Here you see the ruins of a flourishing city; there you cannot even find its ruins. . . .

History, properly speaking, is only a collection of the crimes and misfortunes of mankind. But let us observe that these two evils, moral and physical, do not contain all of history or the whole experience of individuals; everywhere both moral and physical good are to be found, a few examples of virtue, a few examples of happiness—and that is where the problem lies.

2.   Mandeville, The Fable of the Bees

Envy It Self, and Vanity, Were Ministers of Industry

ENVY is that Baseness in our Nature, which makes us grieve and pine at what we conceive to be a Happiness in others. I don't believe there is a Human Creature in his Senses arriv'd to Maturity, that at one time or other has not been carried away by this Passion in good Earnest; and yet I never met with any one that dared own he was guilty of it, but in Jest. That we are so generally ashamed of this Vice, is owing to that strong Habit of Hypocrisy, by the Help of which, we have learned from our Cradle to hide even from our selves the vast Extent of Self-Love, and all its different Branches. It is impossible Man should wish better for another than he does for himself, unless where he supposes an Impossibility that himself should attain to those Wishes; and from hence we may easily learn after what manner this Passion is raised in us. In order to it, we are to consider First, That as well as we think of our selves, so ill we often think of our Neighbour with equal Injustice; and when we

SOURCE: Bernard Mandeville, *The Fable of the Bees: or, Private vices, publick benefits*, ed. F. B. Kaye (Oxford: The Clarendon Press, 1924).

apprehend, that others do or will enjoy what we think they don't deserve, it afflicts and makes us angry with the Cause of that Disturbance. Secondly, That we are ever employ'd in wishing well for our selves, every one according to his Judgment and Inclinations, and when we observe something we like, and yet are destitute of, in the Possession of others; it occasions first Sorrow in us for not having the Thing we like. This Sorrow is incurable, while we continue our Esteem for the Thing we want: But as Self-Defence is restless, and never suffers us to leave any Means untried how to remove Evil from us, as far and as well as we are able; Experience teaches us, that nothing in Nature more alleviates this Sorrow than our Anger against those who are possess'd of what we esteem and want. This latter Passion therefore, we cherish and cultivate to save or relieve our selves, at least in part, from the Uneasiness we felt from the first.

If Envy was not rivetted in Human Nature, it would not be so common in Children, and Youth would not be so generally spurr'd on by Emulation. Those who would derive every Thing that is beneficial to the Society from a good Principle, ascribe the Effects of Emulation in School-boys to a Virtue of the Mind; as it requires Labour and Pains, so it is evident, that they commit a Self-Denial, who act from that Disposition; but if we look narrowly into it, we shall find that this Sacrifice of Ease and Pleasure is only made to Envy, and the Love of Glory. If there was not something very like this Passion mix'd with that pretended Virtue, it would be impossible to raise and increase it by the same Means that create Envy. The Boy, who receives a Reward for the Superiority of his Performance, is conscious of the Vexation it would have been to him, if he should have fall'n short of it: This Reflexion makes him exert himself, not to be out-done by those whom now he looks upon as his Inferiors, and the greater his Pride is, the more Self-denial he'll practise to maintain his Conquest. The other, who, in spite of the Pains he took to do well, has miss'd of the Prize, is sorry, and consequently angry with him whom he must look upon as the Cause of his Grief: But to shew this Anger, would be ridiculous, and of no Service to him, so that he must either be contented to be less esteem'd than the other Boy; or by renewing his Endeavours become a greater Proficient: and it is ten to one, but the disinterested, good-humour'd, and peaceable Lad will choose the first, and so become indolent and unactive, while the covetous, peevish, and quarrelsome Rascal shall take incredible Pains, and make himself a Conqueror in his Turn.

3. La Mettrie, Man a Machine

IN SPITE of all these advantages of man over animals, it is doing him
honor to place him in the same class. For, truly, up to a certain age,
he is more of an animal than they, since at birth he has less instinct.
What animal would die of hunger in the midst of a river of milk?
Man alone. Like that child of olden time to whom a modern writer
refers, following Arnobius, he knows neither the foods suitable for
him, nor the water that can drown him, nor the fire that can reduce
him to ashes. Light a wax candle for the first time under a child's
eyes, and he will mechanically put his fingers in the flame as if to
find out what is the new thing that he sees. It is at his own cost that
he will learn of the danger, but he will not be caught again. Or, put
the child with an animal on a precipice, the child alone falls off; he
drowns where the animal would save itself by swimming. At fourteen or fifteen years the child knows hardly anything of the great
pleasures in store for him, in the reproduction of his species; when
he is a youth, he does not know exactly how to behave in a game
which nature teaches animals so quickly. He hides himself as if he
were ashamed of taking pleasure, and of having been made to be
happy, while animals frankly glory in being cynics. Without
education, they are without prejudices. For one more example, let
us observe a dog and a child who have lost their master on a
highway: the child cries and does not know to what saint to pray,
while the dog, better helped by his sense of smell than the child by
his reason, soon finds his master.

Thus nature made us to be lower than animals or at least to
exhibit all the more, because of that native inferiority, the wonderful efficacy of education which alone raises us from the level of the
animals and lifts us above them. But shall we grant this same distinction to the deaf and to the blind, to imbeciles, madmen, or

SOURCE: Translated by Gertrude C. Bussey in Man a Machine (La
Salle, Ind.: The Open Court Publishing Co., 1912). Reprinted by
permission of the publishers.

savages, or to those who have been brought up in the woods with animals; to those who have lost their imagination through melancholia, or in short to all those animals in human form who give evidence of only the rudest instinct? No, all these, men of body but not of mind, do not deserve to be classed by themselves.

We do not intend to hide from ourselves the arguments that can be brought forward against our belief and in favor of a primitive distinction between men and animals. Some say that there is in man a natural law, a knowledge of good and evil, which has never been imprinted on the heart of animals.

But is this objection, or rather this assertion, based on observation? Any assertion unfounded on observation may be rejected by a philosopher. Have we ever had a single experience which convinces us that man alone has been enlightened by a ray denied all other animals? If there is no such experience, we can no more know what goes on in animals' minds or even in the minds of other men, than we can help feeling what affects the inner part . . .

I will grant that animals, even the best of them, do not know the difference between moral good and evil, that they have no recollection of the trouble taken for them, of the kindness done them, no realization of their own virtues. [I will suppose], for instance, that this lion, to which I, like so many others, have referred, does not remember at all that it refused to kill the man, abandoned to its fury, in a combat more inhuman than one could find among lions, tigers and bears, put together. For our compatriots fight, Swiss against Swiss, brother against brother, recognize each other, and yet capture and kill each other without remorse, because a prince pays for the murder. I suppose in short that the natural law has not been given animals. What will be the consequences of this supposition? Man is not moulded from a costlier clay; nature has used but one dough, and has merely varied the leaven. Therefore if animals do not repent for having violated this inmost feeling which I am discussing, or rather if they absolutely lack it, man must necessarily be in the same condition. Farewell then to the natural law and all the fine treatises published about it! The whole animal kingdom in general would be deprived of it. But, conversely, if man can not dispense with the belief that when health permits him to be himself, he always distinguishes the upright, humane, and virtuous, from those who are not humane, virtuous, nor honorable: that it is easy to tell vice from virtue, by the unique pleasure and the peculiar repugnance that seem to be their natural effects, it follows that animals, composed of the same matter, lacking perhaps only one degree of fermentation to make it exactly like man's, must share the same prerogatives of animal nature, and that thus there exists no soul or sensitive substance . . .

We were not originally made to be learned; we have become so perhaps by a sort of abuse of our organic faculties, and at the expense of the State which nourishes a host of sluggards whom vanity has adorned with the name of philosophers. Nature has created us all solely to be happy—yes, all of us from the crawling worm to the eagle lost in the clouds. For this cause she has given all animals some share of natural law, a share greater or less according to the needs of each animal's organs when in normal condition.

Now how shall we define natural law? It is a feeling that teaches us what we should not do, because we would not wish it to be done to us. Should I dare add to this common idea, that this feeling seems to me but a kind of fear or dread, as salutary to the race as to the individual; for may it not be true that we respect the purse and life of others only to save our own possessions, our honor, and ourselves; like those Ixions of Christianity who love God and embrace so many fantastic virtues merely because they are afraid of hell!

You see that natural law is but an intimate feeling that, like all other feelings (thought included), belongs also to imagination. Evidently, therefore, natural law does not presuppose education, revelation, nor legislator—provided one does not propose to confuse natural law with civil laws, in the ridiculous fashion of the theologians . . .

4. Rousseau, Discourse on the Origin of Inequality

Part I

I FIND in any animal only an ingenious machine to which nature gave senses so that it could wind itself up and protect itself, up to a certain point, from whatever tends to destroy or to disturb it. I see

SOURCE: C. E. Vaughan (ed.), *The Political Writings of Rousseau* (2 vols.; Cambridge: The University Press, 1915), vol. 1. Translated by the editor.

exactly the same things in the human machine; with this difference that in the animal nature alone does everything, whereas man collaborates in his operations insofar as he is a free agent. The one chooses or rejects by instinct; and the other by an act of freedom. In consequence, the animal cannot depart from the rule that has been prescribed to him, even when it would be advantageous to him to do so, whereas man departs from it, frequently to his hurt. Thus a pigeon would die of hunger next to a bowl filled with the best meat, as a cat would near piles of fruits or grain, although either one could be well nourished by the food it disdains, if it could take a notion to try it. Thus dissolute men abandon themselves to excesses which produce fever and death, because the mind depraves the senses, and because the will continues to speak when nature is silent.

Every animal has ideas, since it has senses. It even combines its ideas up to a certain point; and in this regard man differs from the animal only in degree. Some philosophers have even suggested that there is more difference between two given men than between a given man and a given animal. Therefore it is not so much the understanding which is man's specific distinction among animals as it is the quality of being a free agent. Nature commands every animal and the animal obeys. Man experiences the same impulsion, but he knows that he is free to acquiesce or to resist; and it is above all in his consciousness of this freedom that the spirituality of his soul is evident. For physics explains in some fashion the mechanism of the senses and the formation of ideas; but not the power of willing, or rather of choosing, and in the awareness of this power we see only acts of the mind which are in no way explained by the laws of mechanics.

Even if the difficulties involved in all these questions may leave some room for disputation about this difference between man and beast, there is another, very specific quality which separates them, concerning which there can be no argument: it is the faculty of making progress. This faculty which, with the help of circumstances, successively develops all others belongs as much to the species as to the individual; whereas an animal after several months is all that he will be during his whole life, and his species, after a thousand years, is what it was in the first year of that thousand. Why is man alone subject to the loss of his mental faculties? Is it not because he returns to his original state and, whereas the animal, who has learned nothing and has nothing to lose, always retains his instinct, man, losing in consequence of age or other accidents all that his *perfectability* had enabled him to acquire, falls even lower than the animal? It would be sad for us to be forced to admit that this distinctive and almost unlimited faculty is the source of all of man's misfortunes; that it draws him eventually out of that original condition in which he would otherwise pass tranquil and innocent days; that, causing his knowledge and his errors, his vices and his virtues to bloom with the passing of centuries, it makes him, in the end, a tyrant over himself and over nature. It would be frightful to be obliged to praise as a benevolent being the man who first suggested to the inhabitant of the banks of the Orinoco the custom of applying staves to his children's temples in order to conserve at least a part of their original imbecility and happiness. . . .

Whatever these origins may have been, we can at least see, from the little care which nature took to bring men together by mutual needs or to facilitate the use of language, how little she prepared them for sociability, and how little of her work she put in all they have done to establish the bonds of society. Indeed, it is impossible to imagine why, in that primitive state, a man would need another man any more than a monkey or a wolf needs his fellows; nor, if we grant this need, what motive might persuade the other man to satisfy it; nor even, in the latter case, how they could agree on the conditions. I know that we are constantly told that nothing would have been so wretched as man in such a state; and if it is true, as I believe I have proved, that he could have had the desire and the opportunity to leave it only after many centuries, it would be a grievance against nature and not against the man she made thus. However, if I understand this word "wretched," it is a meaningless word, or one which means only a painful privation and the suffering of the body or the soul. Now I should like someone to explain to me what kind of wretchedness could be felt by a free being whose heart is at peace and whose body is healthy. I ask whether civil life or natural life is more likely to become unbearable to those who enjoy it. . . . I ask whether anyone has ever heard of a free savage even thinking of complaining about life and of putting an end to it. Let us judge, then, with less pride, where the true wretchedness lies . . .

It seems, first of all, that men in this state, having no kind of moral relationships or known duties, could have been neither good nor bad, and had neither vices nor virtues; unless, taking those words in a physical sense, we term vices in the individual qualities which may hurt his self-preservation, and virtues, those which may further it; in which case, we should have to call him most virtuous who least resists the simple impulses of nature. However, without departing from the usual meaning, it is proper for us to suspend our judgment about such a situation, and to beware of our prejudices until we have examined, scale in hand, whether there are more virtues than vices among civilized men; or whether their virtues are more beneficial to them than their vices are fatal; or whether the progress of their knowledge is a sufficient indemnity for the hurts they constantly do to each other even as they learn about the good they ought to do to each other; or whether they would not be, all in all, in a happier situation if they had neither evil to fear nor good to hope from anyone, rather than having submitted to universal dependency and obliged themselves to receive everything from those who feel no obligation to give them anything.

Above all, let us not conclude with Hobbes that, because he has no idea of the good, natural man is wicked; or that he is vicious, because he does not know virtue, or that he always refuses his fellows services that he has no feeling of owing to them; nor that because of the right which he correctly attributes to himself over the things he needs, he has the madness to imagine that he is the sole proprietor of the whole universe. Hobbes has clearly seen the flaw in all modern definitions of natural right; but the consequences which he draws from his own show that he takes it in a sense which is no less false. In his reasoning about the principles which he establishes, that writer should have said that the state of nature being the state in which our self-preservation involves least harm to that of others, it is, consequently, the most conducive to peace and the most suited to the human kind. He says exactly the opposite because he improperly injected into the savage's self-preservation the need to satisfy innumerable passions which are the work of society and which have made its laws necessary. The wicked man, he says, is a robust child. There remains to decide whether the savage is a robust child. Even if this were granted, what should he conclude from it? That, being robust, if he were as dependent on others as when he was weak, there is no kind of excesses to which he would not give himself; that he would beat his mother when she was too slow in giving her breast; that he would strangle one of his younger brothers when he was annoyed by him; that he would bite another's leg, when he would be bumped or annoyed by him. However, to be robust and dependent is a contradictory supposition in the state of nature; man is weak when he is dependent, and before he becomes robust, he is emancipated. Hobbes has not seen that the same cause which prevents savages from using their reason, as our jurisconsults claim they do, also prevents them from making abusive use of their faculties, as he claims, so that we may say that savages are not wicked precisely because they do not know what it is to be good; for it is neither the development of knowledge, nor the brake of law, but the absence of passions and ignorance of vice that prevents them from doing evil. . . . There is, moreover, another principle which Hobbes did not grasp, which, having been given to man to soften in certain circumstances the ferocity of his self-love, before its birth, or the desire of self-preservation, moderates his ardor for his wellbeing with an innate repugnance to see his fellow man suffer. I do not think I am falling into contradiction by granting to man the only natural virtue which the most extreme detractor of human virtues was forced to recognize. I speak of pity, a characteristic suitable to beings as weak and subject to as many ills as we are; a virtue which is all the more universal and useful to man in that it is prior in him to all reflection; and so natural, that even animals sometimes show recognizable signs of it.

Part II

At this point all our faculties are developed, memory and imagination are at work, self-love involved, reason active, and the mind has reached almost the limit of development of which it is capable. At this point, all our natural characteristics are in play, the rank and fate of each man established, not only on the basis of wealth and the power of helping or harming others, but on that of intelligence, beauty, strength or skill, merit or talents. These qualities being the only ones that could attract prestige, it soon became necessary either to have them or to affect them; it was necessary, for the individual's advantage, to show himself in a different light from what he really was. Being and appearance became two quite different things; and from this distinction arose imposing pomp, deceitful trickery, and all the vices which follow in their train. On the other hand, man, who had been free and dependent before, is now, because of a multitude of new needs, subjected, so to speak, to all of nature, and especially to his fellow men, whose slave he becomes even as he becomes their master. If he is rich, he needs their services; if he is poor, he needs their help; and a middle place does not put him in a position to get along without them. Consequently, he must constantly strive to get them interested in his fate, and to make them find their own advantage, whether it be real or an illusion, in working for his own. This makes him dishonest and conniving with some, imperious with others, and makes it necessary for him to take advantage of all those he needs when he is unable to make himself feared by them and when it is not in his interest to serve them. Finally, devouring ambition, the drive to enhance their fortune compared with others, less because of a true need than to raise themselves above others, inspire in all men a dark inclination to hurt each other, a secret envy which is all the more dangerous because, in order to strike its blows with greater safety, it often puts on the mask of benevolence; in a word, competition and rivalry on the one hand, conflict of interests on the other, and always the secret desire to profit at the expense of others. All these evils are the first effect of property and the inseparable accompaniment of nascent inequality. . . .

I should like to point out how this universal desire for reputation, honors and recognition, which consumes all of us, stimulates talents and abilities and causes them to be compared; how it arouses and multiplies passions; and how, making all men competitors, rivals, or rather enemies, it causes reverses, successes, and catastrophes of every kind every day, by making so many claimants enter into the lists. I would show that this passion to be talked about, this rage to be distinguished which keeps us almost always alienated from ourselves, is responsible for what is best and for what is worst among men: our virtues and our vices, our knowledge and our errors, our conquerors and our philosophers—that is to say, a throng of bad things and a small number of good ones. I would prove, finally, that if we see a handful of powerful and rich men at the summit of grandeur and wealth, while the masses crawl in obscurity and deprivation, it is because the former esteem the things they enjoy only insofar as the others are deprived of them, and that, without changing their condition, they would cease to be happy if the people ceased being unhappy.

Note i.   Men are wicked; sad and constant experience makes proof unnecessary. Nevertheless, man is naturally good, I think I have proved that. What could have depraved him to such a degree, except the changes that took place in his make up, the progress he has made, and the knowledge he has acquired? Admire human society as much as you wish; it is nonetheless true that it makes men necessarily hate each other in proportion as their interests conflict, and render each other apparent mutual services while hurting each other in every imaginable way. What should we think of a relationship in which each individual's reason dictates to him maxims that are directly contrary to those which the public reason preaches to the social body, and in which each is benefited by the misfortune of others? There is perhaps not a single well-to-do man whose greedy heirs, often his own children, do not secretly wish his death; not a vessel at sea whose shipwreck would not be good news for some merchant; not a house which a dishonest debtor would not like to burn down with all the papers within it; not a nation which does not rejoice at the disaster of its neighbors. Thus we find our advantage in what hurts our fellow men, and one man's loss almost always makes another's profit. But what is even more dangerous is that public calamities are awaited and hoped for by many individuals; some wish for epidemics, others death, others war, others famine. . . . Let us then penetrate beyond our frivolous demonstrations of mutual benevolence to what goes on within our hearts, and let us reflect about what kind of a state of things it is in which men are forced to make a show of love for each other and to destroy each other, in which they are born enemies out of duty and knaves out of self-interest. If you reply that society is so constituted that each man gains by serving others, I will reply that that would be very nice did he not gain still more by harming them. There is no legitimate profit that is not surpassed by the profit we can make by illegitimate means, and the harm we do to our neighbor is always more lucrative than the services we render him. All we have to do is to find the means of protecting ourselves; and that is the end toward which the powerful use all their strength and the weak all their shrewdness.

The savage, when he has dined, is at peace with all of nature and the friend of all his fellow men. . . . The social man is in quite a different situation. For him it is a matter first of acquiring what he needs, and then the superfluities: first come the delights, then immense riches, then subjects, then slaves. He has not a moment of relaxation. The strangest thing is that the less natural and urgent needs are, the greater the passions and, what is worse, the greater the power to satisfy them; so that after lengthy prosperity, after having devoured much treasure and ruined many men, my hero will end up by cutting everyone's throat until he is the sole master of the universe. Such is, in a nutshell, the moral picture, if not of human life, at least of the secret wishes in the heart of every civilized man. . . .

What then? Should we destroy societies, wipe out property, and return to the forests to live with the bears? This is the type of conclusion my adversaries draw, and I should like to forestall it rather than allowing them the shame of drawing it. Oh you who have not heard the heavenly voice, and who see in your species no other purpose except to live out this short life peacefully; you who can abandon in the midst of the city your fatal acquisitions, your worried minds, your corrupted arts, and your frenetic desires; since it depends on you, go back to your ancient and first innocence; go back to the forests, leave behind the sight and the memory of the crimes of your contemporaries, and do not feel that you are lowering your species by giving up its knowledge in order to give up its vices. As for men like me, whose passions have forever destroyed their native simplicity, who can no longer nourish themselves with herbs and acorns, nor do without laws and leaders; . . . as for those, in a word, who are convinced that the divine voice summoned mankind to the knowledge and happiness of the celestial minds—all these, by exercising the virtues they oblige themselves to practice as they learn to know them, will delight in meriting the eternal reward they should expect for it. They will respect the sacred links of the societies to which they belong; they will love their fellow men and serve them with all their power; they will scrupulously obey the laws, and the men who are their authors and administrators. . . . But they will despise nonetheless an order of things which can maintain itself only with the help of so many respectable people (who are sought for more often than they are found), and from which, in spite of all their efforts, more real calamities are born than apparent advantages.

5. Helvétius, On Man

Natural Man Must Be Cruel

WHAT DOES the spectacle of nature reveal to us? A multitude of beings destined to devour each other. Man especially, say the anatomists, has the teeth of a carnivorous animal. He must therefore be voracious, consequently cruel and bloodthirsty. Moreover, flesh is for him the most healthful food, the most fit for his structure. His self-preservation, like that of almost all animal species, depends on his destroying others. Men, scattered by nature across the vast forests, were hunters first. When they drew together and were forced to find nourishment within a smaller space, need made them shepherds. Still more numerous they finally became food growers. In all of these diverse situations man is the born destroyer of animals, either to nourish himself on their flesh, or to defend the cattle, fruits, grains, and legumes necessary to his survival against them.

Natural man is his own butcher, his own cook. His hands are always dripping with blood. Accustomed to killing, he must be deaf to the cry of pity. If the stag at bay moves me, if his tears make mine flow, this spectacle which is so touching by its novelty is a pleasant one to the savage whom custom has hardened to it.

The most pleasant melody to the ears of the Inquisitor are the shrieks of pain. He laughs next to the stake on which the heretic is expiring. This Inquisitor, an assassin authorized by the law, keeps within the civilized community the ferocity of natural man: he is a man of blood. The closer we draw to the natural state, the more we grow accustomed to murder, the easier it is. . . . A man who

SOURCE: Helvétius, *De L'Homme* (London, 1776), an anonymous eighteenth-century translation.

is not accustomed by a good upbringing to see in the sufferings of others those to which he himself is exposed will always be harsh and often bloodthirsty. The common people are like that. They do not have enough wits to be human . . .

Whoever upholds the original goodness of men is trying to deceive them. Shall we deem the consideration which mutual fear inspires in two beings who are about equal in strength to be natural goodness? Civilized man is no longer restrained by this fear; he becomes cruel and barbarous.

Think of the picture of a battlefield at the moment which follows victory, when the plain is still strewn with dead and dying, when avarice and cupidity cast their greedy glances on the blood-stained grounds of the expiring victims of the public weal, when without pity for the wretches whose sufferings they are redoubling, they [the victors] approach them and strip them. The tears, the frightening face of anguish, the piercing cry of pain, nothing moves them. Blind to the tears of these unfortunate victims, they are deaf to their moans. Such is man on the battlefields of victory . . .

Liberated from fear of the laws or of reprisals, man's injustices have no bounds other than those of his power. What then becomes of this original goodness, which M. Rousseau sometimes attributes to man and sometimes denies to him. Let me not be accused of denying the existence of good men. There are men who are tender and compassionate for their fellow man's sufferings; but humanity is the effect of education in them, and not of nature. The same people, had they been born among the Iroquois, would have adopted barbarous and cruel customs. If M. Rousseau is still contradicting himself on this matter, it is because his theories are in contradiction with his own experience; it is because sometimes he writes in accordance with the one, sometimes in accordance with the other. Shall we always forget that, born without ideas, without a character, indifferent to moral good and evil, we have only physical sensitivity as a gift from nature; that man in the cradle is nothing; that his vices, his virtues, his artificial passions, his talents, finally, his prejudices, even as far as self-love—everything is acquired by him.

Self-Interest Daily Denies This Maxim: "Do Not Do to Others What You Would Not Have Them Do to You."

The Catholic priest, persecuted by the Calvinist or the Muslim, denounces persecution as an infraction of natural law. But should this same priest become a persecutor, persecution appears legitimate to him. In him it is the effect of holy zeal and of his love for his neighbor. Thus the same action becomes just or unjust according to whether this priest is executioner or executed.

Shall we read the history of the various Christian religious sects? As long as they are weak they want no other weapons used in theological disputation except reasoning and persuasion. But do these sects become powerful? As I have already said, they turn from being persecuted into persecutors. Calvin burns Servetus; the Jesuits persecute the Jansenists; the Jansenist would like to burn the deist. How self-interest leads us astray in a labyrinth of errors of contradiction! Even self-evidence is obscure.

What does the theater of this world show to us? Nothing but the diverse and perpetual play of self-interest. The more we meditate on this principle the more breadth and fecundity we discover in it.

6.   Voltaire, Candide and Philosophical Dictionary

A. Candide

CHAPTER XX. WHAT BEFELL CANDIDE AND MARTIN ON THEIR VOYAGE

THE OLD SCHOLAR, whose name was Martin, embarked with Candide for Bordeaux. They both had seen and suffered a great deal; and if the ship had been destined to sail from Surinam to Japan round the Cape of Good Hope, they could have found sufficient entertainment for each other during the whole voyage in discoursing upon moral and natural evil.

Candide, however, had one advantage over Martin. He lived in

SOURCE: Voltaire, Candide and Zadig, ed. L. G. Crocker (New York: Washington Square Press, 1962), pp. 74–79. The text is taken from the eighteenth-century translation by Tobias Smollett.

the pleasing hopes of seeing Miss Cunegund once more, whereas the poor philosopher had nothing to hope for. Besides, Candide had money and jewels, and, notwithstanding he had lost a hundred red sheep, laden with the greatest treasure on the earth, and though he still smarted from the reflection of the Dutch skipper's knavery, yet when he considered what he had still left and repeated the name of Cunegund, especially after meal-times, he inclined to Pangloss's doctrine.

"And pray," said he to Martin, "what is your opinion of the whole of this system? What notion have you of moral and natural evil?"

"Sir," replied Martin, "our priests accused me of being a Socinian, but the real truth is I am a Manichaean."

"Nay, now you are jesting," said Candide; "there are no Manichaeans existing at present in the world."

"And yet I am one," said Martin, "but I cannot help it. I cannot for the soul of me think otherwise."

"Surely the devil must be in you," said Candide.

"He concerns himself so much," replied Martin, "in the affairs of this world that it is very probable he may be in me as well as everywhere else; but I must confess, when I cast my eye on this globe, or rather globule, I cannot help thinking that God has abandoned it to some malignant being. I always except El Dorado. I scarce ever knew a city that did not wish the destruction of its neighboring city, nor a family that did not desire to exterminate some other family. The poor, in all parts of the world, bear an inveterate hatred to the rich, even while they creep and cringe to them; and the rich treat the poor like sheep, whose wool and flesh they barter for money. A million of regimented assassins traverse Europe from one end to the other to get their bread by regular depredation and murder, because it is the most gentlemanlike profession. Even in those cities which seem to enjoy the blessings of peace and where the arts flourish, the inhabitants are devoured with envy, care, and anxiety, which are greater plagues than any experienced in a town besieged. Private chagrins are still more dreadful than public calamities. In a word, I have seen and suffered so much, that I am a Manichaean."

"And yet there is some good in the world," replied Candide.

"Maybe," said Martin, "but it has escaped my knowledge."

While they were deeply engaged in this dispute they heard the report of cannon, which redoubled every moment. Each took out his glass, and they spied two ships warmly engaged at the distance of about three miles. The wind brought them both so near the French ship that those on board her had the pleasure of seeing the fight with great ease. At last one of the two vessels gave the other a shot between wind and water, which sank her outright. Then could Candide and Martin plainly perceive a hundred men on the deck of the vessel which was sinking, who, with hands uplifted to heaven, sent forth piercing cries and were in a moment swallowed up by the waves.

"Well," said Martin, "you now see in what manner mankind treat each other."

"It is certain," said Candide, "that there is something diabolical in this affair."

As he was speaking thus, he saw something of a shining red hue, which swam close to the vessel. The boat was hoisted out to see what it might be, when it proved to be one of his sheep. Candide felt more joy at the recovery of this one animal than he did grief when he lost the other hundred, though laden with the large diamonds of El Dorado.

The French captain quickly perceived that the victorious ship belonged to the crown of Spain, that the other which sank was a Dutch pirate and the very same captain who had robbed Candide. The immense riches which this villain had amassed were buried with him in the deep, and only this one sheep saved out of the whole.

"You see," said Candide to Martin, "that vice is sometimes punished. This villain, the Dutch skipper, has met with the fate he deserved."

"Very truly," said Martin, "but why should the passengers be doomed also to destruction? God has punished the knave, and the devil has drowned the rest."

The French and Spanish ships continued their cruise, and Candide and Martin their conversation. They disputed fourteen days successively, at the end of which they were just as far advanced as the first moment they began. However, they had the satisfaction of disputing, of communicating their ideas and of mutually comforting each other. Candide embraced his sheep.

"Since I have found thee again," said he, "I may possibly find my Cunegund once more."

CHAPTER XXI. CANDIDE AND MARTIN, WHILE THUS REASONING WITH
EACH OTHER, DRAW NEAR TO THE COAST OF FRANCE

At length they sighted the coast of France.

"Pray, Mr. Martin," said Candide, "have you ever been in France?"

"Yes, sir," said Martin, "I have been in several provinces of that kingdom. In some, one-half of the people are mad-men; and in some, they are too artful; in others, again, they are in general either very good-natured or very brutal; while in others, they affect to be witty, and in all, their ruling passion is love, the next is slander and the last is to talk nonsense."

"But pray, Mr. Martin, were you ever in Paris?"

"Yes, sir, I have been in that city, and it is a place that contains the several species just described. It is a chaos, a confused multitude, where everyone seeks for pleasure without being able to find it, at least, as far as I have observed during my short stay in that city. At my arrival, I was robbed of all I had in the world by pickpockets and sharpers at the fair of St. Germain. I was taken up myself for a robber and confined in prison a whole week. After that I hired myself as proofreader to a press in order to get a little money toward defraying my expenses back to Holland on foot. I knew the whole tribe of scribblers, intriguers, and religious convulsionaries. It is said the people of that city are very polite; I believe they may be so."

"For my part, I have no curiosity to see France," said Candide. "You may easily conceive, my friend, that, after spending a month at El Dorado, I can desire to behold nothing upon earth but Miss Cunegund. I am going to wait for her at Venice. I intend to pass through France on my way to Italy; will you not bear me company?"

"With all my heart," said Martin. "They say Venice is agreeable to none but noble Venetians, but that, nevertheless, strangers are well received there when they have plenty of money. Now I have none, but you have, therefore I will attend you wherever you please."

"Now we are upon this subject," said Candide, "do you think that the earth was originally sea, as we read in that great book which belongs to the captain of the ship?"

"I believe nothing of it," replied Martin, "any more than I do of the many other chimeras which have been related to us for some time past."

"But then, to what end," said Candide, "was the world formed?"

"To make us mad," said Martin.

"Are you not surprised," continued Candide, "at the love which the two girls in the country of the Oreillons had for those two monkeys?—You know, I have told you the story."

"Surprised!" replied Martin. "Not in the least. I see nothing strange in this passion. I have seen so many extraordinary things, that there is nothing extraordinary to me now."

"Do you think," said Candide, "that mankind always massacred each other as they do now? Were they always guilty of lies, fraud, treachery, ingratitude, inconstancy, envy, ambition, and cruelty? Were they always thieves, fools, cowards, gluttons, drunkards, misers, calumniators, debauchees, fanatics, and hypocrites?"

"Do you believe," said Martin, "that hawks have always been accustomed to eat pigeons when they found them?"

"Yes, of course," said Candide.

"Well then," replied Martin, "if hawks have always had the same nature, why should you pretend that mankind change theirs?"

"Oh!" said Candide, "There is a great deal of difference, for free will . . ."

Reasoning thus, they arrived at Bordeaux.

B. Philosophical Dictionary

WICKED

WE ARE told that human nature is essentially perverse; that man is born a child of the devil, and wicked. Nothing can be more injudicious; for thou, my friend, who preachest to me that all the world is born perverse, warnest me that thou art born such also, and that I must mistrust thee as I would a fox or a crocodile. Oh, no! sayest thou; I am regenerated; I am neither a heretic nor an infidel; you may trust in me. But the rest of mankind, which are either heretic,

SOURCE: Tobias Smollett (ed.), *The Works of Voltaire; a contemporary version with notes*, revised and modernized with new translations by William F. Fleming, introduction Oliver H. G. Leigh (New York: E. R. DuMont, 1901).

or what thou callest infidel, will be an assemblage of monsters, and every time that thou speakest to a Lutheran or a Turk, thou mayest be sure that they will rob and murder thee, for they are children of the devil, they are born wicked; the one is not regenerated, the other is degenerated. It would be much more reasonable, much more noble, to say to men: "You are all born good; see how dreadful it is to corrupt the purity of your being. All mankind should be dealt with as are all men individually." If a canon leads a scandalous life, we say to him: "Is it possible that you would dishonor the dignity of canon?" We remind a lawyer that he has the honor of being a counsellor to the king, and that he should set an example. We say to a soldier to encourage him: "Remember that thou art of the regiment of Champagne." We should say to every individual: "Remember thy dignity as a man."

And indeed, notwithstanding the contrary theory, we always return to that; for what else signifies the expression, so frequently used in all nations: "Be yourself again"? If we are born of the devil, if our origin was criminal, if our blood was formed of an infernal liquor, this expression: "Be yourself again," would signify: "Consult, follow your diabolic nature; be an imposter, thief, and assassin; it is the law of your nature."

Man is not born wicked; he becomes so, as he becomes sick. Physicians present themselves and say to him: "You are born sick." It is very certain these doctors, whatever they may say or do, will not cure him, if the malady is inherent in his nature; besides, these reasoners are often very ailing themselves.

Assemble all the children of the universe; you will see in them only innocence, mildness, and fear; if they were born wicked, mischievous, and cruel, they would show some signs of it, as little serpents try to bite, and little tigers to tear. But nature not having given to men more offensive arms than to pigeons and rabbits, she cannot have given them an instinct leading them to destroy.

Man, therefore, is not born bad; why, therefore, are several infected with the plague of wickedness? It is, that those who are at their head being taken with the malady, communicate it to the rest of men: as a woman attacked with the distemper which Christopher Columbus brought from America, spreads the venom from one end of Europe to the other.

The first ambitious man corrupted the earth. You will tell me that this first monster has sowed the seed of pride, rapine, fraud, and cruelty, which is in all men. I confess, that in general most of our brethren can acquire these qualities; but has everybody the putrid fever, the stone and gravel, because everybody is exposed to it?

There are whole nations which are not wicked: the Philadelphians, the Banians, have never killed any one. The Chinese, the people of Tonquin, Lao, Siam, and even Japan, for more than a hundred years have not been acquainted with war. In ten years we scarcely see one of those great crimes which astonish human nature in the cities of Rome, Venice, Paris, London, and Amsterdam; towns in which cupidity, the mother of all crimes, is extreme.

If men were essentially wicked—if they were all born submissive to a being as mischievous as unfortunate, who, to revenge himself for his punishment, inspired them with all his passions—we should every morning see husbands assassinated by their wives, and fathers by their children; as at break of day we see fowls strangled by a weasel who comes to suck their blood.

If there be a thousand millions of men on the earth, that is much; that gives about five hundred millions of women, who sew, spin, nourish their little ones, keep their houses or cabins in order, and slander their neighbors a little. I see not what great harm these poor innocents do on earth. Of this number of inhabitants of the globe, there are at least two hundred millions of children, who certainly neither kill nor steal, and about as many old people and invalids, who have not the power of doing so. There will remain, at most, a hundred millions of robust young people capable of crime. Of this hundred millions, there are ninety continually occupied in forcing the earth, by prodigious labor, to furnish them with food and clothing; these have scarcely time. In the ten remaining millions will be comprised idle people and good company, who would enjoy themselves at their ease; men of talent occupied in their professions; magistrates, priests, visibly interested in leading a pure life, at least in appearance. Therefore, of truly wicked people, there will only remain a few politicians, either secular or regular, who will always trouble the world, and some thousand vagabonds who hire their services to these politicians. Now, there is never a million of these ferocious beasts employed at once, and in this number I reckon highwaymen. You have therefore on the earth, in the most stormy times, only one man in a thousand whom we can call wicked, and he is not always so.

There is, therefore, infinitely less wickedness on the earth than we are told and believe there is. There is still too much, no doubt; we see misfortunes and horrible crimes; but the pleasure of complaining of and exaggerating them is so great, that at the least scratch we say that the earth flows with blood. Have you been deceived?—all men are perjured. A melancholy mind which has suffered injustice, sees the earth covered with damned people: as a young rake, supping with his lady, on coming from the opera, imagines that there are no unfortunates.

7. *Diderot, Rameau's Nephew and Refutation of Helvétius*, On Man

---

A. *Rameau's Nephew*

MYSELF: But why do you employ such despicable tricks?

HE: Despicable? Why despicable, if you please? Everyone in my situation uses them. There's nothing despicable in doing what everyone else does. After all, I didn't invent them. And it would be very eccentric and stupid of me if I refused to conform. Oh, I know perfectly well that if you go and apply certain general principles to these things, dragged in from this morality they all talk about and never practice, well of course everything that's black turns out to be white and everything white becomes black. But, mister philosopher, there are general principles of morality just as there are general principles of grammar, and then, in every language, the exceptions to those principles, which I believe you scholars call, er . . . help me, can't you, er . . .

MYSELF: Idioms.

HE: Exactly. Well, every occupation has its exceptions to the general principles of morality, which I am tempted to refer to as professional idioms.

MYSELF: I see what you mean. Fontenelle speaks well, writes well, and yet his style teems with French idioms.

SOURCE: Translated by Derek Coltman in *Diderot's Selected Writings*, ed. L. G. Crocker (New York: The Macmillan Company, 1966), pp. 130–37. Reprinted by permission of the publisher.

HE: And the sovereign, the minister, the financier, the magistrate, the soldier, the writer, the lawyer, the attorney, the merchant, the banker, the artisan, the singing master, the dancing master— they are all extremely honest people, yet there is not one of them whose conduct does not depart in some particulars from the general principles of morality and is not full of moral idioms. The longer things have been established, the greater the number of idioms. The worse the times are, the more the idioms increase. A trade is as good as the man who practices it. And the converse of that is: in the long run, a man is no better than his trade. So a man has to make the most out of his trade.

MYSELF: The only thing I understand clearly from all that rigmarole is that there are either few trades that are practiced honestly or few honest people who extend their honesty to their trades.

HE: You've hit it! But in fact there are none. Though on the other hand, there aren't many people who are rogues outside their trade. Everything would really go quite well if it weren't for a certain number of people who are referred to as industrious, trustworthy, rigorous in carrying out their duties, strict, or, which amounts to the same thing, are always in their shops from morning till night, practicing their trades, and doing nothing but that. As a result, they are the only ones who become rich and respected.

MYSELF: By using a great many idioms.

HE: Precisely. I see you've caught on. Now one idiom in almost all trades—because certain idioms, like certain idiocies, are common to all ages and climes—one common idiom is to get the largest clientele you can. Because, you see, one of the common idiocies is to believe that the man with the largest clientele is necessarily the best at his trade. Those are two exceptions to the general principles of morality you just have to accept. It's a kind of credit. It's nothing in itself, but public opinion makes it valuable. "A good name is worth more than a golden belt," so the saying goes. Though having a good name doesn't guarantee you the golden belt, and these days, I notice, no one who has a golden belt ever seems to lack a good name. As far as possible, you should try to have the good name and the belt as well. And that is what I'm aiming at when I try to increase my value in people's eyes with what you call my despicable ruses and my unworthy little tricks. I give my lesson, and I give it well: that's the general principle. I also pretend that I have more lessons to give than there are hours in the day: that's the idiom.

MYSELF: And you say you give the lesson well?

HE: Yes, pretty well, quite passably. My dear uncle's fundamental bass has made all that much simpler now. There was a time when I was stealing my pupils' money, yes, stealing it, there's no doubt about that. Today I earn it—as much as the others do, anyway.

MYSELF: And you stole it without remorse?

HE: Without remorse! What do you think? There's a saying, "When one thief steals from another, the devil laughs." The parents were all bursting with money that God alone knows how they came by. They were all courtiers, financiers, big merchants, bankers, promoters, and so on. I was helping them to make restitution—me and a whole crowd of others they were employing in exactly the same way. In nature, all the species devour each other. And all the different classes devour each other in society. It's a way of squaring accounts without having to drag the law into it. The dancer at the Opéra, for instance—once it was La Deschamps, nowadays it's La Guimard—avenges the sovereign by fleecing the financier; then the purveyor of fashions, the jeweler, the interior decorator, the dressmaker, and the swindler avenge the financier by fleecing La Deschamps. And the only ones who do no harm to anyone and still come out of the whole thing any the worse off are the fools and the layabouts —which is just as it should be. So you see that these exceptions to the general principles of morality, or these moral idioms, which everyone makes such a fuss about and refers to as swindler's tricks, don't amount to a thing, and the main thing, as always, is to keep a sense of perspective.

MYSELF: Yours is certainly astonishing.

HE: And, then, there's poverty. The voice of conscience and the claims of honor are difficult to hear when your insides are yelling for food. But that's all right, because if ever I become rich I shall be obliged to make restitution, and I am quite reconciled to making restitution in every possible way, with good food, with gambling, with wine, and with women.

MYSELF: But I'm afraid you're never going to become rich.

HE: Yes, I rather suspect that too.

MYSELF: But supposing you did, what would you do?

HE: I'd do the same as all the other beggars who suddenly get rich:

I'd turn into the most insolent rogue you've ever seen. I'd remember everything they made me go through, and I'd repay every humiliation I've been made to suffer with a vengeance. I see it all. I love to give orders, and give orders I shall. I love to be praised, and praise me they shall. I shall have all those hangers-on of Vilmorin's on my payroll, and I shall say to them what people used to say to me: "Get to it, you rogues—amuse me!" And they will amuse me. "Tear all the respectable people I know to ribbons!" And they'll tear them to ribbons, if there are any left. And then we'll have some girls in, and I'll treat them all as equals when we've gotten drunk—and we shall get drunk. And then we'll tell lies about people—oh, and we'll be wicked and vicious in all sorts of ways. It will be delightful. We'll prove that Voltaire hasn't a scrap of genius and that Buffon is just an old windbag, always stuck up there on his high horse, and that Montesquieu is nothing but a clever-clever social butterfly; we'll dump d'Alembert back where he belongs, with all that mathematics of his; and we'll make pulp of all those petty upstart Catos, like you, who despise us out of envy, whose modesty is just a cloak for their pride, and whose respectability is merely a result of their poverty. And as for music—ah, such music we'll make then!

MYSELF: From the praiseworthy use to which you would put your riches, I now perceive what a great pity it is that you're a beggar. The way of life you have described would assuredly bring great honor to the human race, great benefits to your fellow citizens, and glorious renown upon yourself.

HE: I have a feeling you're making fun of me. You don't know who it is you're dealing with, mister philosopher. You don't seem to realize that as things stand, I represent the most influential section of both the city and the court. All our rich men, whatever their rank may be, may have admitted to themselves or may not have admitted to themselves all those things I've just confided to you; but the fact is that the life I said I would lead in their place is the life they are actually leading. That's how much you know, you fellows. You think the same sort of happiness is right for everybody. What a bizarre way of seeing things! Your sort of happiness presupposes a certain romantic turn of mind that we just don't have, an exceptional mental outlook, unusual tastes. You dignify this eccentricity with the name of virtue, you call it philosophical. But are virtue and philosophy suited to everyone? They're things you acquire if you get the chance and hang on to if you can. Just imagine what the world would be like if everyone were wise and philosophical—damnably dull, you will agree. Long live philosophy, say I! Long live the wisdom of Solomon: good wine to drink, good food to stuff yourself with, pretty women to tumble, soft beds to lie on. Take all that away and the rest is mere vanity.

MYSELF: What! Fighting for one's country?

HE: Vanity. No one has a country any more. I can see nothing but tyrants and slaves from one pole to the other.

MYSELF: Being of use to one's friends?

HE: Vanity. Who has friends? And even supposing we did, ought we to turn them into ingrates? Because, if you think about it, that's almost always what happens when you help people. Gratitude is a burden, and all burdens are things to be gotten rid of.

MYSELF: To fill a position in society and carry out its duties?

HE: Vanity. The only reason anyone ever wants a position is to become rich. So what does it matter if you have a position or not if you're rich already? And what does doing your duty lead to? Jealousy, anxiety, persecution. Is that any way to get ahead? Bowing and scraping, dammit, that's the way, bowing and scraping. You have to keep your eyes on the people at the top, study their tastes, fall in with their whims, pander to their vices, praise the rotten things they do—that's the secret.

MYSELF: What about supervising your children's education?

HE: Vanity. There are tutors paid to do that.

MYSELF: But suppose the tutor shares your own principles and neglects his duties. Who is going to suffer?

HE: Certainly not me. Perhaps my daughter's husband, one day. Or my son's wife.

MYSELF: But suppose they both rush headlong into debauchery and vice?

HE: With their social position, it's to be expected.

MYSELF: What if they dishonor themselves?

HE: You can't dishonor yourself if you're rich, whatever you do.

MYSELF: Then what if they ruin themselves?

HE: That's their hard luck. . . .

MYSELF: [Rich people in search of pleasure] wear everything out in the end. Their spirits become dulled. They sink into the clutches of boredom. They lie there suffocating in their own affluence, and if someone were to end their lives for them then and there, he would be doing them a favor. Why? Because the only kind of happiness they know is the kind most quickly blunted. I don't despise the pleasures of the senses: I have a palate too, and one that enjoys delicate foods or a fine wine. I have a heart and eyes: I enjoy looking at a pretty woman. I like to feel the firm curves of her breast beneath my hand, to press my lips against hers, to drink deep of pleasure in her eyes, and die of it in her arms. Occasionally, I quite enjoy an evening spent drinking with my friends, even if it gets a little rowdy. But I cannot pretend to you that I don't find it infinitely more pleasant still to have helped the needy, to have settled some particularly thorny problem, to have given a piece of useful advice, to have read an enjoyable book, to have gone for a walk with a man or woman dear to my heart, to have spent a few instructive hours with my children, to have written a good page, to have carried out the duties of my station in society, to have said a few sweet and tender words to the woman I love and felt her answering arms cling mutely around my neck. I can think of some actions that I would give everything I possess to have performed myself. [Voltaire's] *Mahomet* is a sublime work. But I would rather have rehabilitated the memory of the Calas family. A man I know once went away to live in Cartagena. He was a younger son in a country where custom transmits all family wealth to the eldest. While still abroad, he learned that his elder brother, always spoiled by the family, had stripped his too indulgent parents of everything they possessed and thrown them out of their home, so that the good old couple were now dragging out a miserable existence in a small provincial town. So what did he do, this younger son who had been harshly treated by his parents and forced to seek his fortune far from home? He sent them help; he hastily wound up his affairs, returned to his own country a rich man, restored his father and mother to their own home, and saw to it that his sisters married well. Yes, my dear Rameau, and that man still thinks of that period as the happiest in his life. There were tears in his eyes as he told me about it; and I myself, even as I am telling you his story, feel my heart stirring with joy and my tongue faltering with happiness.

HE: What an odd lot of creatures you philosophers are!

MYSELF: And what an unfortunate lot of creatures you and your kind are if you are unable to apprehend that man can rise above his fate, that it is impossible to be unhappy when you are protected by such nobility as I have described.

HE: It's a kind of happiness I would have found rather difficult to study closely; it's not very often you meet it. So according to you, we ought all to behave like decent people?

MYSELF: If you want to be happy? Without a doubt.

HE: Yet I see an infinite number of decent people who are not happy and an infinite number of people who are happy without being decent.

MYSELF: No, you only think you do.

HE: And isn't it precisely because I had one moment of common sense and honesty that I have no place to go for supper tonight?

MYSELF: No, Rameau, no! It's because you haven't had them the rest of the time. It's because you didn't realize early enough that the most important thing in this world is to find a way of life that will free you from slavish dependence on others.

HE: Well, slavishly dependent or not, the way I found is at least the easiest.

MYSELF: And the least reliable, as well as the least honest.

HE: But the most in keeping with my character, since I am an idler, a fool, and a good-for-nothing.

MYSELF: Agreed.

HE: And, then, since I can achieve the happiness I want by using my natural defects—which I acquired without effort and am able to preserve without effort, which fit nicely with the customs of the country I live in, which suit the taste of my protectors and satisfy their private needs better than a lot of virtues that would simply point an accusing finger at them from morning till night—it would be very odd in me to go around tormenting myself like a damned soul in order to twist myself into some other shape, make myself into someone quite different from what I am, and give myself a new character nothing at all like my own. I'll agree that all the new qualities I'd acquire would be very admirable, because I don't want to argue with you, but acquiring them and using them would be a terrible effort, and they would get me exactly nowhere. They might even get me worse than nowhere—by implying a constant criticism of the wealthy people that beggars like myself have to depend on for a living.

People praise virtue, but they hate it, they run away from it. It freezes you to death, and in this world you've got to keep your feet warm. Apart from which, it would make me bad-tempered, inevitably. Why is it that the pious people we see are so often hard and irritable, so difficult to get on with? It's because they're forcing themselves to do something that isn't natural to them. They're unhappy; and when you're unhappy, you make others unhappy too. That's not what I'm looking for, and that's not what my protectors are looking for. I've got to be gay, quick-witted, entertaining, full of buffoonery, funny. Virtue demands respect, and respect makes people uncomfortable. Virtue demands admiration, and admiration doesn't amuse people. I have to deal with people who are bored, and my job is to make them laugh. Therefore, since absurdity and folly are what make people laugh, I have to be absurd and foolish. And even if nature hadn't made me that way, the easiest thing would be to pretend she had. Happily, I have no need to be a hypocrite. . . .

But suppose your friend Rameau should one day start to display contempt for money, for women, for good food, and for an idle life of pleasure, suppose he should ever start to play the stoic, what would he be then? A hypocrite. Rameau must be what he is: a happy robber among wealthy robbers, not a fellow who goes round trumpeting about virtue or even a simple virtuous man gnawing his crust of bread alone or in company with other beggars. To put it bluntly, I have no use for your idea of happiness or that of the handful of visionaries like you. . . .

MYSELF: Whatever the task a man applies himself to, that is the one that nature intended him for.

HE: Then she makes some odd blunders. I'm not one of those people who look down from such a height that differences disappear, so that a man pruning a tree with a pair of shears and a caterpillar nibbling one of the tree's leaves just look like two different insects, each performing its appointed task. But there's nothing to stop you perching up there on the epicycle of Mercury if you want to. You can look down at us like another Réaumur. Just as he classified flies into the sewing kind, the measuring kind, and the clipping kind, so you can classify men as carpenters, cabinetmakers, runners, dancers, singers, and so on. That's your business; I don't want any part of it. I'm down here in this world, and I'm staying here. But if it's natural to be hungry—and if I always come back to hunger, that's because it's a sensation that's always with me—then I don't see how a society in which a person doesn't always have enough to eat can be a good one. What a hell of a system if there are some men with too much of everything while others, with the same demands being made on them by their stomachs, the same ever-returning hunger, can't get as much as one little bite to eat. And the worst part of all is the unnatural posture that our poverty forces on us. The needy man doesn't even walk like anyone else—he hops, he crawls, he wriggles, he drags himself along. His whole life is spent in taking up attitudes.

MYSELF: What do you mean by "attitudes"?

HE: Go and ask Noverre [the choreographer] that. But there are a lot more to be seen in real life than his art can ever imitate.

MYSELF: So now you're up there too, if I may use your own expression—or, rather, Montaigne's—"perched on the epicycle of Mercury" and comtemplating the varied pantomime of humankind.

HE: Not at all. You are wrong, I assure you. I am too heavy to rise so high. I leave those cloudy regions to the cranes. I stick close to earth. I keep watch on all that's going on around me, and I perform my attitudes—or else amuse myself by watching the others performing theirs. I am an excellent mime, as you shall see.

Whereupon, with a smile, he proceeded to give an imitation of a man expressing admiration, a man begging, a man fawning. Right foot forward, left foot back, spine bent, head tilted up and back, eyes apparently hanging on the expression of another pair of eyes, mouth half open, arms stretched out toward some object in front of him, he seemed to be waiting for a command. The command was given; he darted away like an arrow; he came back; the task had been performed; he expressed as much. His eyes were missing nothing; if anything fell to the floor, he picked it up; he slipped a footstool or a pillow under someone's feet; he held out a saucer; he pulled up a chair; he opened a door; he closed a window; he drew the curtains; he watched his master and mistress, motionless, arms hanging at his sides, legs together, listening, straining to interpret the expressions on their faces and saying: Now you've seen my attitudes. Most people's are the same; flatterers, courtiers, lackeys, beggars—they're all like that. .   .   .

MYSELF: But according to you, there are a great many beggars in this world of ours; and I can't think of anyone who doesn't know a few steps of that ballet of yours.

HE: You are right. There is only one man in the whole of any kingdom who walks: that's the king. All the others just go through a series of attitudes.

MYSELF: The king? I'm not so sure about that. Don't you think there may occasionally be a little foot by his side, a little curly head, a little nose that makes him join the dance from time to time? Anyone who needs someone else is a beggar, and a beggar must have an attitude. The king performs his attitudes to his mistress and to God; he dances his ballet for them. The minister, in his turn, dances the role of the courtier, the flatterer, the valet, or the beggar before the king. Then there is the crowd of ambitious climbers, all dancing the steps you've just shown me, all doing their variations, each more despicable than the last, in the front of the minister. The wellborn abbé, in his Geneva collar and his long cloak, humbles himself once every week, at least, in front of the official who hands out the livings. Believe me, what you call the beggar's pantomime is the whole world's ring-around-the-rosy. Everyone has his Bertin and his little Hus.

HE: That's a consoling thought.

B. Refutation of the Work of Helvétius Entitled On Man
[1773–76]

To feel is to judge.[1]

THIS assertion, as it is phrased, does not seem strictly true to me. A stupid man feels but does not necessarily judge. A being totally deprived of memory feels, but it does not judge: judgment presupposes the comparison of two ideas. The difficulty consists in knowing how this comparison is performed, since it presupposes

SOURCE: Denis Diderot, *Oeuvres philosophiques*, ed. Paul Vernière (Paris: Garnier Frères, 1956), pp. 563–67. Translation by the editor.

[1] The italicized passages heading each entry are from Helvétius and are the points against which, in each instance, Diderot proceeds to conduct his polemic.

the simultaneous presence of two ideas in the mind. Helvétius would have removed a terrible stumbling block if he had given a clear explanation of how we entertain two ideas simultaneously or how, if we do not entertain them simultaneously, we can nevertheless still compare them.

Perhaps I will in an ill humor when I read this sixth chapter, but here are my remarks on it—good or bad, I shall set them down just as they came to me at the time. From all the author's metaphysics, there emerges the fact that judgment, or the comparison of objects with each other, presupposes some motive for comparing them. Helvétius then concludes that this motive arises necessarily from the desire for happiness, which, in its turn, arises from physical sensitivity. This conclusion is very far-fetched; it is more applicable to animals in general than to man. To leap suddenly from physical sensitivity, *i.e.*, the fact that I am not a plant, a stone, or a metal, to the desire for happiness, from the desire for happiness to self-interest, from self-interest to attention, from attention to the comparison of ideas—these are generalities I cannot accept. I am a man, and I must have causes particular to man. The author also adds that by climbing two rungs higher or descending one rung lower, he could go on from physical sensitivity to structure, from structure to existence and could then say, "I exist, and I exist in this form; I feel, I judge; I try to be happy because I feel; my self-interest leads me to compare my ideas because I have a will toward happiness." But what possible utility can I derive from a string of consequences that is equally applicable to a dog, a weasel, an oyster, or a dromedary? . . .

Descartes said, "I think, therefore I am."

Helvétius wants us to say, "I feel, therefore I wish to feel pleasantly."

I prefer Hobbes. He claims that if we wish to draw any meaningful conclusion, we must say, "I feel, I think, I judge, therefore a portion of matter organized as I am can feel, think, and judge." . . .

If he had started with the single phenomenon of physical sensitivity, accepting it as either a universal property of all matter or a result of structure, and clearly deduced from it all the operations of the understanding, then he would have done something new, difficult, and extremely fine.

But I shall hold in even greater esteem the man who, by means of experiments or observation, either provides us with rigorous proof that sentience is as essential to matter as impenetrability or demonstrates it irrefutably to be an effect of structure.

I urge all physicists and all chemists to attempt the discovery of what living, sentient, animal substance is.

In the development of the egg and in some other operations of nature, I can clearly see matter that is apparently inert, although possessing structure, passing from this inanimate state to a state of sentience and life as a result of purely physical agents, but the necessary link in this transition escapes me.

Our notions of matter, structure, motion, heat, flesh, sentience, and life must still be very far from complete.

We must all agree on this: the organization or coordination of inert parts most certainly does not produce sentience. Secondly, the presence of universal sentience in all molecules of matter is only a supposition, and a supposition of which the whole strength is derived from the difficulties from which it extricates us; and in good philosophy, that is not enough. But now let us go back to our author.

Is it really true that physical pleasure and pain, which are possibly the only principles of action in animals, are also the only principles of action in men?

It is certainly necessary to possess a structure like ours and to feel in order to act. But it seems to me that those are merely the essential and primal conditions, the data *sine qua non*, and that the immediate and most direct motives of our aversions and desires are something else.

Without alkali and sand, there can be no glass, but are those elements the *cause* of transparency?

Without uncultivated land and without a pair of arms, we cannot clear new land, but are those the *motives* of the farmer when he clears a stretch of forest?

To take conditions for causes is to lay oneself open to childish paralogisms and meaningless conclusions.

If I were to say: One must be in order to feel; one must feel in order to be an animal or a man; one must be an animal or a man in order to be miserly, ambitious, and jealous; therefore jealousy, ambition, and avarice have as their primary causes structure, sentience, and existence—well, would you be able to refrain from laughing at me? And why not? Because I would be confusing the conditions for all animal actions in general with the motives for the actions of one individual taken from one particular species of animal called man.

Admittedly I do everything I do in order to feel pleasure or in order to avoid pain, but has the word "feel" only one connotation?

Is there only physical pleasure in possessing a beautiful woman? Is there only physical pain in losing her, either to death or to another?

Is the distinction between the physical and the moral not as solid as that between the merely feeling animal and the thinking animal?

Is it not true that what appertains to the feeling being and what appertains to the thinking being are sometimes united and at other times separated in almost all the actions that make for happiness or unhappiness in our lives, a happiness and an unhappiness that both presuppose physical sensation as a prerequisite condition—which is to say, quite simply, that it is necessary to be something more than a cabbage?

Thus we see how important it was not to make feeling and judging two perfectly identical operations.

8. D'Holbach, Universal Morality, or the Duties of Man Founded on His Nature

---

On Compassion or Pity

To FEEL compassion for men's sufferings, according to the meaning of the word, is to feel what they feel, to suffer with them, to share their sorrows. It is, in some fashion, to put ourselves in their place in order to feel the painful situation which is tormenting them. Thus compassion in man is a habitual inclination to feel more or less keenly the ills with which others are afflicted.

In order to explain the causes of this sensitivity which interests men in the pains of their fellows, some moralists have had recourse to something called sympathy; that is to say, to a chimerical and

SOURCE: D'Holbach, La Morale universelle (Paris, 1820). Translated by the editor.

occult cause which explains nothing. It is in man's structure, in his sensitivity, in a faithful memory, in an active imagination that we must seek the true cause of compassion. He who has sensitive organs feels pain keenly and recalls the idea of it accurately. His imagination paints it to him strongly when he sees a man who is suffering. At once he is himself troubled, he shudders, his heart is tightened, he feels a real sorrow, which in very sensitive people is sometimes manifested by fainting or convulsions. The natural effect of the pain which the keenly affected person feels, then, is to seek the means to bring to an end in others the painful situation which has been transferred to him. From the alleviation which is given to the one who suffers, there results a real relief for the person who helps him; a very sweet pleasure which reflection further increases by the thought of having done someone good, of having acquired rights to an affection, at having merited his gratitude, of having acted in a way which proves that he has a tender and sensitive heart, an attitude which all men desire to find in their fellows and whose absence would lead to the belief that one has a bad disposition.

Men, being very diverse in their structure and in the strength of their imagination, are not able to feel with equal keenness the ills of their fellow men. There are men in whom pity does not exist, or at least is not strong enough to determine them to put an end to the sufferings they see in others. All too often we come upon men who are so used to well-being, the enjoyment of every comfort, that their lack of ever having felt suffering hardens them to the suffering of others and even prevents them from conceiving it. An unhappy person generally has more compassion than one who has never suffered the blows of fate. He who has undergone the pains of gout or kidney stones is far more disposed than another to pity those whom he sees afflicted with the same illness. The pauper who has often felt the horrors of hunger knows all its strength and pities him who feels it; whereas the rich man, constantly satiated, seems to be unaware of its existing in a world where millions of unfortunates are deprived of the necessities of life.

Some moralists have thought that compassion, or this disposition to share the misfortunes of others which is found in sensitive, well-born, properly brought up persons, should be regarded as the basis of all moral and social virtues. But pity, as everything proves, is very rare in this world; the world is filled with a crowd of insensitive beings whose hearts are moved little or not at all by the misfortunes of their fellow men. In some this feeling does not exist; in others it is so weak that the slightest self-interest, the least passion, the most trivial caprice are capable of stifling it.

Although all men delight in being considered sensitive, there are few who show signs of true sensitivity. If a first impulse moves them greatly, these feelings lead to nothing and are soon aborted. Princes contemplate with dry eyes the misfortunes of a whole people, which could often be remedied by a single word from their mouths. Fathers impassively watch the tears flow from wife, children, and servants whose misfortunes are caused by their own bad humor or follies. Greedy men look pitilessly upon the want of peoples whom they have reduced to beggars by their profiteering. In a word, there are very few people who are sufficiently moved by the misfortunes of others to deign to give them consolation or to stretch out a helping hand to them. Most often they fly from the spectacle of misfortune, which is upsetting, and they look for a thousand excuses not to help an unfortunate man, who is generally looked upon as a bothersome and totally useless being.

I must go beyond this. Most men feel themselves entitled by the weakness or misfortune of others to inflict further outrages upon them without fear of reprisal; they take a barbarous pleasure in adding to their afflictions, in making them feel their superiority, in treating them cruelly, in ridiculing them. Thus, beings who are themselves exposed to the whims of fortune, far from feeling pity for the fate of the unfortunate, further aggravate their suffering by haughty attitudes, cutting mockery, and insulting scorn.

9. De Sade, Philosophy in the Boudoir

Morals

WHAT IS MAN, and what difference is there between him and the other animals of the earth? Decidedly none. Like them he was placed upon this globe by chance. Like them he is born, like them

SOURCE: De Sade, *La Philosophie dans le boudoir*, précédée d'une étude sur le marquis de Sade et le sadisme par Holpey (Paris:

he propagates, increases and decreases. Like them he endures old age and disappears into oblivion at the end of the term which Nature has allotted to each species of animal by reason of the structure of its organs. If the comparisons are so exact that it is impossible for the scrutiny of the philosopher to distinguish any dissimilarity, then it will always be as wrong to kill an animal as to kill a man, or else as unimportant. It is only in the prejudices of our vanity that we discern any degree of significance, and, unfortunately, nothing is so absurd as the prejudices of vanity. But let us press the question. You cannot deny that it is all the same to destroy a man or a beast. But is not the destruction of any living animal decidedly an evil, as the Pythagoreans believed and as certain inhabitants on the banks of the Ganges still believe? Before replying to this, let us remind our readers that we are only examining this question in relation to Nature. We will consider it after in relation to man.

Now I ask what price Nature can place upon individuals which cost her nothing in either suffering or attention? The workman only values his work by virtue of the labor he employs in its creation. Does man cost Nature anything? Even supposing that he does, does he cost any more than a monkey or an elephant? I will go further. What are Nature's regenerating materials? What is the composition of beings who become alive? Are not the three elements that form them originally the product of the destruction of other bodies? If every individual were eternal, would it not become impossible for Nature to create new ones? If the immortality of beings is impossible for Nature, then their destruction becomes one of her laws.

If then this destruction is so useful to her that she cannot possibly dispense with it, and if she cannot progress to new creation without drawing upon the masses of decay prepared for her by death, then from this instant the idea of annihilation that we attach to death ceases to be real. There will no longer be any definable annihilation. What we call the end of the living creature will no longer be a real end, but a simple transmutation, the basis of which is perpetual motion, the veritable essence of matter, which all modern philosophers accept as one of their prime laws. According to these irrefutable principles then, death is nothing more than a

---

private edition; La Société des études sadiques, n. d.). Translated by the editor.

change of form, an imperceptible transition from one existence to another, in fact, what Pythagoras called metempsychosis.

Once you have accepted these truths, I wonder if you can ever propose that destruction is a crime? Will you dare to tell me, with the idea of preserving your absurd prejudices, that transmutation is destruction? Surely not. To do that you would need to prove that there is a moment of inaction in matter, an instant of pause. Now you will never discover this moment. Small creatures are formed the moment that the breath leaves the larger creature, and the life of these small beings is only one of the necessary effects determined by the momentary sleep of the larger. Will you dare to say now that one pleases Nature more than the other? For that you would need to prove an impossible thing, namely that the long or squared form is more useful, more agreeable to Nature than the oblong or triangular form. You would need to prove that with respect to the sublime designs of Nature a lazybones growing fatter and fatter with inactivity and indolence is more useful than a horse, whose service is so essential, or than a bullock, whose body is so precious that not a single part of it is unserviceable. You would need to say that the venomous serpent is more necessary than the faithful dog.

Now, as all these propositions are untenable, you must therefore admit without reservation that it is impossible for us to annihilate the works of Nature; it being certain that all we do when we indulge in destroying is to work an alteration in form which cannot extinguish life, it becomes beyond human powers to prove that there can be anything criminal in the alleged destruction of a creature, of whatever age, sex, or species. You are led on and on by this series of deductions we are making, each one developing out of the others, until at last you must admit that the act you commit in varying the forms of Nature's different works, far from harming her, is advantageous to her by providing her in this way with the raw material for her reconstructions.

Well then, leave it to her, people say. Of course you must leave it to her, but it is her promptings that a man follows when he turns to homicide, it is the advice of Nature that he obeys. The man who destroys his fellow is to Nature what pest or famine is, all equally her agents. She makes use of every possible means to obtain as soon as possible this kind of destruction, which is absolutely essential for her works. Let us condescend for a moment to let the sacred torch of philosophy illuminate our minds. Who else but Nature whispers to us of personal hatreds, vengeances, wars, in fact all the everlasting motives for murder? If she advises them, she must need them. How then can we suppose ourselves guilty toward her when all that we are doing is following her plan?

That is more than enough to convince every enlightened reader that it is impossible for murder ever to outrage Nature.

II

The Problem of Evil

THE EXISTENCE of evil in the world has been a problem to man ever since his alienation from nature; that is, it is seemingly inherent in the human condition. It found its first great poetic expression in the Greek tragedies and in the Book of Job. The renewal of critical rationalism toward the end of the seventeenth century led to a reopening of the question of evil, along with many others. It seemed central to thought about the nature of the universe, man's place in it, his destiny, his morality.

As with so many things, it was Bayle's corrosive skepticism that brought out anew the impossibility of reconciling the belief in a good and almighty God with the existence of evil in the world and in men. The dilemma he propounded (either God is good and not all-powerful, or all-powerful and not good, and in either case is not God) created vast and often furious reaction among the faithful. But all their efforts, which persisted throughout the century, provided no logical escape from the impasse. Leibniz wrote a theodicy ("justification of God") in 1710, expounding the necessity of evil in a world which God had necessarily made "the best of all possible worlds." His rather complex, sometimes abstruse argumentation fails to blunt the fine point of Bayle's simple reasoning. The optimistic deists like Shaftesbury (*The Moralists,* published as part of *Characteristics of Men, Manners, Opinions, Times,* 1711) and Pope (*Essay on Man,* 1732–34) rationalized disharmonies into a universal harmony. Going beyond Leibniz, they denied the existence of significant evil: "Everything that is, is right."

Voltaire, in his gay though not always happy youth, had been seduced by the optimistic view. As he matured, he became more and more sensitive to the existence of evil in his own life, in the world around him, and throughout history. If Bayle's Manicheism was correct and there were two contesting principles in the world, then that of evil, it seemed, had always had the upper hand. Optimism was a mockery of human suffering—even a form of covert pessimism that prevented melioristic action. Voltaire's views received their most poignant expression in his *Poème sur le désastre de Lisbonne* (1756).

Rousseau was a deist, but a sentimental deist, for whom sentiment was more reliable and precious than specious argumentation (at least when the latter failed him). He needed God for his faith in conscience, for his metaphysical and political system, and most of all, for his emotional security. His reply to Voltaire, written for public consumption, combines Voltaire's own weapon of irony with Rousseau's unmatched eloquence. Voltaire never forgave him.

Toward the end of the century, Sade, expressing the nihilistic view, turned back to Bayle. The world is evil and needs evil, and God (if he exists) is a principle of evil. Bayle had suggested that God's connivance in evil furnished an example that men might feel justified in following. This is precisely what Sade proclaimed. His dialogue, *La Philosophie dans le boudoir*, was published in 1795.

10. Bayle, Manicheans

PROPERLY speaking, history is nothing but the crimes and misfortunes of the human race. But let us observe that these two evils, the one moral and the other physical, do not encompass all history or all private experience. Both moral good and physical good are found everywhere, some examples of virtue, some examples of happiness; and this is what causes the difficulty. For if all mankind were wicked and miserable, there would be no need to have recourse to the hypothesis of two principles. It is the mixture of happiness and virtue with misery and vice that requires this hypothesis. It is in this that the strength of the sect of Zoroaster lies . . .

To make people see how difficult it would be to refute this false system, and to make them conclude that it is necessary to have recourse to the light of revelation in order to destroy it, let us suppose here a dispute between Melissus[1] and Zoroaster. They were both pagans and great philosophers. Melissus, who acknowl-

SOURCE: Translated by R. H. Popkin and Craig Brush in Pierre Bayle, *Historical and Critical Dictionary* (Indianapolis, Ind.: The Bobbs-Merrill Co., Inc., 1965), pp. 147–50. Copyright © 1965. Reprinted by permission of the publishers.

[1] Greek philosopher of Samos, disciple of Palmenides, and representative of the Eleatic school; flor. c. 1440 B.C.

edged only one principle, would say at the outset that his theory agrees admirably with the ideas of order. The necessary Being has no limits. He is therefore infinite and all-powerful, and thus he is one. And it would be both monstrous and inconsistent if he did not have goodness and did have the greatest of all vices—an essential malice. "I confess to you," Zoroaster would answer, "that your ideas are well connected; and I shall willingly acknowledge that in this respect your hypothesis surpasses mine. I will renounce an objection that I could employ, which is that infinity ought to comprehend all that is real, and malice is not less real than goodness. Therefore the universe should require that there be wicked beings and good beings. And since supreme goodness and supreme malice cannot subsist in one subject, it is the case that in the nature of things there must be an essentially good being, and another essentially bad being. I renounce, I say, this objection. I allow you the advantage of being more conformable to the notion of order than I am. But by your hypothesis explain a little to me how it happens that man is wicked and so subject to pain and grief. I defy you to find in your principles the explanation of this phenomenon, as I can find it in mine. I then regain the advantage. You surpass me in the beauty of ideas and in a priori reasons, and I surpass you in the explanation of phenomena and in a posteriori reasons. And since the chief characteristic of a good system is its being capable of accounting for experience, and since the mere incapacity of accounting for it is a proof that a hypothesis is not good, however fine it appears to be in other respects, you must grant that I hit the nail on the head by admitting two principles and that you miss it by admitting only one.

"If man is the work of a single supremely good, supremely holy, supremely powerful principle, is it possible that he can be exposed to illnesses, to cold, to heat, to hunger, to thirst, to pain, to vexation? Is it possible he should have so many bad inclinations and commit so many crimes? Is it possible that the supreme holiness would produce so criminal a creature? Is it possible that the supreme goodness would produce so unhappy a creature? Would not the supreme power joined to an infinite goodness pour down blessings upon its work and defend it from everything that might annoy or trouble it?" If Melissus consults the ideas of order, he will answer that man was not wicked when God created him. He will say that man received a happy state from God, but not having followed the lights of his conscience, which according to the intention of his author would have conducted him along the virtuous path, he became wicked, and he deserved that the supremely just and supremely good God made him feel the effects of His wrath. Then it is not God who is the cause of moral evil; but he is the cause of physical evil, that is to say, the punishment of moral evil—punishment which, far from being incompatible with the supremely good principle, necessarily flows from one of God's attributes, I mean that of justice, which is no less essential to man than God's goodness. This answer, the most reasonable that Melissus could make, is basically fine and sound. But it can be combatted by arguments which have something in them more specious and dazzling. For Zoroaster would not fail to set forth that, if man were the work of an infinitely good and holy principle, he would have been created not only with no actual evil but also without any inclination to evil, since that inclination is a defect that cannot have such a principle for a cause. It remains then to be said that, when man came from the hands of his creator, he had only the power of self-determination to evil, and that since he determined himself in that way, he is the sole cause of the crime that he committed and the moral evil that was introduced into the universe. But, (1) we have no distinct idea that could make us comprehend how a being not self-existent should, however, be the master of its own actions. Then Zoroaster will say that the free will given to man is not capable of giving him an actual determination since its being is continuously and totally supported by the action of God. (2) He will pose this question, "Did God foresee that man would make bad use of his free will?" If the answer is affirmative he will reply that it appears impossible to foresee what depends entirely on an undetermined cause. "But I will readily agree with you," he will say, "that God foresaw the sin of his creature; and I conclude from this that he would have prevented it; for the ideas of order will not allow that an infinitely good and holy cause that can prevent the introduction of moral evil does not stop it, especially when by permitting it he will find himself obliged to pour down pains and torments upon his own work. If God did not foresee the fall of man, he must at least have judged that it was possible; therefore, since he saw he would be obliged to abandon his paternal goodness if the fall ever did occur, only to make his children miserable by exercising upon them the role of a severe judge, he would have determined man to moral good as he has determined him to physical good. He would not have left in man's soul any power for carrying himself toward sin, just as he did not leave any power for carrying himself toward misery in so far as it was misery. This is where we are led by the clear and distinct ideas of order when we follow, step by step, what an infinitely good principle ought to do. For, if a goodness as limited as that of a human father necessarily requires that he prevent as much as possible the bad use which his children might make of the goods he gives them, much more will an infinite and all-powerful goodness prevent the bad effects of its gifts. Instead of giving them free will, it will determine its creatures to good; or if it gives them free will, it will always efficiently watch over them to prevent their fall into sin." I very well believe that Melissus would not be silenced at this point, but whatever he might answer would be immediately combatted by reasons as plausible as his, and thus the dispute would never terminate . . .

11.   Leibniz, Theodicy

SOME go even further: not content with using the pretext of necessity to prove that virtue and vice do neither good nor ill, they have the hardihood to make the Divinity accessory to their licentious way of life, and they imitate the pagans of old, who ascribed to the gods the cause of their crimes, as if a divinity drove them to do evil. The philosophy of Christians, which recognized better than that of the ancients the dependence of things upon the first Author and his co-operation with all the actions of creatures, appears to have increased this difficulty. Some able men in our own time have gone so far as to deny all action to creatures, and M. Bayle, who tended a little towards this extraordinary opinion, made use of it to restore the lapsed dogma of the two principles, or two

SOURCE: Austin Farrer (ed.), Theodicy; essays on the goodness of God, the freedom of man, and the origin of evil, trans. E. M. Huggard (New Haven, Conn.: Yale University Press, 1952), pp. 57–61, 128–29, 131, 132. Reprinted by permission of Routledge & Kegan Paul, Ltd., London, England.

gods, the one good, the other evil, as if this dogma were a better solution to the difficulties over the origin of evil. Yet again he acknowledges that it is an indefensible opinion and that the oneness of the Principle is incontestably founded on a priori reasons; but he wishes to infer that our Reason is confounded and cannot meet her own objections, and that one should disregard them and hold fast the revealed dogmas, which teach us the existence of one God altogether good, altogether powerful and altogether wise. But many readers, convinced of the irrefutable nature of his objections and believing them to be at least as strong as the proofs for the truth of religion, would draw dangerous conclusions.

Even though there were no co-operation by God in evil actions, one could not help finding difficulty in the fact that he foresees them and that, being able to prevent them through his omnipotence, he yet permits them. This is why some philosophers and even some theologians have rather chosen to deny to God any knowledge of the detail of things and, above all, of future events, than to admit what they believed repellent to his goodness. The Socinians and Conrad Vorstius lean towards that side; and Thomas Bonartes, an English Jesuit disguised under a pseudonym but exceedingly learned, who wrote a book *De Concordia Scientiae cum Fide*, of which I will speak later, appears to hint at this also.

They are doubtless much mistaken; but others are not less so who, convinced that nothing comes to pass save by the will and the power of God, ascribe to him intentions and actions so unworthy of the greatest and the best of all beings that one would say these authors have indeed renounced the dogma which recognized God's justice and goodness. They thought that, being supreme Master of the universe, he could without any detriment to his holiness cause sins to be committed, simply at his will and pleasure, or in order that he might have the pleasure of punishing; and even that he could take pleasure in eternally afflicting innocent people without doing any injustice, because no one has the right or the power to control his actions.[1] Some even have gone so far as to say that God acts thus indeed; and on the plea that we are as nothing in comparison with him, they liken us to earthworms which men crush without heeding as they walk, or in general to animals that are not of our species and which we do not scruple to ill-treat.

---

[1] Leibniz may possibly be referring to the Jansenists, among others.

I believe that many persons otherwise of good intentions are misled by these ideas, because they have not sufficient knowledge of their consequences. They do not see that, properly speaking, God's justice is thus overthrown. For what idea shall we form of such a justice as has only will for its rule, that is to say, where the will is not guided by the rules of good and even tends directly towards evil? Unless it be the idea contained in that tyrannical definition by Thrasymachus in Plato,[2] which designated as just that which pleases the stronger. Such indeed is the position taken up, albeit unwittingly, by those who rest all obligation upon constraint, and in consequence take power as the gauge of right. But one will soon abandon maxims so strange and so unfit to make men good and charitable through the imitation of God. For one will reflect that a God who would take pleasure in the misfortune of others cannot be distinguished from the evil principle of the Manichaeans, assuming that this principle had become sole master of the universe; and that in consequence one must attribute to the true God sentiments that render him worthy to be called the good Principle.

Happily these extravagant dogmas scarce obtain any longer among theologians. Nevertheless some astute persons, who are pleased to make difficulties, revive them: they seek to increase our perplexity by uniting the controversies aroused by Christian theology to the disputes of philosophy. Philosophers have considered the questions of necessity, of freedom and of the origin of evil; theologians have added thereto those of original sin, of grace and of predestination. The original corruption of the human race, coming from the first sin, appears to us to have imposed a natural necessity to sin without the succour of divine grace: but necessity being incompatible with punishment, it will be inferred that a sufficient grace ought to have been given to all men; which does not seem to be in conformity with experience.

But the difficulty is great, above all, in relation to God's dispositions for the salvation of men. There are few saved or chosen; therefore the choice of many is not God's decreed will. And since it is admitted that those whom he has chosen deserve it no more than the rest, and are not even fundamentally less evil, the goodness which they have coming only from the gift of God, the difficulty

[2] In the *Republic*.

is increased. Where is, then, his justice (people will say), or at the least, where is his goodness? Partiality, or respect of persons, goes against justice, and he who without cause sets bounds to his goodness cannot have it in sufficient measure. It is true that those who are not chosen are lost by their own fault: they lack good will or living faith; but it rested with God alone to grant it them. We know that besides inward grace there are usually outward circumstances which distinguish men, and that training, conversation, example often correct or corrupt natural disposition. Now that God should call forth circumstances favourable to some and abandon others to experiences which contribute to their misfortune, will not that give us cause for astonishment? And it is not enough (so it seems) to say with some that inward grace is universal and equal for all. For these same authors are obliged to resort to the exclamations of St. Paul, and to say: "O the depth!" when they consider how men are distinguished by what we may call outward graces, that is, by graces appearing in the diversity of circumstances which God calls forth, whereof men are not the masters, and which have nevertheless so great an influence upon all that concerns their salvation.

Nor will it help us to say with St. Augustine that, all men being involved in the damnation caused by the sin of Adam, God might have left them all in their misery; and that thus his goodness alone induces him to deliver some of them. For not only is it strange that the sin of another should condemn anyone, but there still remains the question why God does not deliver all—why he delivers the lesser number and why some in preference to others. He is in truth their master, but his wisdom permits not that he exercise that power in an arbitrary and despotic way, which would be tyrannous indeed.

Moreover, the fall of the first man having happened only with God's permission, and God having resolved to permit it only when once he had considered its consequences, which are the corruption of the mass of the human race and the choice of a small number of elect, with the abandonment of all the rest, it is useless to conceal the difficulty by limiting one's view to the mass already corrupt. One must, in spite of oneself, go back to the knowledge of the consequences of the first sin, preceding the decree whereby God permitted it, and whereby he permitted simultaneously that the damned should be involved in the mass of perdition and should not be delivered: for God and the sage make no resolve without considering its consequences. . . .

9. Some adversary not being able to answer this argument will perchance answer the conclusion by a counter-argument, saying that the world could have been without sin and without sufferings; but I deny that then it would have been better. For it must be known that all things are connected in each one of the possible worlds: the universe, whatever it may be, is all of one piece, like an ocean: the least movement extends its effect there to any distance whatsoever, even though this effect become less perceptible in proportion to the distance. Therein God has ordered all things beforehand once for all, having foreseen prayers, good and bad actions, and all the rest; and each thing as an idea has contributed, before its existence, to the resolution that has been made upon the existence of all things; so that nothing can be changed in the universe (any more than in a number) save its essence or, if you will, save its numerical individuality. Thus, if the smallest evil that comes to pass in the world were missing in it, it would no longer be this world; which, with nothing omitted and all allowance made, was found the best by the Creator who chose it.

10. It is true that one may imagine possible worlds without sin and without unhappiness, and one could make some like Utopian or Sevarambian[3] romances: but these same worlds again would be very inferior to ours in goodness. I cannot show you this in detail. For can I know and can I present infinities to you and compare them together? But you must judge with me *ab effectu*, since God has chosen this world as it is. We know, moreover, that often an evil brings forth a good whereto one would not have attained without that evil. Often indeed two evils have made one great good: . . .

16. It must be confessed, however, that there are disorders in this life, which appear especially in the prosperity of sundry evil men and in the misfortune of many good people. There is a German proverb which even grants the advantage to the evil ones, as if they were commonly the most fortunate:

> *Je krummer Holz, je bessre Krücke:*
> *Je ärger Schalck, je grösser Glücke.*[4]

---

[3] Refers to the seventeenth-century utopia, *Histoire des Sévarambes*.
[4] "The more crooked the wood, the better the jug;
 The bigger the fool, the greater good fortune."

17. But even though that should not happen here, the remedy is all prepared in the other life: religion and reason itself teach us that, and we must not murmur against a respite which the supreme wisdom has thought fit to grant to men for repentance . . .

12. Shaftesbury, The Moralists, A Rhapsody

MUCH is alledg'd in answer, to show why Nature errs, and how she came thus impotent and erring from an unerring Hand. But I deny she errs; and when she seems most ignorant or perverse in her Productions, I assert her even then as wise and provident, as in her goodliest Works. For 'tis not then that Men complain of the World's Order, or abhor the Face of Things, when they see various Interests mix'd and interfering. Natures subordinate, of different kinds, oppos'd one to another and in their different Operations submitted, the higher to the lower. 'Tis on the contrary, from this Order of inferiour and superiour Things, that we admire the World's Beauty, founded thus on Contrarietys: whilst from such various and disagreeing Principles, a Universal Concord is established.

Thus in the several Orders of Terrestrial Forms, a Resignation is required, a Sacrifice and mutual yielding of Natures one to another. The Vegetables by their Death sustain the Animals: and Animal-Bodys dissolv'd, enrich the Earth, and raise again the Vegetable World. The numerous Insects are reduc'd by the superiour Kinds of Birds and Beasts: and these again are check'd by Man; who in his turn submits to other Natures, and resigns his Form a Sacrifice in common to the rest of Things. And if in Natures so little exalted or pre-eminent above each other, the Sacrifice of Interests can appear so just; how much more reasonably may all inferiour Natures be subjected to the superiour Nature of the World! That World, Palemon, which even now transported you, when the Sun's fainting Light gave way to these bright Constellations, and left you this wide System to contemplate.

SOURCE: *Characteristicks of Men, Manners, Opinions, Times* (London, 1737).

Here are those Laws which ought not, nor can submit to any thing below. The Central Powers, which hold the lasting Orbs in their just Poize and Movement, must not be controul'd to save a fleeting Form, and rescue from the Precipice a puny Animal, whose brittle Frame, howe'er protected, must of itself so soon dissolve. The ambient Air, the inward Vapours, the impending Meteors, or whatever else is nutrimental or preservative of this Earth, must operate in a natural Course: and other Constitutions must submit to the good Habit and Constitution of the all-sustaining Globe.

Let us not therefore wonder, if by Earthquakes, Storms, pestilential Blasts, nether or upper Fires, or Floods, the animal Kinds are oft afflicted, and whole Species perhaps involv'd at once in common Ruin: But much less let us account it strange, if either by outward Shock, or some interiour Wound from hostile Matter, particular Animals are deform'd even in their first Conception, when the Disease invades the Seats of Generation, and seminal Parts are injur'd and obstructed in their accurate Labours. 'Tis then alone that monstrous Shapes are seen: Nature still working as before, and not perversely or erroneously; not faintly, or with feeble Endeavours; but o'er-power'd by a superiour Rival, and by another Nature's justly conquering Force.

Nor need we wonder, if the interiour Form, the Soul and Temper, partakes of this occasional Deformity, and sympathizes often with its close Partner. Who is there can wonder either at the Sicknesses of Sense, or the Depravity of Minds inclos'd in such frail Bodys, and dependent on such pervertible Organs?

Here then is that Solution you require: and hence those seeming Blemishes cast upon Nature. Nor is there aught in this beside what is natural and good. 'Tis Good which is predominant; and every corruptible and moral Nature by its Mortality and Corruption yields only to some better, and all in common to that best and highest Nature, which is incorruptible and immortal.

13.   Voltaire, The Lisbon Earthquake

An Inquiry into the Maxim, "Whatever Is, Is right."

Oh wretched man, earth-fated to be cursed;
Abyss of plagues, and miseries the worst!
Horrors on horrors, griefs on griefs must show,
That man's the victim of unceasing woe,
And lamentations which inspire my strain,
Prove that philosophy is false and vain.
Approach in crowds, and meditate awhile
Yon shattered walls, and view each ruined pile,
Women and children heaped up mountain high,
Limbs crushed which under ponderous marble lie;
Wretches unnumbered in the pangs of death,
Who mangled, torn, and panting for their breath,
Buried beneath their sinking roofs expire,
And end their wretched lives in torments dire.
Say, when you hear their piteous, half-formed cries,
Or from their ashes see the smoke arise,
Say, will you then eternal laws maintain,
Which God to cruelties like these constrain?
Whilst you these facts replete with horror view,
Will you maintain death to their crimes was due?
And can you then impute a sinful deed
To babes who on their mothers' bosoms bleed?
Was then more vice in fallen Lisbon found,
Than Paris, where voluptuous joys abound?
Was less debauchery to London known,
Where opulence luxurious holds her throne?
Earth Lisbon swallows; the light sons of France

SOURCE: Tobias Smollett (ed.), *The Works of Voltaire; a contemporary version with notes*, revised and modernized with new translations by William F. Fleming, introduction Oliver H. G. Leigh (New York: E: R: DuMont, 1901).

Protract the feast, or lead the sprightly dance.
Spectators who undaunted courage show,
While you behold your dying brethren's woe;
With stoical tranquillity of mind
You seek the causes of these ills to find;
But when like us Fate's rigors you have felt,
Become humane, like us you'll learn to melt.
When the earth gapes my body to entomb,
I justly may complain of such a doom.
Hemmed round on every side by cruel fate,
The snares of death, the wicked's furious hate,
Preyed on by pain and by corroding grief
Suffer me from complaint to find relief.
'Tis pride, you cry, seditious pride that still
Asserts mankind should be exempt from ill.
The awful truth on Tagus' banks explore,
Rummage the ruins on that bloody shore,
Wretches interred alive in direful grave
Ask if pride cries, "Good Heaven thy creatures save."
If 'tis presumption that makes mortals cry,
"Heaven on our sufferings cast a pitying eye."
All's right, you answer, the eternal cause
Rules not by partial, but by general laws.
Say what advantage can result to all,
From wretched Lisbon's lamentable fall?
Are you then sure, the power which could create
The universe and fix the laws of fate,
Could not have found for man a proper place,
But earthquakes must destroy the human race?
Will you thus limit the eternal mind?
Should not our God to mercy be inclined?
Cannot then God direct all nature's course?
Can power almighty be without resource?
Humbly the great Creator I entreat,
This gulf with sulphur and with fire replete,
Might on the deserts spend its raging flame,
God my respect, my love weak mortals claim;
When man groans under such a load of woe,
He is not proud, he only feels the blow.
Would words like these to peace of mind restore

The natives sad of that disastrous shore?
Grieve not, that others' bliss may overflow,
Your sumptuous palaces are laid thus low;
Your toppled towers shall other hands rebuild;
With multitudes your walls one day be filled;
Your ruin on the North shall wealth bestow,
For general good from partial ills must flow;
You seem as abject to the sovereign power,
As worms which shall your carcasses devour.
No comfort could such shocking words impart,
But deeper wound the sad, afflicted heart.
When I lament my present wretched state,
Allege not the unchanging laws of fate;
Urge not the links of the eternal chain,
'Tis false philosophy and wisdom vain.
The God who holds the chain can't be enchained;
By His blest will are all events ordained:
He's just, nor easily to wrath gives way,
Why suffer we beneath so mild a sway:
This is the fatal knot you should untie,
Our evils do you cure when you deny?
Men ever strove into the source to pry,
Of evil, whose existence you deny.
If he whose hand the elements can wield,
To the winds' force makes rocky mountains yield;
If thunder lay oaks level with the plain,
From the bolts' strokes they never suffer pain.
But I can feel, my heart oppressed demands
Aid of that God who formed me with His hands.
Sons of the God supreme to suffer all
Fated alike; we on our Father call.
No vessel of the potter asks, we know,
Why it was made so brittle, vile, and low?
Vessels of speech as well as thought are void;
The urn this moment formed and that destroyed,
The potter never could with sense inspire,
Devoid of thought it nothing can desire.
The moralist still obstinate replies,
Others' enjoyments from your woes arise,
To numerous insects shall my corpse give birth,

When once it mixes with its mother earth:
Small comfort 'tis that when Death's ruthless power
Closes my life, worms shall my flesh devour.
Remembrances of misery refrain
From consolation, you increase my pain:
Complaint, I see, you have with care repressed,
And proudly hid yor sorrows in your breast.
But a small part, I no importance claim
In this vast universe, this general frame;
All other beings in this world below
Condemned like me to lead a life of woe,
Subject to laws as rigorous as I,
Like me in anguish live and like me die.
The vulture urged by an insatiate maw,
Its trembling prey tears with relentless claw:
This it finds right, endowed with greater powers
The bird of Jove the vulture's self devours.
Man lifts his tube, he aims the fatal ball
And makes to earth the towering eagle fall;
Man in the field with wounds all covered o'er,
Midst heaps of dead lies weltering in his gore,
While birds of prey the mangled limbs devour,
Of Nature's Lord who boasts his mighty power.
Thus the world's members equal ills sustain,
And perish by each other born to pain:
Yet in this direful chaos you'd compose
A general bliss from individuals' woes?
Oh worthless bliss! Injured reason's sight,
With faltering voice you cry, "What is, is right"?
The universe confutes your boasting vain,
Your heart retracts the error you maintain.
Men, beasts, and elements know no repose
From dire contention; earth's the seat of woes:
We strive in vain its secret source to find.
Is ill the gift of our Creator kind?
Do then fell Typhon's cursed laws ordain
Our ill, or Arimanius[1] doom to pain?

[1] Ahriman, principle of evil, opposed to Ormazd, both lay figures in Zoroastrianism.

Shocked at such dire chimeras, I reject
Monsters which fear could into gods erect.
But how conceive a God, the source of love,
Who on man lavished blessings from above,
Then would the race with various plagues confound,
Can mortals penetrate His views profound?
Ill could not from a perfect being spring,
Nor from another, since God's sovereign king;
And yet, sad truth! in this our world 'tis found,
What contradictions here my soul confound!
A God once dwelt on earth amongst mankind,
Yet vices still lay waste the human mind;
He could not do it, this proud sophist cries,
He could, but he declined it, that replies;
He surely will, ere these disputes have end,
Lisbon's foundations hidden thunders rend,
And thirty cities' shattered remnants fly,
With ruin and combustion through the sky,
From dismal Tagus' ensanguined shore,
To where of Cadiz' sea the billows roar.
Or man's a sinful creature from his birth,
And God to woe condemns the sons of earth;
Or else the God who being rules and space,
Untouched with pity for the human race,
Indifferent, both from love and anger free,
Still acts consistent to His first decree:
Or matter has defects which still oppose
God's will, and thence all human evil flows;
Or else this transient world by mortals trod,
Is but a passage that conducts to God.
Our transient sufferings here shall soon be o'er,
And death will land us on a happier shore.
But when we rise from this accursed abyss,
Who by his merit can lay claim to bliss?
Dangers and difficulties man surround,
Doubts and perplexities his mind confound.
To nature we apply for truth in vain,
God should His will to human kind explain.
He only can illume the human soul,

Instruct the wise man, and the weak console.
Without Him man of error still the sport,
Thinks from each broken reed to find support.
Leibnitz can't tell me from what secret cause
In a world governed by the wisest laws,
Lasting disorders, woes that never end
With our vain pleasures real sufferings blend;
Why ill the virtuous with the vicious shares?
Why neither good nor bad misfortune spares?
I can't conceive that "what is, ought to be,"
In this each doctor knows as much as me.
We're told by Plato, that man, in times of yore,
Wings gorgeous to his glorious body wore,
That all attacks he could unhurt sustain,
By death ne'er conquered, ne'er approached by pain.
Alas, how changed from such a brilliant state.
He crawls 'twist heaven and earth, then yields to fate.
Look round this sublunary world, you'll find
That nature to destruction is consigned.
Our system weak which nerves and bone compose,
Cannot the shock of elements oppose;
This mass of fluids mixed with tempered clay,
To dissolution quickly must give way.
Their quick sensations can't unhurt sustain
The attacks of death and of tormenting pain,
This is the nature of the human frame,
Plato and Epicurus I disclaim.
Nature was more to Bayle than either known:
What do I learn from Bayle, to doubt alone?
Bayle, great and wise, all systems overthrows,
Then his own tenets labors to oppose.
Like the blind slave to Delilah's commands,
Crushed by the pile demolished by his hands.
Mysteries like these can no man penetrate,
Hid from his view remains the book of fate.
Man his own nature never yet could sound,
He knows not whence he is, nor whither bound.
Atoms tormented on this earthly ball,
The sport of fate, by death soon swallowed all,

But thinking atoms, who with piercing eyes
Have measured the whole circuit of the skies;
We rise in thought up to the heavenly throne,
But our own nature still remains unknown.
This world which error and o'erweening pride,
Rulers accursed between them still divide,
Where wretches overwhelmed with lasting woe,
Talk of a happiness they never know,
Is with complaining filled, all are forlorn
In seeking bliss; none would again be born.
If in a life midst sorrows past and fears,
With pleasure's hand we wipe away our tears,
Pleasure his light wings spreads, and quickly flies,
Losses on losses, griefs on griefs arise.
The mind from sad remembrance of the past,
Is with black melancholy overcast;
Sad is the present if no future state,
No blissful retribution mortals wait,
If fate's decrees the thinking being doom
To lose existence in the silent tomb.
All may be well; that hope can man sustain,
All now is well; 'tis an illusion vain.
The sages held me forth delusive light,
Divine instructions only can be right.
Humbly I sigh, submissive suffer pain,
Nor more the ways of Providence arraign.
In youthful prime I sung in strains more gay,
Soft pleasure's laws which lead mankind astray.
But times change manners; taught by age and care
Whilst I mistaken mortals' weakness share,
The light of truth I seek in this dark state,
And without murmuring submit to fate.
A caliph once when his last hour drew nigh,
Prayed in such terms as these to the most high:
"Being supreme, whose greatness knows no bound,
I bring thee all that can't in Thee be found;
Defects and sorrows, ignorance and woe."
Hope he omitted, man's sole bliss below.

14.   Rousseau, Letter to Voltaire

August 18, 1756

I DO NOT SEE how we can look for the source of moral evil elsewhere than in man, who is free, who has progressed and thereby become corrupted. As for physical evils, if it is a contradiction, as it seems to me, that matter should be both sensitive and insensitive, they are inevitable in any system of which man is a part, and then the question is not why man is not perfectly happy, but why he exists. Moreover, I think I have showed that with the exception of death, which is scarcely an evil except by the preparations with which we precede it, most of our physical ills are once again our own doing. Without leaving your subject, the Lisbon earthquake, admit, for example, that nature had not brought together there twenty thousand six- or seven-story houses, and that if the inhabitants of that great city had been dispersed more evenly and less densely lodged, the damage would have been much less and perhaps there would have been none. Everybody would have run away at the first tremor, and the next day would have found them twenty leagues away, just as gay as if nothing had occurred. But it is necessary for them to remain, to stay stubbornly around their huts, to expose themselves to new shocks, because what is left behind is more valuable than what can be carried away. How many wretches perished in that disaster because one wanted to take his clothing, another his papers, another his money? Do we not realize that the person of each man has become the least part of himself and that it is not worth while saving it, if all the rest is lost?

You would have preferred—and who would not have preferred it!—that the earthquake take place in the recesses of a desert rather than in Lisbon. Can we doubt that they also take place in deserts?

SOURCE: R. A. Leigh (ed.), *Correspondance complète de Jean-Jacques Rousseau* (Geneva: Institut et Musée Voltaire, 1965), vol. IV. Translated by the editor.

But we do not talk about those, because they do no harm to our city gentlemen, the only men whom we value. They do little harm even to animals and to savages who dwell scattered across those distant places and who fear neither the collapse of roofs nor the burning of houses. But what would such a privilege signify? Do you intend that the order of the world should change to suit our caprices, that nature should be submitted to our laws, and that to forbid an earthquake in some place we have only to build a city there?

There are events which often strike us more or less according to the viewpoint from which we consider them and which lose much of the horror they inspire in us at a first glance when we decide to look at them closely. I learned in Zadig,[1] and nature each day confirms it to me, that premature death is not always a real evil and that it may sometimes be held a relative good. Among so many men crushed under the ruins of that unhappy city, several, without doubt, have escaped greater misfortunes, and, despite the fact that such a description is touching and congenial to poetry, it is not certain that a single one of those victims has suffered more than if, according to the ordinary course of events, he would have waited in lengthy anguish for the death which caught him suddenly there. Is there a sadder end than that of a dying man who is tormented by useless fuss, who is harassed by a notary and by heirs, whom the doctors slowly murder in his bed, while barbarous priests artfully attempt to make his death a pleasure? As for me, I see everywhere that the evils to which nature subjects us are much less cruel than those which it pleases us to add to hers.

But, however ingenious we may be in fomenting our own sufferings through our fine institutions, we have not yet been able to progress to the point of making life generally unbearable and of preferring nothingness to being; otherwise, discouragement and despair would not have waited to take possession of most men, and the human race could not have long survived. Now if it is better for us to be than not to be, that itself would suffice to justify our existence even if we had no recompense to expect for the ills we have to suffer, and even if those ills were as great as you depict them. But it is difficult to find men of good faith on this subject and accurate calculations among the philosophers, because the latter are

[1] A tale by Voltaire.

always forgetting in comparing goods and ills the sweet pleasure of existing independently of any other sensation, and that men are impelled to calumniate life out of the vainglory of despising death, somewhat like those women who with a spotted dress and scissors claim to prefer holes to spots.

You think with Erasmus that few people would like to live their life over again under the conditions of their present life; but such a one who boasts loudly of his wares would come down a peg if he had some hope of making a bargain. Besides, sir, whom am I supposed to believe you have consulted on this subject? Rich men, perhaps, satiated with false pleasures but ignorant of the true ones, always bored by life and always fearing to lose it, men of letters, perhaps of all classes of men the most sedentary, the most unhealthy, the most cogitative, and consequently the unhappiest. Do you wish to find men of better composition, or at least generally more sincere, and who, making up the greater number, should, if only for that reason, be listened to in preference? Ask an honest bourgeois, who has spent an obscure and tranquil life without projects and ambition; a good artisan who lives comfortably from his trade; even a peasant—not in France, where they say it is necessary to starve them to death in order to live off them, but one, for instance, in the country where you are,[2] and in general in any free country . . .

That a man's cadaver nourishes worms, wolves, or plants is, I admit, no compensation for that man's death; but if in the system of this universe it is necessary for the self-preservation of the human species that there be a circulation of substance among men, animals, and plants, then the particular evil suffered by an individual contributes to the general good. I die, I am eaten by worms, but my brothers and my children will live as I have lived, and I am doing, according to the natural order for all men, what Codrus, Curtius, Leonidas, the Decii, the Philenes,[3] and a thousand others have voluntarily done for a small part of mankind.

To come back, sir, to the society you are attacking, I believe that it cannot be properly examined without carefully discriminating between personal evil, the existence of which has been denied by no philosopher, and general evil, which optimism denies. The

[2] Rousseau's own country, Switzerland.
[3] Decii, prominent family of Roman patriots during the Republic; Philenes, or Philaeni, Carthaginian heroes.

question is not whether each one of us suffers or not; but whether it is good that the universe exists and whether our sufferings are inevitable in its constitution. Thus the addition of an article would, it seems, make the proposition more accurate, and instead of *everything is good*, it would perhaps be better to say, *the whole is good*,[4] or *everything is good for the whole*. It becomes quite evident then that no man could furnish direct proofs either for or against; for these proofs would require a perfect knowledge of the constitution of the world, of its author's purpose, and that knowledge is incontestably above human intelligence. The true principles of optimism can be drawn neither from the properties of matter, nor from the mechanics of the universe, but only from an induction of the perfections of the divinity who presides over everything . . .

I cannot forbear remarking, in conclusion, a strange contrast between you and me in regard to the subject of this letter. Satiated with glory, disillusioned about vain grandeur, you live a free man in the midst of abundance; certain of immortality, you philosophize peacefully about the nature of the soul, and if your body or your heart suffers, you have Tronchin for doctor and friend. And yet you see only evil on earth. And I, an obscure man, poor, lonely, tormented by an incurable malady, I meditate with pleasure in my retreat and find that all is good. Whence these apparent contradictions? You yourself have given the explanation: you enjoy, but I hope, and hope makes everything beautiful.

[4] In French, *tout est bien, le tout est bien.*

15. De Sade, Philosophy in the Boudoir

DOLMANCÉ—IT IS demonstrated that man owes his existence to nothing but Nature's irresistible schemes. If man is thus proven to have been in this world as long as the world has existed, he is like

SOURCE: De Sade, *La Philosophie dans le boudoir*, précédée d'une étude sur le Marquis de Sade et le sadisme par Holpey (Paris: private edition; La Société des études Sadiques, n. d.). Translated by the editor.

the oak, like grain, like the minerals to be found in the earth's entrails, which are bound only to reproduce, reproduction being required by the globe's existence, which owes its own existence to nothing whatsoever. If it is demonstrated that this God, whom fools consider the author and maker of all we know there to be, is merely the *ne plus ultra* of human reason, the phantom created at the moment when this reason can advance its operations no further; if it is proven that this God's existence is impossible, and that Nature, forever in action, always moving, has of herself what it pleases idiots to award to God gratuitously; if it is certain that on the supposition of this inert being's existence, he would be the most ridiculous of all things, since he would have been useful only a single time and, thereafter and throughout millions of centuries, fixed in a contemptible immobility and inactivity; and that, supposing him to exist as religions portray him to us, he would be the most detestable of creatures, since it would be God who permits evil to be on earth while his omnipotence could prevent it; if, I say, all that is admitted to be proven, as incontestably it is, do you believe, Eugénie, that this piety which binds man to an idiotic, inadequate, atrocious, and contemptible creator is a very necessary virtue?

EUGÉNIE, TO MADAME DE SAINT-ANGE—What! Is God's existence an illusion, then?

MADAME DE SAINT-ANGE—And without doubt one of the most deplorable.

DOLMANCÉ—To believe in it one must first have gone out of one's mind. Fruit of the terror of some and of the weakness of others, that abominable phantom, Eugénie, is of no use to the earthly scheme and would infallibly be injurious to it, since the will of God would have to be just and should never be able to compromise with the necessary injustices decreed by Nature; since he would have constantly to will the good, while Nature must desire it only as compensation for the evil which serves her laws; since it would be necessary that he, God, exert his influence at all times, while Nature, one of whose laws is perpetual activity, could only find herself in competition with him, and in unceasing opposition to him. Will you reply that God and Nature are one? That's an absurdity. The thing created cannot be its creator's equal. Can the pocket watch be the clock tower? Very well, it will be argued, Nature is nothing, God is all. Another stupidity. There are necessarily two things in the universe: the creative agent and the individual created; now, the single obstacle one must overcome, the one question to which one must provide a reply is the identity of this creative agent. If matter acts, and is moved by combinations unknown to us, if movement is inherent in Nature; if, in short, she alone, by reason of her energy, is able to create, produce, preserve, maintain in equilibrium within the immense bounds of space all the spheres that stand before our sight and whose uniform march, unvarying, fills us with respect and admiration, what then becomes of the need to seek out an agent, since this active faculty essentially is to be found in Nature herself, which is nothing else than matter in action? Well, now; do you suppose your deific chimera will shed light upon anything? I defy anyone to prove him to me. Suppose that I am mistaken about matter's internal faculties. I have, at least, nothing worse than a difficulty. What do you do for me when you offer your God to me? And how would you have me acknowledge as cause of what I do not understand, something that I understand even less? Will it be by means of the Christian religion that I shall examine . . . that I shall obtain a view of your frightful God? Then let's glance at the God Christianity portrays. What do I see in the God of that infamous sect if not an inconsistent and barbarous being, today the creator of a world of destruction he repents of tomorrow. What do I see there? A weak being forever unable to master man and force him to bend a knee. This creature, although emanated from him, dominates him, knows how to offend him and thereby merit eternal torments. What a weak fellow, this God! How was he able to fashion all that we know and yet fail to form man in his own guise? You will answer that had man been created so, he would have been little deserving of his author. What a platitude is this! And why should it be necessary that man be deserving of his God? If God had made him entirely good, he should never have been able to do evil, and only then would the work be worthy of a God. To allow man to choose was to tempt him; and God's infinite powers very well forewarned him of what would be the result. As soon as the being was created, it was to pleasure God doomed the creature he had himself formed. A horrible God, this God of yours, a monster! Is there a criminal more worthy of our hatred and our implacable vengeance than he! However, little content with a task so sublimely executed, he drowns man to convert him, he burns him, he curses him, and nothing in all that changes him one iota. The Devil, more powerful than this villainous God, a being still in possession of his power, forever able to brave his author, incessantly succeeds, by his seductions, in debauching the herd that the Eternal reserved unto himself.

III

Science and Materialism

PHYSICS in the eighteenth century exploited the triumphs of the seventeenth. Chemistry was not to separate itself from medieval ideas and alchemy and enter the modern world until Priestley and Lavoisier did their work. The former discovered oxygen in 1774; the latter explained its role in combustion, distinguished elements and compounds, and introduced quantitative methods. The humanistic thinkers, interested in exploring the universe, man's place in it, and the nature of life, turned to biology and physiology. They were also concerned with the methodology and, to a limited extent, the philosophy of science. The first kind of inquiry led the more original speculators to a theory of materialism. La Mettrie's *L'Homme machine* (1747) is generally considered to be the fountainhead of modern materialism. It sets forth a theory of a godless universe in which there are only physical events and everything, from the motion of bodies to the development of the embryo and human decisions, is determined by a rigorous necessity and by built-in, natural "goals." Nature "has used only a single dough," and man differs from other animals only by the greater complexity of his physical structure. All animals are machines which are self-regulating and self-sustaining systems, and man can be understood in no other way.

Buffon was a scientist-poet, studying and describing animals in faultless prose. But he was also a theorist of scientific method and a bold speculator who, concealing his atheism in order to hold his post as keeper of the Jardin du Roi, tried to account for life in naturalistic terms. He developed an evolutionary theory of the earth, but, holding man to be a unique creature and the king of the animal world, fell short of conceiving a theory of organic evolution. Buffon's great work, *Histoire naturelle,* spans the most significant years of the century. We have chosen a selection from its beginning (1749) and another from its conclusion. Starting on his vast project, Buffon examines the problem of scientific knowledge. He rejects both skepticism and the Cartesian model of self-evident knowledge; all reference to the divine is eliminated. That knowledge which is possible for man is upheld as valid. The second passage, from *Les Epoques de la nature* (1778), tries to sum up the results of long study and reflection in an overall vision

of science, knowledge, and nature; it is an effort to reconstitute nature's course and the course that must be taken in the study of natural
history.

Diderot was neither a physician like La Mettrie nor a practicing
investigator like Buffon. As an amateur, he was a keen student of
medicine and the sciences of his time. He was also an amateur philosopher and a great humanist, deeply involved in the dilemmas created by
the monistic materialism of his time. He was interested in scientific
method (*Pensées sur l'interprétation de la nature*, 1753), but he was
more interested in "interpreting" nature, in providing a framework for
an approach to the problems of human life and values. A true adven-
turer or experimenter in ideas, he embarks on intellectual voyages of
discovery in his brilliant dialogues which sometimes lead him to
opposing conclusions. In *Le Rêve de d'Alembert* (1769, publ. 1830), he
develops a complete system of materialism, extending from cosmology
to morals and combining science, philosophy, and poetry. It will be
obvious that, although he is not completely detached from the earlier
mechanical philosophy, his conception is much broader than that of
La Mettrie.

16.   La Mettrie, Man a Machine

MAN IS so complicated a machine that it is impossible to get a clear
idea of the machine beforehand, and hence impossible to define it.
For this reason, all the investigations have been vain, which the
greatest philosophers have made a priori, that is to say, in so far as
they use, as it were, the wings of the spirit. Thus it is only a
posteriori or by trying to disentangle the soul from the organs of
the body, so to speak, that one can reach the highest probability
concerning man's own nature, even though one can not discover
with certainty what his nature is.

Let us then take in our hands the staff of experience, paying no
heed to the accounts of all the idle theories of philosophers. To be
blind and to think that one can do without this staff is the worst

SOURCE: Translated by Gertrude C. Bussey in *Man a Machine* (La
Salle, Ind.: The Open Court Publishing Co., 1912). One passage,
omitted by Miss Bussey in a more prudish age, has been added by
the editor. Reprinted by permission of the publisher.

kind of blindness. How truly a contemporary writer says that only vanity fails to gather from secondary causes the same lessons as from primary causes! One can and one even ought to admire all these fine geniuses in their most useless works, such men as Descartes, Malebranche, Leibniz, Wolff and the rest, but what profit, I ask, has any one gained from their profound meditations, and from all their works? Let us start out then to discover not what has been thought, but what must be thought for the sake of repose in life.

There are as many different minds, different characters, and different customs, as there are different temperaments. Even Galen knew this truth which Descartes carried so far as to claim that medicine alone can change minds and morals, along with bodies. (By the writer of *L'histoire de l'âme*, this teaching is incorrectly attributed to Hippocrates.[1]) It is true that melancholy, bile, phlegm, blood etc.—according to the nature, the abundance, and the different combination of these humors—make each man different from another.

In disease the soul is sometimes hidden, showing no sign of life; sometimes it is so inflamed by fury that it seems to be doubled: sometimes, imbecility vanishes and the convalescence of an idiot produces a wise man. Sometimes, again, the greatest genius becomes imbecile and loses the sense of self. Adieu then to all that fine knowledge, acquired at so high a price, and with so much trouble! Here is a paralytic who asks if his leg is in bed with him; there is a soldier who thinks that he still has the arm which has been cut off. The memory of his old sensations, and of the place to which they were referred by his soul, is the cause of his illusion, and of this kind of delirium. The mere mention of the member which he has lost is enough to recall it to his mind, and to make him feel all its motions; and this causes him an indefinable and inexpressible kind of imaginary suffering. This man cries like a child at death's approach, while this other jests. What was needed to change the bravery of Caius Julius, Seneca, or Petronius into cowardice or faintheartedness? Merely an obstruction in the spleen, in the liver, an impediment in the portal vein? Why? Because the imagination is obstructed along with the viscera, and this gives rise to all the singular phenomena of hysteria and hypochondria.

[1] The writer is La Mettrie, who is correcting an earlier statement.

What can I add to the stories already told of those who imagine themselves transformed into wolf-men, cocks or vampires, or of those who think that the dead feed upon them? Why should I stop to speak of the man who imagines that his nose or some other member is of glass? The way to help this man regain his faculties and his own flesh-and-blood nose is to advise him to sleep on hay, lest he break the fragile organ, and then to set fire to the hay that he may be afraid of being burned—a fear which has sometimes cured paralysis. But I must touch lightly on facts which everybody knows.

Neither shall I dwell long on the details of the effects of sleep. Here a tired soldier snores in a trench, in the middle of the thunder of hundreds of cannon. His soul hears nothing; his sleep is as deep as apoplexy. A bomb is on the point of crushing him. He will feel this less perhaps than he feels an insect which is under his foot.

On the other hand, this man who is devoured by jealousy, hatred, avarice, or ambition, can never find any rest. The most peaceful spot, the freshest and most calming drinks are alike useless to one who has not freed his heart from the torment of passion.

The soul and the body fall asleep together. As the motion of the blood is calmed, a sweet feeling of peace and quiet spreads through the whole mechanism. The soul feels itself little by little growing heavy as the eyelids droop, and loses its tenseness, as the fibres of the brain relax; thus little by little it becomes as if paralyzed and with it all the muscles of the body. These can no longer sustain the weight of the head, and the soul can no longer bear the burden of thought; it is in sleep as if it were not.

Is the circulation too quick? the soul can not sleep. Is the soul too much excited? the blood can not be quieted: it gallops through the veins with an audible murmur. Such are the two opposite causes of insomnia. A single fright in the midst of our dreams makes the heart beat at double speed and snatches us from needed and delicious repose, as a real grief or an urgent need would do. Lastly, as the mere cessation of the functions of the soul produces sleep, there are, even when we are awake (or at least when we are half awake), kinds of very frequent short naps of the mind, vergers' dreams, which show that the soul does not always wait for the body to sleep. For if the soul is not fast asleep, it surely is not far from sleep, since it can not point out a single object to which it has attended, among the uncounted number of confused ideas which, so to speak, fill the atmosphere of our brains like clouds.

Opium is too closely related to the sleep it produces, to be left out of consideration here. This drug intoxicates, like wine, coffee, etc., each in its own measure and according to the dose. It makes a man happy in a state which would seemingly be the tomb of feeling, as it is the image of death. How sweet is this lethargy! The soul would long never to emerge from it. For the soul has been a prey to the most intense sorrow, but now feels only the joy of suffering past, and of sweetest peace. Opium even alters the will, forcing the soul which wished to wake and to enjoy life, to sleep in spite of itself. I shall omit any reference to the effect of poisons.

Coffee, the well-known antidote for wine, by scourging the imagination, cures our headaches and scatters our cares without laying up for us, as wine does, other headaches for the morrow. But let us contemplate the soul in its other needs.

The human body is a machine which winds its own springs. It is the living image of perpetual movement. Nourishment keeps up the movements which fever excites. Without food, the soul pines away, goes mad, and dies exhausted. The soul is a taper whose light flares up the moment before it goes out. But nourish the body, pour into its veins life-giving juices and strong liquors, and then the soul grows strong like them, as if arming itself with a proud courage, and the soldier whom water would have made flee, grows bold and runs joyously to death to the sound of drums. Thus a hot drink sets into stormy movement the blood which cold water would have calmed.

To what excesses cruel hunger can bring us! We no longer regard even our own parents and children. We tear them to pieces eagerly and make horrible banquets of them; and in the fury with which we are carried away, the weakest is always the prey of the strongest . . .

[And what of that other fury in a man or a woman pursued by continence and good health! That timid and modest girl doesn't stop at losing all her shame and modesty; incest frightens her no more than adultery frightens a loose woman. If her needs do not find prompt satisfaction, they will not stop at such indispositions as uterine fever, mania, etc.; that unfortunate girl will die of a sickness for which there are so many doctors.]

One needs only eyes to see the necessary influence of old age on reason. The soul follows the progress of the body, as it does the progress of education. In the weaker sex, the soul accords also with delicacy of temperament, and from this delicacy follow tenderness,

affection, quick feelings due more to passion than to reason, prejudices, and superstitions, whose strong impress can hardly be
effaced. Man, on the other hand, whose brain and nerves partake of
the firmness of all solids, has not only stronger features but also a
more vigorous mind . . .

That is, at least, much more than was said by the physician
Diderot, in his *Pensées philosophiques*, a sublime work that will not
convince a single atheist. What reply can, in truth, be made to a
man who says, "We do not know nature; causes hidden in her
breast might have produced everything. In your turn, observe the
polyp of Trembley;[2] does it not contain in itself the causes which
bring about regeneration? Why then would it be absurd to think
that there are physical causes by reason of which everything has
been made, and to which the whole chain of this vast universe is so
necessarily bound and held that nothing which happens, could
have failed to happen,—causes, of which we are so invincibly
ignorant that we have had recourse to a God, who, as some aver, is
not so much as a logical entity? Thus to destroy chance is not to
prove the existence of a supreme being, since there may be some
other thing which is neither chance nor God—I mean, nature. It
follows that the study of nature can make only unbelievers; and
the way of thinking of all its more successful investigators proves
this."

The weight of the universe therefore far from crushing a real
atheist does not even shake him. All these evidences of a creator,
repeated thousands and thousands of times, evidences that are
placed far above the comprehension of men like us, are self-evident
(however far one push the argument) only to the anti-Pyrrho-
nians, or to those who have enough confidence in their reason to
believe themselves capable of judging on the basis of certain
phenomena, against which, as you see, the atheists can urge others
perhaps equally strong and absolutely opposed. For if we listen to
the naturalists again, they will tell us that the very causes which, in
a chemist's hands, by a chance combination, made the first mirror,
in the hands of nature made the pure water, the mirror of the
simple shepherdess; that the motion which keeps the world going
could have created it, that each body has taken the place assigned

---

[2] In 1740, the Swiss naturalist, Abraham Trembley, discovered that a hydra
cut into parts would regenerate itself.

to it by its own nature, that the air must have surrounded the earth, and that iron and the other metals are produced by internal motions of the earth, for one and the same reason; that the sun is as much a natural product as electricity, that it was not made to warm the earth and its inhabitants, whom it sometimes burns, any more than the rain was made to make the seeds grow, which it often spoils; that the mirror and the water were no more made for people to see themselves in, than were all other polished bodies with this same property; that the eye is in truth a kind of glass in which the soul can contemplate the image of objects as they are presented to it by these bodies, but that it is not proved that this organ was really made expressly for this contemplation, nor purposely placed in its socket, and in short that it may well be that Lucretius, the physician Lamy, and all Epicureans both ancient and modern were right when they suggested that the eye sees only because it is formed and placed as it is, and that, given once for all, the same rules of motion followed by nature in the generation and develop-ment of bodies, this marvelous organ could not have been formed and placed differently . . .

But since all the faculties of the soul depend to such a degree on the proper organization of the brain and of the whole body, that apparently they are but this organization itself, the soul is clearly an enlightened machine. For finally, even if man alone had received a share of natural law, would he be any less a machine for that? A few more wheels, a few more springs than in the most perfect animals, the brain proportionally nearer the heart and for this very reason receiving more blood—any one of a number of unknown causes might always produce this delicate conscience so easily wounded, this remorse which is no more foreign to matter than to thought, and in a word all the differences that are supposed to exist here. Could the organism then suffice for everything? Once more, yes; since thought visibly develops with our organs, why should not the matter of which they are composed be susceptible of remorse also, when once it has acquired, with time, the faculty of feeling? . . .

Let us then conclude boldly that man is a machine, and that in the whole universe there is but a single substance differently modified . . .

17. Buffon, Discourse on Studying and Treating Natural History and The Epochs of Nature

A. Discourse on the Manner of Studying and Treating Natural History (1749)

IT SHOULD NOT be imagined even today that in the study of natural history we should limit ourselves to making exact descriptions and verifying only particular facts. That is indeed, as we have said, the essential purpose with which we must start out. But we must try to rise to something greater and worthier of our concern: that is, to combine observations, to generalize facts, to link them by analogies, and to try to reach that high degree of knowledge at which we are able to judge that particular effects depend on more general ones, at which we can compare nature to herself and to her grand operations, and at which we can at least open paths to the perfectioning of the definite parts of natural science. Good memory, application, and attention suffice to reach the first goal; but for the latter we need something more. We need general ideas, keen observation, and a type of reasoning based more on reflection and study; we need, finally, that quality of mind which enables us to grasp distant relationships, to bring them together, and to form from them a body of systematic ideas, after having carefully estimated and weighed the probabilities.

It is here that we need a method to guide our thinking, not the method of which we have spoken, which is useful only to arrange words arbitrarily, but a method to support the very order of things which should guide our reasoning, illumine our views, extend them, and prevent us from going astray.

The greatest philosophers have felt the need of this method and they have even tried to give us principles and examples of it. But some have left us only the history of their own thoughts, and others the fables created by their imaginations. If some have risen

SOURCE: Buffon, *Oeuvres philosophiques*, ed. Jean Piveteau (Paris: Presses Universitaires de France, 1954). Translated by the editor.

to that high point of metaphysics at which the principles, relationships, and the ensemble of the sciences can be seen, none has given
us his ideas about all that, none has given us advice; and the method
of proper inquiry in the sciences is still to be found. For lack of
precepts we have been offered examples; instead of principles,
definitions have been used, and instead of verified facts, venture-
some suppositions.

Even in this century in which the sciences seem to be carefully
cultivated, I think it is easy to say that their philosophy is neglected
and perhaps more so than in any other century. The arts that
people call scientific have taken its place: the methods of calculus
and geometry, those of botany and natural history, formulas, in a
word, and dictionaries occupy nearly everyone. People imagine
they know more because they have increased the number of
symbolic expressions and learned phrases, and they do not realize
that all these arts are only scaffolding whose purpose is to reach
knowledge, and not knowledge itself, and that they ought not to
be utilized when we can dispense with them, and that we should
always be prepared for their failing us when we wish to apply
them to constructions.

Truth, that metaphysical entity of which everyone should have
a clear idea, seems to me to be entangled in such a large number of
foreign objects which are given its name that I am not surprised we
have trouble in recognizing it. Prejudices and false applications
have multiplied in proportion as our hypotheses have been more
learned, more abstract, and more perfected; therefore it is more
difficult than ever to recognize what we are able to know, and to
distinguish it clearly from that of which we must remain ignorant.
The following reflections will at least serve as an opinion about this
important subject.

The word "truth" evokes only a vague idea. It has never had a
precise definition, and definition itself, taken in a general and
absolute sense, is merely an abstraction which exists only in virtue
of some supposition. Instead of trying to construct a definition of
truth, let us, then, seek to make an enumeration; let us examine
what are commonly called truths, and try to form clear ideas about
them.

There are three kinds of truths. It is customary to put mathematical truths in the first category; yet they are only truths of
definition; these definitions bear on simple but abstract supposi-

tions, and all truths of this class are only composite, still abstract consequences of these definitions. We have made the suppositions, combined them in every way; this body of combinations is mathematical science. There is therefore nothing in that science except what we have put into it; and the truths we draw from it can only be different expressions representing the same suppositions which we have used. Thus mathematical truths are only the exact repetition of definitions or suppositions. The last consequence is true only because it is identical with the preceding one and because the latter is identical with the one preceding it, and so on, going back to the first supposition. And, since definitions are the only principles on which everything is built, and since they are arbitrary and relative, all the consequences that may be drawn from them are equally arbitrary and relative. What are called mathematical truths are therefore reduced to identities of ideas and have no reality. We make suppositions, we reason about our suppositions, we draw consequences from them, we can conclude; the conclusion or last consequence is a true proposition relatively to our supposition; but this truth is no more real than the supposition itself. This is not the place to discuss the uses of the mathematical sciences or the abuses to which they are subject; it suffices for us to have proven that mathematical truths are only truths of definition or, if you prefer, different expressions of the same thing and that they are truths only relatively to our own definitions; for this reason they have the advantage of always being exact and demonstrative, but they are abstract, intellectual, and arbitrary.

Physical truths, on the other hand, are not at all arbitrary and do not depend on us. Instead of being founded on suppositions we have made, they rest on facts alone. A succession of similar facts, or if you prefer, a frequent repetition, an uninterrupted series of the same events is what constitutes the essence of physical truth. What is called physical truth is, then, only a probability, but so great a probability that it is equivalent to certainty. In mathematics we make suppositions; in physics we propound and establish. In the first, we have definitions, in the second we have facts. In the abstract sciences, we go from definition to definition; in the real sciences, we go from observation to observation. In the first, we arrive at self-evidence; in the second, at certainty. The word "truth" comprehends both and therefore corresponds to two different ideas; its meaning is vague and composite. It was not possible, then, to give a general definition of it; it was necessary, as we have just done, to separate it into classes in order to form a clear idea of it.

I shall not speak about the other classes of truths. Those of ethics, for example, which are in part real and in part arbitrary, but require a long discussion that would take us away from our purposes, all the more because their object and aim are only proprieties and probabilities.

Mathematical evidence and physical certitude are, consequently, the only two points under which we need to consider truth. As soon as it departs from the one or the other, it is only probability and likelihood. Let us then examine what we may know about evident or certain knowledge, after which we shall see what we can know only by conjecture, and finally, what we cannot know.

We know or are able to know, as evident knowledge, all the properties or rather all the relationships of numbers, lines, surfaces, and all other abstract quantities. We shall be able to know them more completely as we undertake to resolve new questions, and more surely as we seek out the causes of difficulties. As we are the creators of this science, and as it includes absolutely nothing but what we have ourselves imagined, it can contain no obscurities or paradoxes which are real or impossible of solution. The solutions will always be found by carefully examining the principles that are supposed and by following all the steps taken to reach them. Since the combinations of these principles and of the ways of using them are innumerable, there is in mathematics an immense field of acquiring knowledge and of knowledge yet to be acquired, which we shall always be the master to cultivate when we wish to and in which we shall always harvest the same abundant crop of truths.

But these truths would always have been matters of pure speculation, mere curiosity and utter uselessness, if we had not found the means of associating them with physical truths. Before considering the advantages of this union, let us see what we may hope to know in this category.

The phenomena which present themselves daily to our eyes, which follow and repeat each other uninterruptedly and constantly, are the foundation of our physical knowledge. It suffices that the thing should always occur in the same way for it to constitute a certitude or truth for us. All the facts of nature that we have observed, or that we shall be able to observe, are as many truths.

Thus we can increase their number as much as it pleases us to, by multiplying our observations. Our knowledge is limited only by the limits of the universe.

But when, after we have carefully observed the facts by repeated observations; when, after having established new truths by precise experiments, we seek out the reasons for these same facts, the causes of these effects, we suddenly find ourselves stopped—reduced to trying to deduce the effects from more general effects, and obliged to admit that the causes are and will ever be unknown to us, because our senses, being themselves the effects of causes that we cannot know, can give us ideas *of effects only*, and never of causes. We are therefore reduced to calling a general effect a cause, and we must give up any understanding beyond that limit. These general effects are for us the true laws of nature. All phenomena which we shall recognize as depending on these laws will be for us so many facts that are explained, so many truths that are understood. Those phenomena that we cannot connect with them will be merely facts that we have to keep in reserve until a greater number of observations and longer experimentation teach us other facts and uncover the physical cause, that is to say, the general effect from which derive these special effects. It is here that the union of the two sciences, mathematics and physics, can yield the greatest advantages. The one gives us the "how much," the other the "how" of things. Since what is involved here is combining and calculating the probabilities in order to judge whether an effect depends on one cause rather than on another, when you have imagined the "how" through physics, that is to say, when you have seen that such an effect may indeed depend on such a cause, then you apply calculation to determine the "how much" [i.e. probability?] of that effect, given its cause; and if you find that the result agrees with the observations, the probability that you have guessed correctly increases so greatly that it becomes a certitude; whereas, without this help, it would have remained a simple probability.

B. *The Epochs of Nature (1778)*

Just as in civil history one consults titles, searches for medals, or deciphers ancient inscriptions in order to determine the epochs of human revolutions, and in order to determine the dates of moral

Source: *Ibid.*

events, so too in natural history it is necessary to search the archives of the world, to draw old monuments out of the entrails of the earth, collect their debris, and assemble in a body of proofs all the evidences of physical changes which can enable us to reach back to the several ages of nature. This is the only way of setting a few landmarks in the immensity of space and of placing a certain number of mileposts along the eternal road of time. The past is like distance; our vision gradually weakens and would be completely lost if history and chronology had not placed lanterns or torches at the darkest turning points. But, despite these lights of the written tradition, if we go back only a few centuries, how many factual uncertainties do we encounter! How many errors concerning the course of events! And what profound darkness enshrouds the periods beyond that tradition! It has, moreover, transmitted to us only the deeds of a few nations, that is to say, the accounts of a very small part of the human race. All the rest of mankind remains a blank for us, a blank for posterity. They came out of their nothingness, only to pass like shadows which leave no traces. Would to God that the names of all those so-called heroes whose crimes or bloody fame has been celebrated were equally buried in the night of the forgotten!

Thus civil history, limited in one dimension by the darkness of a time which is rather close to our own, extends in the other dimension only to the small portions of the earth which people interested in being remembered have successively occupied. Natural history, on the other hand, embraces all places and all times and has no limits other than those of the universe.

Since nature is contemporaneous with matter, space, and time, its history is that of all substance, of all places, of all ages. Although it may appear at first sight that its great works do not suffer alteration or change, and that even in its most fragile and fleeting productions it shows itself constantly and ever the same, since at each instant its first models reappear to us in new forms; nevertheless, on looking at nature closely we shall see that its course is not absolutely uniform; we shall recognize that it admits of noticeable variations, that it undergoes successive alterations, that it even lends itself to new combinations, to mutations of matter and of form; and finally, that as constant as it appears as a whole, so is it variable in each of its parts; and if we conceive of it in the fullness of its extent, we shall not be able to doubt that it is quite different today from what it was in the beginning and from what it has become through the periods of time. It is these diverse changes that we call epochs. Nature has come through a variety of states. The surface of the earth has taken on a succession of different forms. Even the heavens have changed, and all things in the physical universe are, like those in the moral world, in a continual process of unending variations. For instance, the state in which we see nature today is as much our work as her own. We have been able to temper it, to modify it, to bend it to our needs and our desires; we have settled, cultivated, fertilized the earth. Its present appearance is then quite different from that of ages which preceded the invention of the arts. The golden age of morality, or rather of fable, was only the iron age of physics and truth. The half-savage men of those times, dispersed, few in number, did not feel their power or know their real wealth; the treasure of their intelligence was buried. They were ignorant of the power of united wills and never dreamed that, by means of society and their persistent and concerted enterprise, they would one day imprint their ideas on the entire face of the universe.

Consequently, it is necessary for us to seek out and examine nature in those newly discovered regions, in those lands which have always remained uninhabited, in order for us to derive an idea of its former state. That former state is relatively quite modern compared with the state when our terrestrial continents were covered by water, when fish lived on our plains and our mountains formed the reefs of the seas. How many changes and different states must have followed each other since those ancient times (which were still not the first) until the dawn of history! How many things have been buried! How many events entirely forgotten! How many revolutions of men! The human mind has needed a long series of observations, it has needed thirty centuries of culture to recognize only the present state of things. The earth still has undiscovered regions; only recently have we determined its shape; only in our own day have we developed a theory of its internal form and demonstrated the order and arrangement of the materials of which it is composed. Therefore it is only from this moment on that we can begin to compare nature with itself and to go back from its present and known state to several epochs of an older state.

Since, however, it is a matter of piercing the night of time, of recognizing through the inspection of existing things the former existence of things that have been annihilated, and of going backward through the sole power of remaining facts to the historical truth of buried facts; since, in a word, it is a matter of judging not only the recent past but the most ancient past from the present alone, and since in order to rise to this perspective we need to unite all our powers, we shall use three great means: (1) the facts that may bring us close to the origins of nature; (2) the relics that may be considered as witnesses of its earliest ages; (3) the traditions which may give us some ideas of subsequent ages. After this we shall try to link everything together by analogy and to form a chain which will descend from the top of the ladder of time unto ourselves.

18. Diderot, D'Alembert's Dream

D'ALEMBERT: I'd very much like you to tell me what difference there is, according to you, between a man and a statue, between marble and flesh.

DIDEROT: Not a great deal. Flesh can be made into marble, and marble into flesh.

D'ALEMBERT: But they are not the same.

DIDEROT: In the sense that what you call vital energy is not the same as what you call inanimate energy.

D'ALEMBERT: I don't understand.

DIDEROT: I'll make it clearer. The displacement of a body from one place to another cannot in itself be termed motion; it is merely the effect of motion. Motion exists equally both in a moving body and in a stationary body.

D'ALEMBERT: That's a new way of looking at things.

DIDEROT: But true, for all that. Remove the obstacle that is oppos-

SOURCE: Translated by Derek Coltman in *Diderot's Selected Writings*, ed. L. G. Crocker (New York: The Macmillan Company, 1966), pp. 180–85, 186–89. Reprinted by permission of the publishers.

ing the displacement of a stationary body and it will be displaced. Remove the air surrounding the trunk of that huge oak by some instantaneous process of rarefaction and the water contained in the trunk will immediately expand, bursting it into countless pieces. And the same, I should like to add, is true of your own body.

D'ALEMBERT: Very well. But what relation is there between motion and the capacity for sensation? Do you mean, by any chance, that you recognize two different kinds of sentience, analogous to animate force and inanimate force? So that there is an animate force that expresses itself in the movement of bodies, an inanimate force that manifests itself as pressure, an active sentience that is characterized by certain observable behavior in animals, and perhaps also in plants, and an inactive sentience whose existence would be revealed to us only when it became active?

DIDEROT: Precisely. You've expressed it beautifully.

D'ALEMBERT: The statue, then, possesses only an inactive kind of sentience; whereas man, animals, perhaps even plants are endowed with active sentience.

DIDEROT: That difference between the block of marble and living tissue does undoubtedly exist; but, as you are of course aware, it is not the only one.

D'ALEMBERT: Of course. Whatever the resemblance between the external forms of the man and the statue, there is no resemblance whatever between their internal structures. The chisel of even the most gifted sculptor cannot even create skin. But there is a very simple means of transforming an inanimate force into an animate one; it is an experiment we see repeated before our eyes a hundred times a day; whereas, on the other hand, I'm not at all sure I see how a body can be made to pass from a state of inactive sentience to a state of active sentience.

DIDEROT: That's because you're not looking hard enough. It's just as common a phenomenon.

D'ALEMBERT: Then what is it, this common phenomenon, if you please?

DIDEROT: Very well, since you seem to want me to put you to shame, I'll tell you. It occurs every time you eat.

D'ALEMBERT: Every time I eat!

DIDEROT: Yes. For what are you doing when you eat? You are removing the obstacles that were preventing the food from exercising an active capacity for sensation. You are assimilating it into yourself, turning it into flesh, making it animal, making it actively sentient. And what you do to your food, I can do any time I choose to marble.

D'ALEMBERT: And how will you do it?

DIDEROT: How? By making it edible.

D'ALEMBERT: Making marble edible? That doesn't sound too easy a task to me.

DIDEROT: Then it's up to me to show you how it's done. I take this statue here. I put it in a mortar. And then I have at it with my pestle. . . . When the block of marble has been reduced to the finest of powder, then I mix that powder with humus or leaf mold; I knead them well together; I sprinkle water on the mixture, then I leave it to decompose for a year, two years, a century—time means nothing to me. When the whole mass has finally been transformed into a more or less homogeneous substance, into humus, do you know what I do with it?

D'ALEMBERT: I'm sure you don't eat the humus.

DIDEROT: No, but there does exist a means of uniting myself with, of appropriating, the humus. A latus, as the chemists would say.

D'ALEMBERT: And that latus, is it plant life?

DIDEROT: Well done. I sow beans, peas, cabbages, and other vegetables in the humus. The plants feed on the soil, and I feed on the plants.

D'ALEMBERT: Well, whether it's true or false, I must say I like this idea of marble changing into humus, humus into plant life, and then plant life into animal life, into flesh in fact.

DIDEROT: So you see, I've made flesh—or soul, as my daughter put it: a form of matter with an active capacity for sensation. And though I may not have solved the problem you set me, I have at least got very near to doing so; for you will admit that there is a much greater difference between a piece of marble and a sentient being than between a sentient being and one that can think.

D'ALEMBERT: Yes, I agree there. But the fact remains that the sentient being is still not a thinking being.

DIDEROT: Before we go on to the next step, let me tell you the life story of one of Europe's greatest geometricians.[1] Now, what was this marvelous being to begin with? Nothing.

---

[1] Diderot refers to d'Alembert himself, an illegitimate child.

D'ALEMBERT: Nothing! What do you mean? Nothing can be made from nothing.

DIDEROT: You are taking my words too literally. My meaning is this, that before his mother, the beautiful and wicked canoness Mme de Tencin, had reached the age of puberty and before the soldier La Touche had reached his adolescence, the molecules that were destined to form the first rudiments of my geometrician were still scattered here and there throughout the delicate bodies of both these young people. They then filtered through those bodies with their lymph and circulated in their blood until they finally reached the organs of storage from which they were destined to emerge and unite: the ovaries of the mother and the testicles of the father. So our precious seed has been formed. And now, according to widely held opinion, it is brought down through one of the Fallopian tubes into the womb, to which it is attached by a long cord; and there it stays, continually growing and finally developing into a fetus. Now comes the moment for it to emerge from its dark prison; it is born, then abandoned on the steps of Saint-Jean-le-Rond, which was to provide it with its name; rescued from the foundlings' home; put to the breast of Mme Rousseau, the glazier's good wife; suckled; and finally, after having grown in body and mind, we behold it a man of letters, an engineer, and a geometrician. How was all this made to happen? Merely by eating and by other purely mechanical operations. The general formula is, put as briefly as possible: Eat, digest, and distill *in vasi licito, et fiat homo secundum artem.*[2] And anyone expounding to the Academy the process by which a man or an animal is formed need concern himself with none but material agents, whose successive results would be: an inert being, a sentient being, a thinking being, a being solving the problem of the precession of the equinoxes, a sublime being, a marvelous being, a being aging, degenerating, dying, passing through dissolution, and returning finally to humus.

D'ALEMBERT: So you don't believe in preexisting germs?

DIDEROT: No.

D'ALEMBERT: Ah, I'm glad to hear it.

DIDEROT: Such an idea is contrary to both experience and reason: contrary to experience because no amount of experiment would

---

[2] "Into the appropriate vessel, and in this way let man be made."

ever discover those germs in an egg or in most animals before a certain age; against reason because, although there may be no limit to the divisibility of matter in the mind, there is such a limit in nature; and the mind rejects the notion of an elephant already completely formed inside that one, and so on to infinity.

D'ALEMBERT: But without these preexisting germs, there is no way of explaining how the very first generation of animals was produced.

DIDEROT: If you're bothered by the "Which came first, the chicken or the egg?" problem, then that means you're supposing that animals have always been as they are now. What folly! We know no more about what they were like originally than we know about what they are to become in the future. The worm wriggling in the mud, so tiny that we cannot see it, may be on the way to becoming a huge animal; the enormous animal that now strikes terror into us because of its size may be on the way to becoming a tiny worm; it may be only a particular and ephemeral production of this planet.

D'ALEMBERT: I didn't quite follow that.

DIDEROT: I said . . . But it would only lead us away from the subject of our discussion.

D'ALEMBERT: What does that matter? We can get back to it later—or not, as we please.

DIDEROT: Will you allow me to anticipate time by a few thousand years?

D'ALEMBERT: Why not? Time means nothing to nature.

DIDEROT: Have you any objections to my snuffing out our sun?

D'ALEMBERT: None at all. After all, we know it won't be the first to have been snuffed out.

DIDEROT: The sun once extinguished, then, what will happen? The plants will perish, the animals will perish, and the earth will become a silent, an unpeopled planet. Relume that star: immediately, you have reestablished the cause that will necessarily produce an infinity of new forms of life, among which, as the centuries passed, I should not dare to guarantee that our plants and our animals, as we see them today, would either recur or not recur.

D'ALEMBERT: But why should the same scattered elements, when they came together, not yield the same results?

DIDEROT: Because in nature everything is indissolubly linked, and anyone who supposes the creation of a new phenomenon or brings back a moment of the past is creating a new and different world.

[At a later point, the interlocutors move on to problems of psychology.]

D'ALEMBERT: So it seems to me; there is only one remaining difficulty.

DIDEROT: You're wrong there: there are a great many more than one.

D'ALEMBERT: But one principal one. And it is this: it seems to me that we are able to think of only one thing at a time and that, in order to formulate even a simple proposition, to say nothing of much vaster logical sequences that must embrace thousands of individual ideas in the course of their development, it would seem that we must have at least two objects present in our minds at the same time: the object, which seems to remain in the mind's eye, and also the quality that the mind is considering whether or not to attribute to that object.

DIDEROT: I think as you do here, and it has sometimes led me to compare the fibers of our organs to vibrating and sensitive strings that continue to vibrate and produce sound long after they have been plucked. It is this vibration, this inevitable resonance, as it were, that keeps us constantly aware of the object's presence, while the mind occupies itself with deciding what qualities that object possesses. But vibrating cords also have another property: that of making other strings vibrate; and it is in this way that a first idea summons up a second, those two a third, those three together a fourth, and so on, without our being able to set a limit to the number of ideas awakened, then linked together in the mind of the philosopher as he meditates or listens to his own thoughts in silence and darkness. The mind is an instrument capable of astonishing leaps, and an awakened idea will sometimes set another string vibrating whose harmonic will produce a wholly incomprehensible interval between itself and the first. But if this phenomenon can be observed between resonating strings that are inanimate and disjunct, why should it not take place between points that are animate and linked together, between continuous and sentient fibers?

D'ALEMBERT: Well, it's certainly a very ingenious idea—even if it isn't true. But I am now rather inclined to think that you are slipping, by imperceptible degrees, into the difficulty that you set out to avoid.

DIDEROT: What is that?

D'ALEMBERT: You are opposed to the notion that we are composed of two different substances, are you not?

DIDEROT: I make no secret of that.

D'ALEMBERT: Well, if you look into the matter closely, you will see that you are making the philosopher's understanding distinct from the instrument. You are making it into a sort of musician who listens to the sounds emanating from the cords and then decides whether they are producing concords or discords.

DIDEROT: Possibly I did lay myself open to this objection, but you might not have made it if you had considered the difference between the philosopher-instrument and the harpsichord-instrument. The philosopher-instrument is sentient: he is, simultaneously, both the musician and the instrument. As a sentient being, he has a moment-by-moment awareness of the sounds he is producing. As an animal, he retains a memory of them. It is this faculty of the physical organism that, by linking the sounds together, produces and stores up the melody. Imagine a harpsichord with the faculties of sensation and memory. Will it not be able to repeat the tunes that you have played upon it all by itself? We are all instruments endowed with feeling and memory. Our senses are so many strings that are struck by surrounding objects and that also frequently strike themselves. That, as I see the matter, is all that happens in a harpsichord constructed like you or me. First, an impression is created by some cause either inside or outside the instrument; this impression gives rise to a sensation, a sensation that has duration, for it is impossible to conceive that it could be caused and then fade away again all in one indivisible moment; another impression then follows, similarly created by sensation; then voices, which express the sensations in either natural or conventionally formulated sounds.

D'ALEMBERT: I understand. So, therefore, if this sentient and animate harpsichord were also endowed with the capacity to feed and reproduce itself, it would be a living creature and would engender, either by itself or with its female counterpart, young harpsichords, also living and capable of vibration.

DIDEROT: Undoubtedly. What else, in your opinion, is a chaffinch,

a nightingale, a musician, or a man? And what other difference
do you find there to be between a bird and a bird-organ? Do
you see this egg? With this you can topple every theological
theory, every church or temple in the world. What is it, this egg,
before the seed is introduced into it? An insentient mass. And
after the seed has been introduced into it? What is it then? An
insentient mass. For what is that seed itself other than a crude
and inanimate fluid? How is this mass to make the transition to a
different structure, to sentience, to life? Through heat. And
what will produce that heat in it? Motion. What will the successive effects of that motion be? Instead of answering that, sit
down, and let us follow them with our eyes, moment by moment. First, there is a dot that quivers; then a little thread that
grows longer and takes on color; flesh is being formed; a beak,
rudimentary wings, eyes, and feet appear; a yellowish substance
empties out and produces intestines: it is an animal. The animal is
moving about, struggling, emitting cries; I can hear its cries
through the shell; it becomes covered in down; it can see. The
weight of its head, as it moves it about, brings its beak into
repeated contact with the inner surface of its prison wall; the
wall breaks; the bird emerges, it walks, it flies, it becomes angry,
it flies away, it comes back again, it complains, it suffers, it loves,
it desires, it feels pleasure; it has all the same affections as you
yourself; it performs the same actions. Are you going to claim, as
Descartes did, that it is nothing but an imitative machine? Little
children will laugh at you if you do, and philosophers will tell
you that if this bird is a machine, then you are one too. If you
admit that the only difference between you and the bird is one
of structure, then you will be showing good sense, for the
admission will be both reasonable and honest. But your opponents will then point out that what you are saying is this: that
from a piece of inanimate matter, arranged in a certain way,
impregnated with a further quantity of inanimate matter, then
with heat and motion, there can result sentience, life, memory,
consciousness, passion, and thought. You therefore have only
one of two courses left open to you: either you suppose an
element[3] hidden in the inanimate mass of the egg that waited for
that mass to develop further before manifesting its presence or

[3] The soul, a nonphysical or vitalistic entity.

you suppose that this invisible element crept in through the shell at some fixed point during that development. But what is this element? Did it occupy space or not? How did it come or how did it escape without moving? Where was it before? What was it doing there? Or anywhere? Was it created at the very instant that the need for it arose? Was it already in existence? Was it waiting for a host? Was it of the same substance as that host? Or of a different substance? If it was of the same substance, then it was material. If it was of a different substance, then it is impossible for us to conceive either its inert state before the development of the egg or its present activity in the finished animal. You will only have to listen to yourself to pity yourself. You will realize that in order to avoid admitting one simple supposition that explains everything—to wit, that sentience is a general property of matter or a product of physical structure—you are renouncing all common sense and plunging headlong into an abyss of mysteries, contradictions, and absurdities.

IV

Morals

THE METAPHYSICAL and religious climate of the age obliged eighteenth-century thinkers to make a fresh inquiry into the nature and validity of moral obligation. Why do we consider certain actions to be right or wrong and why should such judgments be binding on us? Innumerable books were written on these themes, and many theories and solutions propounded, probably with little effect on the conduct of men—thus substantiating Hume's view that you cannot rationally convince a man that he ought to be a moral being if he does not want to be one. The selections that follow represent several directions of eighteenth-century thought.

Bayle's article on Pyrrho (the Greek founder of a school of absolute skepticism) points up the metaphysical quandary of the moralist who rejects supernaturalism and revelation. Bayle advances the thesis, which at the other end of the century Sade was to develop, that moral evil is part of the universe and that God connives in it. If we justify God, then all moral knowledge and judgment become impossible.

Hume was in some ways Bayle's disciple. But his moral philosophy in the *Treatise of Human Nature* (1739) and in *Inquiry concerning the Principles of Morals* (1751) was more systematic and searching. In the *Treatise* (less mature but more influential than the *Inquiry*), he endeavored to show that moral judgments do not rest on *a priori*, rational truths, but are reactions of pleasure or displeasure, related to the utility of actions and based on "sympathy"—a notion which embraces what we now call "empathy." They are not subject to rational proof. Reason, Hume maintains, is powerless, except to further ends which derive from the "passions," and these ends are not amenable to rational justification or control. Hume was a moralist and thought that moral judgments were necessary and (relatively) valid. He was trying to dispel errors and illusions, but his skepticism may well have substantiated the position of egotistic immoralists who came after him.

Adam Smith, best known today as the author of *The Wealth of Nations* (1776), the primer of laissez-faire economic theory, was earlier reputed as a moralist, and his *Theory of Moral Sentiments* (1759) was widely read. Like Hume, he saw the roots of moral experience in sympathy, but he emphasized the existence in each of us of "an impartial, well-informed spectator," whose approbation we need, whose disapproval we avoid. On this basis, he was critical of the utilitarian element in Hume's ethics and claimed that moral judgment is *sui generis*, not reducible to utility. Mandeville's cynical amoralism aroused the Scotsman's wrath—even as it appealed to certain French writers.

Moral skepticism reached an early peak in the *Discours préliminaire*, which La Mettrie, the most consistent of materialists, wrote in 1751 for his collected writings. Men are properly governed by the law of nature, which determines them to seek pleasure and happiness in whatever ways their constitution dictates. Moral categories and restrictions are artificial inventions of society, and have no other basis and no quality of obligation. They are as necessary to society as the egoistic rebellion against them is proper to the individual. The result is a perpetual conflict—one which Rousseau's political theory is designed to obviate. La Mettrie (along with Helvétius, d'Holbach, and Rousseau in *Discourse on Inequality*) sets the theoretical basis for the nihilism of Sade, who acknowledges his debt.

Helvétius, in *De l'Esprit* (*On the Mind*, 1758), affirms and develops what many in the eighteenth century considered to be the universal law of human behavior, comparable to Newton's law of gravitation: search for pleasure, avoidance of pain. Self-interest is the only motive of all actions; its requirements in society (as Rousseau had said in the *Discourse on Inequality*) involve the desire for prestige and power, and often the hurt of others. Moral judgments, according to Helvétius, are made from the viewpoint of society, and the utility of actions to society is their sole criterion. Intention (reduced to self-interest, regardless of the act) is irrelevant. Fortunately, the mind is a *tabula rasa;* conditioning and habituation make it possible for those who control political power to govern behavior. Helvétius's theories receive an even more radical development in his posthumous work, *De l'homme* (1772). His utilitarianism had a deep influence on Bentham. It contrasts with the theories of Hume and Smith, for whom moral approbation goes beyond self-interest.

Diderot was a great experimenter in ideas. He was passionately devoted to the love of virtue and the teaching of morality. At other times (or at the same time), he had a lucid awareness both of the amoral character of human behavior in society (and in this he agreed with Rousseau) and of the difficulty, or indeed the impossibility, of rationally justifying moral restrictions to the ego. Both tendencies are illustrated in the following selections. The article "Natural Right" appeared in the *Encyclopédie* in 1755; it attempted to defend a naturalistic or empirical natural law doctrine. Apparently Diderot later considered it a failure. It was refuted in the unpublished first version of the *Contrat social*, in which Rousseau pointed to a new way of "answering" the moral nihilist: control of behavior. Diderot's great dialogues, *Le Neveu de Rameau* (1762) and *Le Rêve de d'Alembert* (1769), represent his

"secret doctrine," denounced by Rousseau, as does the remark taken
from his *Eléments de physiologie* (1774–80). This aspect of Diderot's
thought is logically connected to his materialism. He rebelled, however,
in humanistic fashion against the consequences of materialism as expounded by Helvétius (*Réfutation d'Helvétius*, 1773). Only the first of
these selections was published in the eighteenth century; Diderot be-
queathed his "secret doctrine" to posterity.

While some materialists evolved amoralistic theories publicly or in
private, others defended a social, utilitarian morality, at least as a
pragmatic necessity. D'Holbach (*Système de la nature*, 1770), like
Diderot, exemplifies the dilemmas of the moralist who accepts the
"natural," especially the need for pleasure and happiness, as the highest
value and end in life and at the same time wishes to convince men that
the social demand for virtue (the sacrifice of egoistic aims) is valid and
binding. (Supernatural imperatives are of course excluded.) The proposed solutions are always self-defeating, for as forms of utilitarianism
they are always reducible to self-interest—enlightened self-interest, an
immediate virtue-happiness equivalence, self-esteem, or public esteem.
Such solutions are self-defeating, because they are not moral at all, but
forms of prudential behavior or happiness seeking, and because as such
they are empirically unverifiable, to put it at best, or even contrary to
personal and historical experience.

Voltaire's writings span most of the century. In an early work which
he left unpublished, the *Traité de métaphysique* (1734), he reveals his
concern with the challenge of the immoralist and, like Diderot in
"Natural Right," provides an unsatisfactory reply. A deist, he was to
alternate all his life between an abiding belief in natural law (supposedly
not "innate," but nonetheless necessarily developed in all men) and an
increasing emphasis on social utilitarianism. The article "Just and Unjust" comes from his *Dictionnaire philosophique* (1765, first published
in 1764 as the *Dictionnaire portatif*).

Immanuel Kant, well read in the writings of the Enlightenment,
grasped more clearly than any of the Christian apologists had done the
fundamental contradictions and flaws in the ethics of the French
moralists. He made his objections clear in one of his earlier works,
Fundamental Principles of the Metaphysic of Morals (1785), and they
are repeated in his later masterpiece, *Critique of Practical Reason*
(1788). Kant's reaction was notably humanistic, but excessively rigoris-
tic and absolutist. Yet there is a tenuous relationship between the
passage we have selected and Diderot's thinking in "Natural Right,"
as well as with Rousseau's ideas on the conscience in *Emile*.

If the moralism of the French writers was philosophically unacceptable to Kant, it was also rejected by Sade, whose personal inclinations
and reasoning led him in an entirely contrary direction—to the complete liberation of the ego from restraints, which, being created and
imposed by culture in opposition to nature, he holds to be invalid.
Sade's writings were condemned and officially suppressed. But their

influence on the course of later cultural history was great, and he has the merit of courageously exposing hidden depths and evil potentialities in the human psyche. Nevertheless, his system of nihilism is not only destructive and dangerous, but philosophically contradictory and untenable. The selection presented here comes from his novel, *Histoire de Juliette; ou, les Prospérités du vice* (1791).

19. Bayle, Historical and Critical Dictionary

Pyrrho

LET US turn to ethics. (1) It is evident that we ought to prevent evil if we can and that we sin if we allow it when we can prevent it. However, our theology shows us that this is false. It teaches us that God does nothing unworthy of his perfections when he permits all the disorders in the world which he could easily have prevented. (2) It is evident that a creature who does not exist cannot be an accomplice in an evil action. (3) And that it is unjust to punish him as an accomplice of that action. Nevertheless, our doctrine of original sin shows us the falsity of these evident truths. (4) It is evident that we ought to prefer what is righteous to what is profitable; and that the more holy a being is, the less it is allowed to prefer what is profitable to what is righteous. Nevertheless, our theologians tell us that God, having to choose between a world perfectly regulated, adorned with every virtue, and a world like ours, where sin and disorder predominate, preferred ours to the other as suiting better the interest of his glory. You are going to tell me that the duties of the creator should not be measured by our standards. But, if you do this, you fall into the nets of your adversaries. This is where they want you. Their major aim is to prove that the absolute nature of things is unknown to us and that we can know them only relatively. We do not know, they say, if sugar is sweet in itself. We know only that it appears sweet when it

SOURCE: Translated by R. H. Popkin and Craig Brush in Pierre Bayle, *Historical and Critical Dictionary* (New York: The Bobbs-Merrill Co., Inc., 1965), pp. 202–03. Copyright © 1965. Reprinted by permission of the publishers.

is placed on our tongues. We do not know if a certain action is righteous in itself and by its nature. We only believe that with regard to such a person, with respect to certain circumstances, it has the appearance of righteousness. But it is something else in other respects and other relations. Behold then what you are exposed to when you say that the ideas we have of justice and righteousness admit of exceptions and are relative. Consider also that the more you elevate the power or right of God not to act according to our ideas, the more you destroy the one means you have left for proving the existence of bodies, namely, that God does not deceive us, and that he would if there were no corporeal world. To show a whole people a sight or spectacle that does not exist outside their minds would be a deception. You might wish to answer that one should distinguish two cases. If a king did it, it would be a deception; but if God does it, it is not; for the obligations of a king and of God are quite different. Besides this, if the exceptions you make to the principles of morality are based on the infinite incomprehensibility of God, then I can never be sure of anything. For I can never be able to comprehend the whole extent of the rights and privileges of God.

20.   Hume, Treatise of Human Nature

Book II   Of the Passions

SECTION V. OF THE INFLUENCING MOTIVES OF THE WILL

Since reason alone can never produce any action or give rise to volition, I infer that the same faculty is as incapable of preventing volition or of disputing the preference with any passion or emotion. This consequence is necessary. It is impossible reason could have the latter effect of preventing volition, but by giving an impulse in a contrary direction to our passions; and that impulse, had it operated alone, would have been ample to produce volition.

SOURCE: H. D. Aiken (ed.), *Hume's Moral and Political Philosophy* (New York: Hafner Publishing Co., Inc., 1948), pp. 24–26, 37–43, 134–36.

Nothing can oppose or retard the impulse of passion but a contrary impulse; and if this contrary impulse ever arises from reason, that latter faculty must have an original influence on the will and must be able to cause as well as hinder any act of volition. But if reason has no original influence, it is impossible it can withstand any principle which has such an efficacy, or ever keep the mind in suspense a moment. Thus it appears that the principle which opposes our passion cannot be the same with reason, and is only called so in an improper sense. We speak not strictly and philosophically when we talk of the combat of passion and of reason. Reason is, and ought only to be, the slave of the passions, and can never pretend to any other office than to serve and obey them. As this opinion may appear somewhat extraordinary, it may not be improper to confirm it by some other considerations.

A passion is an original existence or, if you will, modification of existence, and contains not any representative quality which renders it a copy of any other existence or modification. When I am angry, I am actually possessed with the passion, and in that emotion have no more a reference to any other object than when I am thirsty, or sick, or more than five feet high. It is impossible, therefore, that this passion can be opposed by, or be contradictory to, truth and reason; since this contradiction consists in the disagreement of ideas, considered as copies, with those objects which they represent.

What may at first occur on this head is that as nothing can be contrary to truth or reason, except what has a reference to it, and as the judgments of our understanding only have this reference, it must follow that passions can be contrary to reason only so far as they are accompanied with some judgment or opinion. According to this principle, which is so obvious and natural, it is only in two senses that any affection can be called unreasonable. First, when a passion, such as hope or fear, grief or joy, despair or security, is founded on the supposition of the existence of objects which really do not exist. Secondly, when, in exerting any passion in action, we choose means sufficient for the designed end, and deceive ourselves in our judgment of causes and effects. Where a passion is neither founded on false suppositions, nor chooses means insufficient for the end, the understanding can neither justify nor condemn it. It is not contrary to reason to prefer the destruction of the whole world to the scratching of my finger. It is not contrary to reason for me to choose my total ruin to prevent the least uneasiness of an Indian, or person wholly unknown to me. It is as little contrary to reason to prefer even my own acknowledged lesser good to my greater, and have a more ardent affection for the former than the latter. A trivial good may, from certain circumstances, produce a desire superior to what arises from the greatest and most valuable enjoyment; nor is there anything more extraordinary in this than in mechanics to see one pound weight raise up a hundred by the advantage of its situation. In short, a passion must be accompanied with some false judgment in order to its being unreasonable; and even then it is not the passion, properly speaking, which is unreasonable, but the judgment.

Book III   Of Morals

PART I. OF VIRTUE AND VICE IN GENERAL

SECTION II. MORAL DISTINCTIONS NOT DERIVED FROM REASON

If the thought and understanding were alone capable of fixing the boundaries of right and wrong, the character of virtuous and vicious either must lie in some relations of objects, or must be a matter of fact which is discovered by our reasoning. This consequence is evident. As the operations of human understanding divide themselves into two kinds—the comparing of ideas and the inferring of matter of fact—were virtue discovered by the understanding, it must be an object of one of these operations; nor is there any third operation of the understanding which can discover it. There has been an opinion very industriously propagated by certain philosophers that morality is susceptible of demonstration; and though no one has ever been able to advance a single step in those demonstrations, yet it is taken for granted that this science may be brought to an equal certainty with geometry or algebra. Upon this supposition vice and virtue must consist in some relations, since it is allowed on all hands that no matter of fact is capable of being demonstrated. . . .

First, as moral good and evil belong only to the actions of the mind, and are derived from our situation with regard to external objects, the relations from which these moral distinctions arise must lie only betwixt internal actions and external objects, and must not be applicable either to internal actions, compared among themselves, or to external objects, when placed in opposition to other external objects. For as morality is supposed to attend certain relations, if these relations could belong to internal actions considered singly, it would follow that we might be guilty of crimes in ourselves, and independent of our situation with respect to the universe; and in like manner, if these moral relations could be applied to external objects, it would follow that even inanimate beings would be susceptible of moral beauty and deformity. Now, it seems difficult to imagine that any relation can be discovered betwixt our passions, volitions, and actions, compared to external objects, which relation might not belong either to these passions and volitions, or to these external objects, compared among themselves.

But it will be still more difficult to fulfil the second condition requisite to justify this system. According to the principles of those who maintain an abstract rational difference betwixt moral good and evil, and a natural fitness and unfitness of things, it is not only supposed that these relations, being eternal and immutable, are the same when considered by every rational creature, but their effects are also supposed to be necessarily the same; and it is concluded they have no less, or rather a greater, influence in directing the will of the Deity than in governing the rational and virtuous of our own species. These two particulars are evidently distinct. It is one thing to know virtue, and another to conform the will to it. In order, therefore, to prove that the measures of right and wrong are eternal laws, obligatory on every rational mind, it is not sufficient to show the relations upon which they are founded; we must also point out the connection betwixt the relation and the will, and must prove that this connection is so necessary that in every well-disposed mind it must take place and have its influence, though the difference betwixt these minds be in other respects immense and infinite. Now, besides what I have already proved, that even in human nature no relation can ever alone produce any action—besides this, I say, it has been shown, in treating of the understanding, that there is no connection of cause and effect, such as this is supposed to be, which is discoverable otherwise than by experience, and of which we can pretend to have any security by the simple consideration of the objects. All beings in the universe, considered in themselves, appear entirely loose and independent of each other. It is only by experience we learn their influence and connection; and this influence we ought never to extend beyond experience.

Thus it will be impossible to fulfil the first condition required to the system of eternal rational measures of right and wrong, because it is impossible to show those relations upon which such a distinction may be founded; and it is as impossible to fulfil the second condition, because we cannot prove a priori that these relations, if they really existed and were perceived, would be universally forcible and obligatory.

But to make these general reflections more clear and convincing, we may illustrate them by some particular instances, wherein this character of moral good or evil is the most universally acknowledged. Of all crimes that human creatures are capable of committing, the most horrid and unnatural is ingratitude, especially when it is committed against parents, and appears in the more flagrant instances of wounds and death. This is acknowledged by all mankind, philosophers as well as the people. The question only arises among philosophers, whether the guilt or moral deformity of this action be discovered by demonstrative reasoning, or be felt by an internal sense and by means of some sentiment which the reflecting on such an action naturally occasions. This question will soon be decided against the former opinion, if we can show the same relations in other objects without the notion of any guilt or iniquity attending them. Reason or science is nothing but the comparing of ideas, and the discovery of their relations; and if the same relations have different characters it must evidently follow that those characters are not discovered merely by reason. To put the affair, therefore, to this trial, let us choose any inanimate object, such as an oak or elm, and let us suppose that by the dropping of its seed it produces a sapling below it which, springing up by degrees, at last overtops and destroys the parent tree: I ask if in this instance there be wanting any relation which is discoverable in parricide or ingratitude? Is not the one tree the cause of the other's existence; and the latter the cause of the destruction of the former in the same manner as when a child murders his parent? It is not sufficient to reply that a choice or will is wanting. For in the case of parricide, a will does not give rise to any different relations, but is only the cause from which the action is derived; and consequently produces the same relations that in the oak or elm arise from some other principles. It is a will or choice that determines a man to kill his parent; and they are the laws of matter and motion that determine a sapling to destroy the oak from which it sprung. Here then the same relations have different causes; but still the relations are the same; and as their discovery is not in both cases attended with a notion of immorality, it follows that that notion does not arise from such a discovery.

But to choose an instance still more resembling; I would fain ask anyone why incest in the human species is criminal, and why the very same action and the same relations in animals have not the smallest moral turpitude and deformity? If it be answered that this action is innocent in animals, because they have not reason sufficient to discover its turpitude, but that man being endowed with that faculty which ought to restrain him to his duty, the same action instantly becomes criminal to him. Should this be said, I would reply that this is evidently arguing in a circle. For before reason can perceive this turpitude, the turpitude must exist, and consequently is independent of the decisions of our reason, and is their object more properly than their effect. According to this system, then, every animal that has sense, and appetite, and will, that is, every animal must be susceptible of all the same virtues and vices for which we ascribe praise and blame to human creatures. All the difference is that our superior reason may serve to discover the vice or virtue, and by that means may augment the blame or praise; but still this discovery supposes a separate being in these moral distinctions, and a being which depends only on the will and appetite, and which, both in thought and reality, may be distinguished from reason. Animals are susceptible of the same relations with respect to each other as the human species, and therefore would also be susceptible of the same morality if the essence of morality consisted in these relations. Their want of a sufficient degree of reason may hinder them from perceiving the duties from existing; since they must antecedently exist in order to their being perceived. Reason must find them, and can never produce them. This argument deserves to be weighed as being, in my opinion, entirely decisive.

Nor does this reasoning only prove that morality consists not in any relations that are the objects of science; but, if examined, will prove with equal certainty that it consists not in any matter of fact which can be discovered by the understanding. This is the second part of our argument; and if it can be made evident, we may conclude that morality is not an object of reason. But can there be any difficulty in proving that vice and virtue are not matters of fact whose existence we can infer by reason? Take any action allowed to be vicious—wilful murder, for instance. Examine it in all lights, and see if you can find that matter of fact or real existence which you call vice. In whichever way you take it, you find only certain passions, motives, volitions, and thoughts. There is no other matter of fact in the case. The vice entirely escapes you, as long as you consider the object. You never can find it till you turn your reflection into your own breast and find a sentiment of disapprobation which arises in you towards this action. Here is a matter of fact; but it is the object of feeling, not of reason. It lies in yourself, not in the object. So that when you pronounce any action or character to be vicious, you mean nothing, but that from the constitution of your nature you have a feeling or sentiment of blame from the contemplation of it. Vice and virtue, therefore, may be compared to sounds, colours, heat, and cold, which, according to modern philosophy, are not qualities in objects but perceptions in the mind: and this discovery in morals, like that other in physics, is to be regarded as a considerable advancement of the speculative sciences; though, like that too, it has little or no influence on practice. Nothing can be more real, or concern us more, than our own sentiments of pleasure and uneasiness; and if these be favourable to virtue, and unfavourable to vice, no more can be requisite to the regulation of our conduct and behaviour.

Part III. Of the Other Virtues and Vices

Section I. of the Origin of the Natural Virtues and Vices

Thus it appears that sympathy is a very powerful principle in human nature, that it has a great influence on our taste of beauty, and that it produces our sentiment of morals in all the artificial virtues. From thence we may presume that it also gives rise to many of the other virtues, and that qualities acquire our approbation because of their tendency to the good of mankind. This presumption must become a certainty, when we find that most of those qualities which we naturally approve of have actually that tendency and render a man a proper member of society; while the qualities which we naturally disapprove of have a contrary tendency and render any intercourse with the person dangerous or disagreeable. For having found that such tendencies have force enough to produce the strongest sentiment of morals, we can never reasonably, in these cases, look for any other cause of approbation or blame; it being an inviolable maxim in philosophy that where any particular cause is sufficient for an effect, we ought to rest satisfied with it, and ought not to multiply causes without necessity. We have happily attained experiments in the artificial virtues, where the tendency of qualities to the good of society is the sole cause of our approbation, without any suspicion of the concurrence of another principle. From thence we learn the force of that principle. And where that principle may take place, and the quality approved of is really beneficial to society, a true philosopher will never require any other principle to account for the strongest approbation and esteem.

That many of the natural virtues have this tendency to the good of society, no one can doubt of. Meekness, beneficence, charity, generosity, clemency, moderation, equity, bear the greatest figure among the moral qualities, and are commonly denominated the social virtues, to mark their tendency to the good of society. This goes so far that some philosophers have represented all moral distinctions as the effect of artifice and education, when skillful politicians endeavoured to restrain the turbulent passions of men, and make them operate to the public good, by the notions of honour and shame. This system, however, is not consistent with experience. For, first, there are other virtues and vices beside those which have this tendency to the public advantage and loss. Secondly, had not men a natural sentiment of approbation and blame, it could never be excited by politicians; nor would the words laudable and praiseworthy, blamable and odious, be any more intelligible than if they were a language perfectly unknown to us, as we have already observed. But though this system be erroneous, it may teach us that moral distinctions arise in a great measure from the tendency of qualities and characters to the interests of society, and that it is our concern for that interest which makes us approve or disapprove of them. Now, we have no such extensive concern for society but from sympathy; and consequently it is that principle which takes us so far out of ourselves as to give us the same pleasure or uneasiness in the characters of others, as if they had a tendency to our own advantage or loss.

The only difference betwixt the natural virtues and justice lies in this, that the good which results from the former rises from every single act, and is the object of some natural passion; whereas a single act of justice, considered in itself, may often be contrary to the public good; and it is only the concurrence of mankind in a general scheme or system of action which is advantageous. When I relieve persons in distress, my natural humanity is my motive; and so far as my succour extends, so far have I promoted the happiness of my fellow creatures. But if we examine all the questions that come before any tribunal of justice, we shall find that, considering each case apart, it would as often be an instance of humanity to decide contrary to the laws of justice as conformable to them. Judges take from a poor man to give to a rich; they bestow on the dissolute the labour of the industrious; and put into the hands of the vicious the means of harming both themselves and others. The whole scheme, however, of law and justice is advantageous to the society; and it was with a view to this advantage that men, by their voluntary conventions, established it. After it is once established by these conventions, it is naturally attended with a strong sentiment of morals which can proceed from nothing but our sympathy with the interests of society. We need no other explication of that esteem which attends such of the natural virtues as have a tendency to the public good. . . .

This theory may serve to explain why the same qualities, in all cases, produce both pride and love, humility and hatred; and the same man is always virtuous or vicious, accomplished or despicable to others, who is so to himself. A person in whom we discover any passion or habit which originally is only incommodious to himself becomes always disagreeable to us merely on its account; as, on the other hand, one whose character is only dangerous and disagreeable to others can never be satisfied with himself as long as he is sensible of that disadvantage. Nor is this observable only with regard to characters and manners, but may be remarked even in the most minute circumstances. A violent cough in another gives us uneasiness, though in itself it does not in the least affect us. A man will be mortified if you tell him he has a stinking breath, though it is evidently no annoyance to himself. Our fancy easily changes its situation; and, either surveying ourselves as we appear to others or considering others as they feel themselves, we enter by that means into sentiments which no way belong to us, and in which nothing but sympathy is able to interest us. And this sympathy we sometimes carry so far as even to be displeased with a quality commodious to us, merely because it displeases others and makes us disagreeable in their eyes, though, perhaps, we never can have any interest in rendering ourselves agreeable to them.

21. Adam Smith, The Theory of Moral Sentiments

Of Licentious Systems

THERE IS, however, another system, which seems to take away altogether the distinction between vice and virtue, and of which the tendency is, upon that account, wholly pernicious; I mean the system of Dr. Mandeville. Though the notions of this author are in almost every respect erroneous, there are, however, some appearances in human nature which, when viewed in a certain manner, seem at first sight to favor them. These, described and exaggerated by the lively and humorous, though coarse and rustic eloquence of Dr. Mandeville, have thrown upon his doctrines an air of truth and probability which is very apt to impose upon the unskillful.

Dr. Mandeville considers whatever is done from a sense of propriety, from a regard to what is commendable and praisworthy, as being done from a love of praise and commendation, or, as he calls it, from vanity. Man, he observes, is naturally much more interested in his own happiness than in that of others, and it is impossible that in his heart he can ever really prefer their prosperity to his own. Whenever he appears to do so, we may be assured that he imposes upon us, and that he is then acting from the same selfish motives as at all other times. Among his other selfish passions, vanity is one of the strongest, and he is always easily flattered and greatly delighted with the applauses of those about him. When he appears to sacrifice his own interest to that of his companions, he knows that this conduct will be highly agreeable to their self-love; and that they will not fail to express their satisfaction by bestowing upon him the most extravagant praises. The pleasure which he expects from this overbalances, in his opinion, the interest which he abandons in order to procure it. His conduct, therefore, upon this occasion is, in reality, just as selfish and arises from just as mean a motive as upon any other. He is flattered,

SOURCE: H. W. Schneider (ed. and intro.), *Adam Smith's Moral and Political Philosophy* (New York: Hafner Publishing Co., Inc., 1948), pp. 43–45, 219–23 *passim*.

however, and he flatters himself with the belief that it is entirely disinterested; since, unless this was supposed, it would not seem to merit any commendation either in his own eyes or in those of others. All public spirit, therefore, all preference of public to private interest, is, according to him, a mere cheat and imposition upon mankind; and that human virtue which is so much boasted of, and which is the occasion of so much emulation among men, is the mere offspring of flattery begot upon pride.

Whether the most generous and public-spirited actions may not, in some sense, be regarded as proceeding from self-love, I shall not at present examine. The decision of this question is not, I apprehend, of any importance towards establishing the reality of virtue, since self-love may frequently be a virtuous motive of action. I shall only endeavour to show that the desire of doing what is honourable and noble, of rendering ourselves the proper objects of esteem and approbation, cannot, with any propriety, be called vanity. Even the love of well-grounded fame and reputation, the desire of acquiring esteem by what is really estimable, does not deserve that name. The first is the love of virtue, the noblest and the best passion of human nature. The second is the love of true glory, a passion inferior, no doubt, to the former, but which in dignity appears to come immediately after it. He is guilty of vanity who desires praise for qualities which are either not praiseworthy in any degree, or not in that degree in which he expects to be praised for them, who sets his character upon the frivolous ornaments of dress and equipage or upon the equally frivolous accomplishments of ordinary behavior. He is guilty of vanity who desires praise for what, indeed, very well deserves it, but what he perfectly knows does not belong to him. The empty coxcomb who gives himself airs of importance which he has no title to, the silly liar who assumes the merit of adventures which never happened, the foolish plagiary who gives himself out for the author of what he has no pretensions to, are properly accused of this passion. He, too, is said to be guilty of vanity who is not contented with the silent sentiments of esteem and approbation, who seems to be fonder of their noisy expressions and acclamations than of the sentiments themselves, who is never satisfied but when his own praises are ringing in his ears, and who solicits, with the most anxious importunity, all external marks of respect, is fond of titles, of compliments, of being visited, of being attended, of being taken notice of in public places with the appearance of deference and attention. This frivolous passion is altogether different from either of the two former, and is the passion of the lowest and the least of mankind, as they are of the noblest and the greatest.

But though these three passions, the desire of rendering ourselves the proper objects of honour and esteem, or of becoming what is honourable and estimable; the desire of acquiring honour and esteem by really deserving those sentiments; and the frivolous desire of praise at any rate, are widely different, though the two former are always approved of, while the latter never fails to be despised; there is, however, a certain remote affinity among them which, exaggerated by the humorous and diverting eloquence of this lively author, has enabled him to impose upon his readers. There is an affinity between vanity and the love of true glory, as both these passions aim at acquiring esteem and approbation. But they are different in this, that the one is a just, reasonable, and equitable passion, while the other is unjust, absurd, and ridiculous. The man who desires esteem for what is really estimable desires nothing but what he is justly entitled to, and what cannot be refused him without some sort of injury. He, on the contrary, who desires it upon any other terms demands what he has no just claim to. The first is easily satisfied, is not apt to be jealous or suspicious that we do not esteem him enough, and is seldom solicitous about receiving many external marks of our regard. The other, on the contrary, is never to be satisfied, is full of jealousy and suspicion that we do not esteem him so much as he desires, because he has some secret consciousness that he desires more than he deserves.

Of the Beauty Which the Appearance of Utility Bestows upon the Characters and Actions of Men; and How Far the Perception of This Beauty May Be Regarded as One of the Original Principles of Approbation

The same ingenious and agreeable author who first explained why utility pleases,[1] has been so struck with this view of things as to resolve our whole approbation of virtue into a perception of this species of beauty which results from the appearance of utility. No qualities of the mind, he observes, are approved of as virtuous, but

---

[1] Adam Smith is referring to Hume.

such as are useful or agreeable either to the person himself or to others; and no qualities are disapproved of as vicious, but such as have a contrary tendency. And Nature, indeed, seems to have so happily adjusted our sentiments of approbation and disapprobation, of the convenience both of the individual and of the society, that after the strictest examination it will be found, I believe, that this is universally the case. But still I affirm that it is not the view of this utility or hurtfulness which is either the first or principal source of our approbation and disapprobation. These sentiments are, no doubt, enhanced and enlivened by the perception of the beauty or deformity which results from this utility or hurtfulness. But still, I say, they are originally and essentially different from this perception.

For, first of all, it seems impossible that the approbation of virtue should be a sentiment of the same kind with that by which we approve of a convenient and well-contrived building; or, that we should have no other reason for praising a man than that for which we commend a chest of drawers.

And, secondly, it will be found upon examination that the usefulness of any disposition of mind is seldom the first ground of our approbation, and that the sentiment of approbation always involves in it a sense of propriety quite distinct from the perception of utility. We may observe this with regard to all the qualities which are approved of as virtuous, both those which, according to this system, are originally valued as useful to ourselves, as well as those which are esteemed on account of their usefulness to others.

The qualities most useful to ourselves are, first of all, superior reason and understanding, by which we are capable of discerning the remote consequences of all our actions, and of foreseeing the advantage or detriment which is likely to result from them; and, secondly, self-command, by which we are enabled to abstain from present pleasure, or to endure present pain, in order to obtain a greater pleasure or to avoid a greater pain in some future time. In the union of those two qualities consists the virtue of prudence, of all the virtues that which is most useful to the individual.

With regard to the first of those qualities, it has been observed on the former occasion that superior reason and understanding are originally approved of as just and right and accurate, and not merely as useful or advantageous. It is in the abstruser sciences, particularly in the higher parts of mathematics, that the greatest and most admired exertions of human reason have been displayed. But the utility of those sciences, either to the individual or to the public, is not very obvious, and to prove it requires a discussion which is not always very easily comprehended. It was not, therefore, their utility which first recommended them to the public admiration. This quality was but little insisted upon, till it became necessary to make some reply to the reproaches of those who, having themselves no taste for such sublime discoveries, endeavoured to depreciate them as useless.

That self-command, in the same manner, by which we restrain our present appetites in order to gratify them more fully upon another occasion, is approved of, as much under the aspect of propriety as under that of utility. When we act in this manner, the sentiments which influence our conduct seem exactly to coincide with those of the spectator. The spectator does not feel the solicitations of our present appetites. To him the pleasure which we are to enjoy a week hence, or a year hence, is just as interesting as that which we are to enjoy this moment. When for the sake of the present, therefore, we sacrifice the future, our conduct appears to him absurd and extravagant in the highest degree, and he cannot enter into the principles which influence it. On the contrary, when we abstain from present pleasure in order to secure greater pleasure to come, when we act as if the remote object interested us as much as that which immediately presses upon the senses, as our affections exactly correspond with his own, he cannot fail to approve of our behaviour, and, as he knows from experience how few are capable of this self-command, he looks upon our conduct with a considerable degree of wonder and admiration. Hence arises that eminent esteem with which all men naturally regard a steady perseverance in the practice of frugality, industry, and application, though directed to no other purpose than the acquisition of fortune. . . .

The pleasure which we are to enjoy ten years hence interests us so little in comparison with that which we may enjoy today, the passion which the first excites is naturally so weak in comparison with that violent emotion which the second is apt to give occasion to, that the one could never be any balance to the other unless it was supported by the sense of propriety, by the consciousness that we merited the esteem and approbation of everybody by acting in the one way, and that we became the proper objects of their contempt and derision by behaving in the other. . . .

We never are generous except when in some respect we prefer some other person to ourselves, and sacrifice some great and important interest of our own to an equal interest of a friend or of a superior. The man who gives up his pretensions to an office that was the great object of his ambition because he imagines that the services of another are better entitled to it; the man who exposes his life to defend that of his friend which he judges to be of more importance, neither of them act from humanity, or because they feel more exquisitely what concerns that other person than what concerns themselves. They both consider those opposite interests, not in the light in which they naturally appear to themselves, but in that in which they appear to others. To every bystander the success or preservation of this other person may justly be more interesting than their own, but it cannot be so to themselves. When to the interest of this other person, therefore, they sacrifice their own, they accommodate themselves to the sentiments of the spectator, and by an effort of magnanimity act according to those views of things which they feel must naturally occur to any third person. The soldier who throws away his life in order to defend that of his officer would perhaps be but little affected by the death of that officer if it should happen without any fault of his own; and a very small disaster which had befallen himself might excite a much more lively sorrow. But when he endeavours to act so as to deserve applause, and to make the impartial spectator enter into the principles of his conduct, he feels that to everybody but himself his own life is a trifle compared with that of his officer, and that, when he sacrifices the one to the other, he acts quite properly and agreeably to what would be the natural apprehensions of every impartial bystander. . . .

All such sentiments suppose the idea of some other being, who is the natural judge of the person that feels them; and it is only by sympathy with the decisions of this arbiter of his conduct that he can conceive either the triumph of self-applause or the shame of self-condemnation.

22. La Mettrie, Preliminary Discourse and Discourse on Happiness

A. Preliminary Discourse

SUCH IS morality: the arbitrary fruit of politics, which may properly demand a return of its usurped rights. We shall see later why it has merited being placed among the branches of philosophy to which it is evident that it does not really belong.

When men decided to live together it was necessary to form a system of political morals to assure the safety of their relations. Since they are unruly animals, difficult to control, and running spontaneously toward their satisfactions, *per fas & nefas*,[1] those who were worthy, by their wisdom and talents, of being placed at the head of the others wisely called religion to the support of rules and laws; they were too sensible to attempt to exercise absolute authority over the impetuous imagination of a turbulent and frivolous people. It [religion] appeared to them with their eyes covered with a sacred blindfold, and soon it was surrounded by that whole multitude who listen, mouth agape and with a stupefied look, to the marvels for which they are so eager; marvels which control them—oh prodigy!—all the more as they understand them less.

To the double brake of morals and religion, that of punishments was prudently added. Good actions, and especially great actions, did not go without reward nor the bad ones without punishment, and the example of the guilty restrained those who were about to become guilty. Without scaffolds, the wheel, the gibbet, without those vile men, the rejects of nature, who would hang the universe for money, despite the play of all those other marvelous devices, the weak would not have been protected from the strong.

SOURCE: *Oeuvres philosophiques de M. de la Mettrie*, 3 vols. (Amsterdam, 1774), vol. 1. Translated by the editor.

[1] What is allowed and what is forbidden.

Since moral laws have their origin in politics, just as laws and executioners do, it follows that they are not the work of nature, nor consequently of philosophy, nor of reason, which are all synonymous terms. . . .

The philosopher deals with what seems to him true or false, regardless of consequences. The legislator, little interested in truth, perhaps (for lack of philosophy, as we shall see) fearing that it be known, cares only about right and wrong, moral good and evil. On the one hand, whatever seems to be in nature is called "true"; and the term "false" is given to whatever is not in nature, to whatever is contradicted by observation and experience. On the other hand, whatever is beneficial to society is decorated with the terms "right," "equitable," etc., and whatever hurts its interests is branded with the name "wrong." In a word, morals lead to equity, justice, etc., and philosophy to truth—so different are their objects.

The morality of nature, or of philosophy, is therefore as different from that of religion and politics as nature is from art. Diametrically opposed to each other, what can we conclude except that philosophy is absolutely irreconcilable with morals, religion, and politics, which are its triumphant rivals in society, while they are shamefully humiliated in the solitude of the study and before the torch of reason—humiliated above all by the vain efforts which many clever people have exerted to reconcile them.

B.   Discourse on Happiness

IF MAN's tendency to evil is such that it is easier for the good to become wicked than for the latter to become better, let us forgive humanity's inhuman inclination. Let us not lose sight of the hindrances and chains that we receive on birth and which follow us throughout life's slavery. Look at those trees planted at the top and at the bottom of a mountain. The ones are small, the others tall. Not only do they differ according to their seed, but according to the more or less warm soil in which they are planted. Man grows according to the same laws. He depends on the climate in which he lives as well as on the parent from whom he comes. All the elements control this weak machine; it does not think in a damp and heavy atmosphere as it does in a pure and dry one. Depending

SOURCE: *Ibid.*

thus on so many external causes and even more on so many internal ones, how could we help being what we are? How could we regulate springs which are unknown to us? But who would believe it? Well-being is our motive even in wickedness. It drives the treacherous, the tyrant, and the assassin, just like the virtuous man. The will is necessarily determined to desire and to seek what may constitute the present advantage of body and soul. . . . When I do good or evil; when, virtuous in the morning, I am vicious in the evening, it is my blood that causes it . . . I think I have made a choice; I congratulate myself on my freedom. Our freest actions are no different. An absolutely necessary determination impels us, and yet we do not wish to be slaves. What madmen we are! And unhappier madmen because we constantly reproach ourselves for not having done what it was not within our power to do!

Since we are mechanically borne toward our well-being, and are born with this tendency and invincible inclination, it follows that each individual, in preferring himself to all others, as do so many useless beings crawling on the surface of the earth, does nothing but follow nature's order, in which one would have to be quite peculiar and unreasonable not to believe in the possibility of happiness. If evildoers can be happy, as is beyond doubt; if they are not only without remorse, but without fear of suffering torture as punishment for their crimes, it is all the more certain that those who merely refrain from doing good (not believing themselves obliged to keep a promise that others made for them) will be able to have a happiness that may depend on their comfort and on their way of feeling in general. "Either reason is a mockery" (as Montaigne well says) "or its only aim is our contentment and its only work to tend to make us live pleasantly . . ."

Our feeling of pleasure being the true source of happiness, it is then quite evident that good and evil are in themselves quite unrelated to happiness; and that a person who finds greater satisfaction in doing evil will be happier than whoever has less satisfaction in doing good. This explains why so many scoundrels are happy in this world and shows that there is a special and individual happiness which exists not only without virtue but in crime itself.

A source of happiness, which I do not think is any purer because in most men's minds it is held to be nobler and finer, is that which derives from the social order. The more the natural character of man has seemed vicious and monstrous relative to society, the more people have tried to apply various correctives. The ideas of generosity, greatness, and humanity have been linked to actions which are important to social intercourse. Esteem and prestige have been given to him who would do no harm despite the advantages he might derive from it; respect, honors, and glory have been given to him who would serve country, friendship, love, or mankind, even at his own expense. By these stimulants, so many animals with a human face have become heroes. Far from abandoning men to their own nature—alas, too sterile to bear fruit—it has been necessary to cultivate them and to graft them, so to speak, at the time when the sap could best flow into the branch that was being grafted onto them.

It is obvious that I do not tire of going back to education, which alone is capable of giving us feelings and a kind of happiness contrary to those we should have had without it. Such is the effect of the modification or change it works on our instinct or way of feeling. The educated soul no longer wants, follows, or does what it formerly did when it was guided only by itself. Enlightened by a thousand new sensations, what it thought good it now thinks bad; what it blamed in others it now praises. True weather vanes, we turn ceaselessly in the direction of our education and then turn back to our first point when our organs, restored to their natural tone, reclaim us and make us follow their primitive inclinations. Then the old determining factors reassert themselves. Those produced by art are effaced; we are not even enough the masters to profit from our education as much as we might, for the good of society.

This materialism deserves consideration. It should be the source of indulgence, excuses, forgiveness, pardons, praise, moderation in punishments, which should be reluctantly imposed, and of the rewards due to virtue, which cannot be too generously bestowed. Virtue being a kind of *hors d'oeuvre*, a foreign ornament always ready to leave us or to fail us for lack of support, the public interest nonetheless deserves to be consulted, for we must indeed kill mad dogs and trample on snakes.

It is clear that the only difference between wicked men and good is that the former prefer their own interest to the general interest, while the latter sacrifice their self-interest to that of a friend or of the community. . . .

Although in general happiness should not be placed in sensual delight, nevertheless there are people for whom voluptuousness is so urgent a need, who have such a powerful hunger and thirst for coitus, that without the venereal act, which they must repeat several times a day, they would be unhappy and much to be pitied. On the contrary, if they give free reign to their sexual appetites, they are happy, not only in and through sensual fulfillment, but in the midst of debauchery, madness, and disorderliness. What proof would you like? Their days flow by almost without their realizing it, because they feel and do not think. Always gay and satisfied, they breathe only joy and carry it with them everywhere. It is, so to speak, the daily coin of our hearts; it is the substitute for thought, more agreeable than thought itself, and more within reach of everyone. How could it be otherwise in the midst of parties and banquets? Joy is in their midst; it laughs with the celebrants, who are delighted by it. They make joy circulate within the group and almost to foam, and they drink it thirstily in various exquisite wines. At the same time, they are being ruined by debts and loss of honor. So true is it that virtue and honesty are foreign to our nature, the ornaments and not the substance of happiness. How many others are virtuous, honorable, chaste, sober—and unhappy! Their candor, their wisdom, their benevolence stand any test; nonetheless, they drag with them the boredom of loneliness, the harshness of their character, and the onerous weight of an unsmiling reason. As harsh and severe as they are grave and taciturn, as cold and sad as they are sure and true, their melancholy and atrabilious countenance frightens away, by their very appearance, laughter and play. They are respected and avoided—that is the fate of virtue—while those likable reprobates who are despised are everywhere eagerly sought out—such is the fate of urbanity and the graces. . . . They are capable, you will say, only of enjoying sensuality and the delights of sweet pruriency. Well then! Are they the less happy? Do they not follow that instinct and that taste by which each animal tends to its well-being? Do they not have the only kind of happiness which is really suitable to their temperament?

So it is with all evildoers. They are perfectly able to be happy if they can be wicked without feeling remorse. I shall go further. He who will have no remorse and is in such familiarity with crime that vices are virtues to him will be happier than another who, after doing a fine deed, is sorry he has done it and who thereby loses all its value. Such is the marvelous empire of unruffled tranquillity.

Oh you who are commonly called a wretch, and you are one from society's viewpoint, you may within yourself be tranquil. You have only to stifle remorse by reflection, if it is strong enough, or by developing habits that are contrary and much more powerful. If you had been brought up without the ideas that are at the base of remorse, you would have been free from having to fight that enemy. That is not all. You must despise life as much as esteem or public hatred. If you do that, I maintain that although you are a parasite, incestuous, a thief, a scoundrel, an infamous reprobate, and the just object of the hatred of all good people, you will nonetheless be happy. For what unhappiness or displeasure can be caused by actions which, however black and horrible they may be imparted to be, would leave (according to my hypothesis) no trace of criminal feeling in the criminal's heart? But if you want to live, be on guard: the government is not so easy as my philosophy. *Justice* is its tutor. Hangmen and gibbets are at its command. Therefore, fear them more than your conscience or the gods.

The first men who have had others to govern felt the weakness of these two brakes. That is the origin of the need to shock a part of the citizenry in order to preserve the rest, as we cut off a gangrenous limb for the health of the body.

Enjoy, too, since a wayward nature allows you to, oh cruel and cowardly prince! enjoy tyranny to the full. Erostratus wanted to immortalize himself through fire; immortalize yourself by your bloodthirstiness. Be as ingenious in the inventions of torture as a woman chaser is in his sensual delights, and find the same pleasure in them if you can. The only pleasure of which you are capable is to hurt others; to do good would be to torture yourself. I do not snatch you away from the cursed inclination which impels you. Could I? It is the source of your wretched happiness. Bears, lions, tigers love to rend other animals. Fierce like them, it is only just that you should yield to the same inclinations. I pity you, nonetheless, for feeding thus on public misery; but who would not pity even more a state in which there would not be one man virtuous enough to deliver it, at the cost of his life, from a monster like you?

And you too, voluptuary, since without keen pleasures you

cannot obtain the happy life, forget your soul and Seneca. For you, all the Stoic virtues are nonsense; think only of your body. Whatever you may have of a soul is indistinguishable from it. Prejudices, pedants, fanatics will rise up against you, but even if all the elements joined in, what matters? What did Tibullus care in the arms of his Cloris about rain, hail, and the unleashed winds? They added to the happiness which defied them. So enjoy the good weather whenever it comes; enjoy the present; forget the past which is no more, and do not fear the future. . . . Let pollution and debauchery, lubricous rivals, following each other and making you melt into ecstasy day and night, make your soul, if it is possible, as sticky and lascivious as your body . . . or if, not content with excelling in the great art of sexuality, lewdness and debauchery are not strong enough for you, then filth and infamy are your lot. Wallow in them like swine, and you will be happy as they are. Besides, I am only telling you what you tell yourself and what you do. I would waste my time and trouble if I used another tone: to speak of temperance to a libertine is to speak of humaneness to a tyrant.

Let it not be said that I am urging people to crime. I am urging them only to be tranquil in crime. Man in general seems a deceitful, tricky, dangerous, perfidious animal; he seems to follow the heat of his blood and passions rather than the ideas which were given to him in childhood and which are the basis of natural law and remorse. That is the sum and substance of what I am saying. . . . If, despite prejudices, so many wicked people violate the actions which they were brought up to do and are not always unhappy, is it not obvious that they would be even less unhappy if we suppose either that they could throw off the yoke, or, above all, if they had never borne it? I say only what seems true to me and express only a philosophical hypothesis. Heaven forbid that I should support wickedness, which is contrary to my character. I sympathize with it, because I find its excuse in natural temperament, which is sometimes difficult or even impossible to dominate. Horses are not the only animals who take the bit in their teeth. Let each one look at himself; let him recall his old fits of anger, his vengeances, his quarrels, and so many other impulses which carried him away, and he will realize that he is a horse like any other. Any passionate and violent man is one.

23.   Helvétius, On the Mind and A Treatise on Man

A. On the Mind

OF PROBITY RELATIVE TO AN INDIVIDUAL

IT IS NOT real Probity, that is Probity with regard to the public, that I consider in this chapter, but merely Probity considered relative to each individual.

In this point of view, I say that each individual calls Probity in another only the habit of actions which are useful to him: I say habit, because it is not one single honest action, more than one single ingenious idea, that will gain us the title of virtuous and witty. There is not that penurious wretch on earth who has not once behaved with generosity; nor a liberal person who has not once been parsimonious; no villain who has not done a good action; no person so stupid who has not uttered one smart sentence; and, in fine, no man who, on inspecting certain actions of his life, will not seem possessed of all the opposite virtues and vices. A greater uniformity in the behaviour of men would suppose in them a continuity of attention which they are incapable of; differing from one another only more or less. The man of absolute uniformity has no existence; so that no perfection, either with regard to vice or virtue, is to be found on the earth.

It is therefore to the habit of actions advantageous to him that an individual gives the name of Probity: I say of actions, because we cannot judge of intentions. How would it be possible? It is seldom or never that action is the effect of a sentiment; we ourselves are often ignorant of the motives by which we are determined. A rich man bestows a comfortable subsistence on a worthy man reduced to poverty. Doubtless he does a good action; but is this action simply the effect of a desire of rendering a man happy? Pity, the hopes of gratitude, vanity itself; all these different motives separately, or aggregately, may they not, unknown to himself, have

SOURCE: The translation was published anonymously in Paris by Durand, 1776.

determined him to that commendable action? Now if a man be, in general, ignorant himself of the motives of his generous action, how can the public be acquainted with them? Thus it is only from the actions of men that the public can judge of their Probity. A man, for instance, has twenty degrees of passion for virtue; but he has thirty degrees of love for a woman; and this woman would instigate him to be guilty of murder. Upon this supposition, it is certain, that this person is nearer guilt than he, who with only ten degrees of passion for virtue, has only five degrees of love for so wicked a woman. Hence I conclude, that of two men, the more honest in his actions has sometimes the lesser passion for virtue.

Every philosopher also agrees, that the virtue of men greatly depends on the circumstances in which they are placed. Virtuous men have too often sunk under a strange series of unhappy events.

He who will warrant his virtue in every possible situation is either an impostor or a fool—characters equally to be mistrusted.

After determining the idea I affix to this word Probity, considered in relation to every individual, we must, to assure ourselves of the propriety of this definition, have recourse to observation; and this will inform us, that there are men whom a happy disposition, a strong desire of glory and esteem, inspire with the same love for justice and virtue, which men in general have for riches and honours.

The actions personally advantageous to these virtuous men are so truly just, that they tend to promote the general welfare, or, at least not to lessen it.

But the number of these men is so small, that I only mention them in honour of humanity. And the most numerous class, which alone comprehends the far greater part of mankind, is that of men so entirely devoted to their own interest, that they never consider the welfare of the whole. Concentrated, if I may be allowed the expression, in their own happiness (a), these men call only those actions honest, which are advantageous to themselves. A judge acquits a criminal, a minister prefers an unworthy person; yet both are just, if those they have favoured may be credited. But should the judge punish, and the minister refuse, the criminal and the party denied will always consider them as unjust.

If the monks, who, during the first dynasty, were intrusted to write the lives of our kings, have only given those of their benefactors, indicating the other reigns only with these words, NIHIL

FECIT;[1] and if they have given the name of slothful kings to some princes truly worthy of esteem; it is because a monk is a man, and every man, in his judgment, consults only his own interest.

The Christians, who justly branded with the name of barbarity and guilt the cruelties inflicted on them by the pagans, did not they give the name of zeal to the cruelties they, in their turn, inflicted on those same pagans? It will, on examination, be found, that there is not a crime but is placed among honest actions, by the societies to which this crime is advantageous; nor an action of public benefit that is not censured by some particular society to which it is detrimental.

In effect, what man, if he sacrifices the pride of styling himself more virtuous than others to the pride of being more sincere; and if, with a scrupulous attention, he searches all the recesses of his soul, will he not perceive that his virtues and vices are wholly owing to the different modifications of personal interest; that all equally tend to their happiness; that it is the diversity of the passions and tastes, of which some are agreeable and others contrary to the public interest, which terms our actions either virtues or vices? Instead of despising the vicious man, we should pity him, rejoice in our own happy disposition, thank heaven for not having given us any of those tastes and passions which would have forced us to have sought our happiness in the misery of another. For, after all, interest is always obeyed; hence the injustice of all our judgments, and the appellations of just and unjust are lavished on the same actions, according to the advantage resulting from them to individuals.

If the physical universe be subject to the laws of motion, the moral universe is equally so to those of interest. Interest is, on earth, the mighty magician which to the eyes of every creature changes the appearance of all objects. The innocent sheep, which feeds in our fields, is it not an object of dread and horror to those imperceptible insects which live upon the leaves of herbs? "Let us," say they, "hasten from hence: that voracious and cruel animal is coming, whose enormous throat swallows at once both us and our cities. Why does not he act like the lion and tiger? Those benign animals do not destroy our habitations; they do not feed on our blood; but, as just avengers of guilt, punish in the sheep the

[1] "He did nothing."

cruelties it inflicts on us." Thus different interests metamorphose objects: we consider the lion as a cruel animal, whereas among the insects, it is the sheep; and what Leibnitz said of the physical universe may be applied to the moral: That this world being constantly in motion, every instant offered a new and different phenomenon to each of its inhabitants.

This principle is so agreeable to experience, that, without entering into a farther discussion, I think myself warranted to conclude that personal interest is the only and universal estimator of the merit of human actions; and, therefore, that Probity, with regard to an individual is, according to my definition, nothing more than the habit of actions personally advantageous to this individual.

B. A Treatise on Man

Chapter X. Individuals, Like Nations, Esteem Justice Solely for the Consideration and Power It Procures Them

THE LOVE man has for power is such, that in all cases the exercise of it is agreeable to him, because it makes him recollect his possession of it. Every man would have great power, and every man knows that it is almost impossible to be at once constantly just and powerful. Man makes, without doubt, a better or worse use of his power, according to the education he has received. But be it as good as it may, there is no great man who does not commit some acts of injustice. The abuse of power is connected with its existence, as the effect with the cause. Corneille says,

> Qui peut tout ce qu'il veut, veut plus que ce
> qu'il doit.
> He who can do whatever he will, wills more
>   than he ought.

This verse is a moral axiom confirmed by experience; and yet no one refuses a great place for fear of exposing himself to the temptation of injustice.

Our love of equity, therefore, is always subordinate to our love of power. Man, solely anxious for himself, seeks nothing but his own happiness. If he respects equity, it is want that compels him to it.

SOURCE: Translated by W. Hooper (London, 1777, Printed for B. Law and G. Robinson, Issue 27).

If a difference arise between two men nearly equal in power, each of them, restrained by a reciprocal fear, has recourse to justice; each of them submits to its decision; that he may interest the public in his favour, and by that mean acquire a certain superiority over his adversary.

But let one of these two men be greatly superior in power to the other, so that he can rob him with impunity; and then, deaf to the voice of justice, he does not litigate, but command. It is not equity, nor even the appearance of equity, that determines between the weak and the powerful; but force, crime, and tyranny. It is thus the Sultan gives the name of seditious to the remonstrances of the impotent, whom it oppresses.

24.   Diderot, Natural Right; Rameau's Nephew; D'Alembert's Dream; and Elements of Physiology

A. "Natural Right" (Encyclopedia)

WE ARE SO accustomed to using this expression that there is almost no one who is not convinced in his own mind that he understands it immediately, without any need for thought. This inner conviction is shared by the philosopher and the unthinking man alike, with this single difference: that upon hearing the question "What is right?" the latter, immediately bereft of all words and ideas, will refer you to the tribunal of conscience and remain mute; whereas the former will be reduced to silence and deeper reflection only after having turned in a vicious circle that either brings him back to the same point from which he set out or throws him into some other problem no less difficult of resolution than the one from which he had thought to free himself by his original definition.

The philosopher, when questioned, says, "Right is the foundation or prime reason of justice." But what is justice? "It is the

SOURCE: The selections A through D translated by Derek Coltman in Diderot's Selected Writings, ed. L. G. Crocker (New York: The Macmillan Co., 1966), pp. 40–45, 139–40, 210–12, 281–82. Reprinted by permission of the publishers.

obligation to render to each exactly what is due to him." But what is there that belongs to one rather than another in a state of things in which everything belongs to everyone and in which a distinct idea of obligation does not yet exist? And what would a man owe to others if he allowed them everything and asked nothing of them in exchange? It is at this point that the philosopher begins to feel that *natural right* is of all our moral notions both one of the most important and one of the most difficult to determine. We shall therefore consider that we have accomplished a great deal in this article if we succeed in establishing clearly a few principles with whose aid the most considerable objections ordinarily raised against the notion of *natural right* may be resolved. In order to achieve this, we must begin our argument again from the very beginning and take care not to advance any argument that is not established by evidence—by the kind of evidence, that is, of which moral questions are capable and that will satisfy any reasonable man.

1. It is evident that if man is not free or if his instantaneous decisions or even his vacillations are caused by some material thing external to his self, so that his choice is not the pure act of an immaterial substance and of a simple faculty of that substance, then there can be no rational goodness or wickedness, even though there may be animal goodness and wickedness: there can be neither moral good nor moral evil, neither justice nor injustice, neither obligation nor rights. From which it is at once apparent, we may add in passing, how important it is to establish solidly in our minds the reality not merely of *free will* but also of *liberty*, which is only too often confused with *free will*.

2. Our existence is mean, contentious, and full of care. We have passions, and we have needs. We wish to be happy, and yet the unjust and passionate man is constantly feeling himself impelled to do unto others what he does not desire they should do unto him. This is a verdict he pronounces in the depths of his own soul, and one from which he cannot escape. He sees his wickedness, and he must either admit it to himself or else allow everyone else the same authority he arrogates to himself.

3. But what reproach can we make to the man who is tormented by such violent passions that life itself becomes an unbearable burden to him if he does not satisfy them and who, in order to acquire the right of doing as he pleases with the existence of others, gives up his own into their hands? What shall we answer if he has

the audacity to say, "I realize that I am bringing terror and confusion to the human race; but I must either be unhappy or the cause of unhappiness in others, and no one is dearer to me than I myself. Do not blame me for this abominable predilection; it is not a matter of free choice. It is the voice of nature, which never argues more strongly within me than when it is speaking on my own behalf. But is it only in my heart that it makes itself heard with such violence? Oh, men! I call you all to witness: which of you, when at the point of death, would not buy back his life at the expense of the majority of the human race, if he were sure he could do so with impunity and in secret? And yet," he will continue, "I am equitable and honest. If my happiness demands that I rid myself of all the existences obstructing my desires, then any other individual must be able to rid himself of mine if it obstructs his. Reason requires as much, and I subscribe to it, I am not so unjust as to demand from another any sacrifice that I am not prepared to make for him"?

4. There is one thing I perceive at the very outset that seems to me to be acknowledged by the good man and the wicked man alike—namely, that we must, in all things, make use of our reason, because man is not merely an animal, but an animal with the power of reason. It follows, therefore, that means of discovering the truth of the present problem do exist; that whoever refuses to seek that truth has forfeited his right to be called a man and should be treated by the rest of his kind as a wild beast; and that once the truth has been discovered, whoever refuses to conform to it is either insane or morally evil.

5. What, then, shall we reply to this savage reasoner of ours before we deprive him of speech forever? That his whole speech may be reduced to a single question, namely, whether or not he acquires any right over the lives of others by abandoning his own life to them; for he does not merely wish to be happy, he also wishes to be equitable and to use his equity as a means of protecting himself from the epithet "wicked"; for if he did not so wish, then we should have to hang him without answering him. We shall point out to him, therefore, that even if what he yields up to others belonged to him so completely that he was able to dispose of it as he pleased and even if the condition he is proposing to the others was actually to their advantage, he would still have no legitimate authority to make them accept it; that he who says, "I wish to live," has just as much right on his side as he who says, "I want to

die"; that the latter has only one life and that by abandoning it, he is making himself the master of innumerable lives; that the exchange he wants to make would scarcely be equitable even if there were only himself and one other evil person on the face of the earth; that it is absurd to assume that others want what he wants, since it is uncertain that the peril to which he is exposing his fellow men is equal to the peril to which he is consenting to expose himself; that the value of what he is risking may not be proportionate to the value of what he is forcing me to risk; that the question of *natural right* is much more complicated than it appears to him; that he is constituting himself both claimant and judge; and that his court may not perhaps be competent to judge this case.

6. But if we deny the individual the right to decide about the nature of justice and injustice, from whom are we to seek a judgment on this great question? From whom? From mankind; it is for mankind alone to decide this question, because the good of all is its only passion. Private wills are not to be trusted: they can be either good or evil; but the general will is always good: it has never deceived, and it never will deceive. If the animal order were more or less on a level with ourselves; if there existed reliable means of communication between them and us; if they could transmit their feelings and thoughts to us clearly and be made aware of ours with equal certainty; in a word, if they were capable of voting in a world parliament, then they would have to be summoned to take part in it, and the question of *natural right* would then be debated not merely by *mankind* but by *animalkind*. But the animals are cut off from us by unchangeable and eternal barriers, and we are dealing here with an order of knowledge and ideas peculiar to the human species, things that both emanate from and constitute its station in the world.

7. In order to know how far he ought to be a man, a citizen, a subject, a father, or a child and when it is proper for him to live or die, the individual should address himself to the general will of mankind. It is for the general will alone to fix the limits of every duty. You have the most sacred *natural right* to everything that is not forbidden to you by the species as a whole. And it is the general will that must enlighten you as to the nature of your thoughts and your desires. Everything that you conceive, every course of action you consider, will be good, great, noble, sublime if it is in accordance with the general and common interest. There is

no quality essential to your species other than the one you require in all your fellow men for your own happiness and theirs. It is the degree of this conformity between you and all of them and between all of them and you that will make it clear to you when you are transgressing the bounds of your species and when you are remaining within them. So that you must never lose sight of it; for if you do, you will perceive that the notions of goodness, of justice, of humanity, of virtue begin to decay in your understanding. Say to yourself often, "I am a man, and I possess no truly inalienable *natural rights* other than those possessed by all mankind."

8. But, you will say, where is the depository of this general will; where can I consult it? . . . In the principles embodied by the written law of every civilized nation; in the social behavior of savage and barbarous peoples; in the tacit agreements obtaining among the enemies of humankind; and even in indignation and resentment, those two passions that nature seems to have placed even in animals to compensate for a lack of social law and public vengeance.

9. If you reflect carefully on all the preceding sections, you will stand convinced: (1) that the man who heeds only his personal wishes is the enemy of mankind; (2) that the general will is in each individual member of mankind a pure act of the understanding, which reasons in the silence of the passions as to what a man may demand from his fellow man and what his fellow man has the right to require of him; (3) that this attention to the general will of the species and its common desire is the rule that must govern the conduct of one individual toward another in the same society, of the individual toward the society of which he is a member, and of the society of which he is a member toward other societies; (4) that submission to the general will is the bond that holds all societies together, even including those created by crime. Alas, virtue is so attractive that robbers will respect its image even in the depths of their caves! (5) that laws must be made for all men and not for one, otherwise that solitary being would be no different from the violent reasoner we hanged in section five; (6) that since of the two wills, the general and the private, the general never errs, there is no difficulty in perceiving to which of them the legislative power should belong for the sake of mankind's happiness or what veneration we owe to those august mortals whose private will unites both the authority and the infallibility of the general; (7) that even if

we supposed the notion of species to be in perpetual flux, the nature of *natural right* would not change, since it would always be dependent on the general will and on the common desire of the entire species; (8) that equity is to justice as cause is to effect, or that justice can be nothing but the utterance of equity; (9) lastly, that all these consequences are evident to anyone who uses his reason and that anyone who refuses to use his reason, thereby forfeiting his status as a man, ought to be treated as an unnatural being.

B. Rameau's Nephew

HE: . . . I want my son to be happy, or, what amounts to the same thing, respected, rich and powerful. I know something about the easiest ways of reaching that goal, and I shall teach them to him early. And though all you wise people may blame me, I shall be absolved by the crowd and by his success. He will have money, I guarantee that. If he has a lot of it, then he will lack for nothing, not even your esteem and respect.

MYSELF: You might be mistaken.

HE: Or he'll do without it, like a lot of other people. In all that he told me, there were a great many of those things that people think, that they allow to determine their actions, but that they never admit in words. And that, truth to tell, is the only really noticeable difference between this fellow of mine and most of the people we see all around us. He was admitting all his vices— and everyone else's vices—but he was not a hypocrite. He was being neither more nor less despicable than they. He was merely being more honest, more willing to face facts, and occasionally profound in his depravity. . . .

MYSELF: . . . True, a man who is prepared to stop at nothing in order to be rich ·must be pretty ineffectual if he fails. But it so happens that there are people, like myself, who do not look upon wealth as the most desirable thing in the world: eccentrics.

HE: Very eccentric. No one is born thinking that way. It's something you have to acquire; it doesn't exist in nature.

MYSELF: Not in human nature?

HE: Not in human nature either. Everything living, man not excepted, seeks its own good at the expense of whoever is at hand. And I am sure that if I let my little savage grow up without ever mentioning such things to him, he would still want to be finely dressed, magnificently fed, made much of by men, adored by women, and showered with all the things that make for happiness in life.

MYSELF: If your little savage were left entirely to himself, if his childish ignorance were left intact, if he were allowed to acquire all the violent passions of a grown man while still remaining as deficient in reason as he had been in his cradle, than he would end up strangling his father and going to bed with his mother.

HE: That proves the necessity of a good upbringing, and who denies that? But what is a good upbringing if it is not one that teaches us how to enjoy all sorts of pleasures without danger and without inconvenience?

MYSELF: I am in almost complete agreement there, but we'd better not go into it any further.

HE: Why not?

MYSELF: Because I'm afraid we only appear to be in agreement. If we enter into a discussion of what the dangers and inconveniences to be avoided are, there is a risk that our opinions might diverge . . .

C. D'Alembert's Dream

[The doctor and Mlle de Lespinasse then go on to discuss sleep and dreams with D'Alembert, who is now awake.]

D'ALEMBERT: . . . What are the will and the liberty of a dreaming man?

BORDEU: What are they? Exactly what they are in a man who is awake: the most recent impulse of desire or aversion, the most recent result of all that he has been from birth to that precise moment. And I defy even the subtlest mind to perceive the slightest difference between them.   •

D'ALEMBERT: Do you think that's true?

BORDEU: And you are the one who asks me that! You have spent a waking dream, acting quite involuntarily, yes, involuntarily, far more involuntarily than in your dream. In your dream you were in control, you were giving orders, you were being obeyed; you were displeased or satisfied, you found yourself being contradicted, you encountered obstacles, you became annoyed, you loved, you hated, you cast blame, you expressed approval, you denied things, you wept, you came, you went. But on days when you have been absorbed in meditation, scarcely were your eyes open in the morning than you were once more in the grip of the idea that had been occupying you the day before; you got dressed, you sat down at your table, you pondered, you drew figures, you made calculations, you ate your dinner, you went back to your problems, sometimes you left the table in order to verify them; you spoke to others, gave orders to your servant, ate supper, went to bed, fell asleep, and all that without having performed a single voluntary action. You existed only as a single point; you were acting, but you were not exercising your will. Can the will be exercised of itself? Will is always brought into action by some interior or exterior motive, by some present impression or some memory from the past, by some passion or intention projected into the future. After which, I have nothing to say about liberty except this: that our most recent action is always the necessary effect of a single cause—ourself; a very complex cause, but a single one.

MLLE DE LESPINASSE: And does that mean the action is inevitable?

BORDEU: Without a doubt. Try to imagine any other action resulting from that cause, assuming that the being performing the action is the same.

MLLE DE LESPINASSE: He's right. Since it is I who act in that particular way, then anyone who could act in a different way would no longer be me. And to say that at the moment when I am saying or doing something, I could be saying or doing another is to say that I am both myself and someone else as well. But, Doctor, what about vice and virtue? "Virtue," a word so sacred in every language, an idea so revered by every nation.

BORDEU: We must replace it with that of doing good, and its opposite with that of doing harm. We are born fortunate or unfortunate; we are carried along, without our being aware of it, in the general torrent that leads one man to glory and another to disgrace.

MLLE DE LESPINASSE: And self-respect and shame and remorse?

BORDEU: They are puerile emotions with no foundation but the ignorance and vanity of a being who attributes to himself the merit or the blame for an inevitable instant in time.

MLLE DE LESPINASSE: And rewards and punishments?

BORDEU: They are means of correcting those beings we refer to as wicked, though they are still capable of alteration, and of encouraging those that we call good.

MLLE DE LESPINASSE: But isn't such a doctrine dangerous?

BORDEU: Is it true or is it false?

MLLE DE LESPINASSE: I think it's true.

BORDEU: Then you are saying that you think there are advantages in falsehood and disadvantages in truth.

MLLE DE LESPINASSE: Yes, I do think that.

BORDEU: And so do I; but the advantages of falsehood are only transitory, whereas those of truth are eternal; the unfortunate consequences of truth, when there are any, soon pass, whereas those produced by a lie last as long as the lie itself. Consider the effects of falsehood on a man's mind and on his conduct. In his mind, either the falsehood becomes mixed up, higgledy-piggledy, with the truth—which makes him incapable of logical thought—or else it is completely and logically linked up with further falsehood—which makes him logically consistent but in error. And what sort of conduct can you expect from a man who is either incapable of logical thought or else logically committed to error?

MLLE DE LESPINASSE: The latter defect, though less contemptible, is possibly more to be feared than the former.

D.   Elements of Physiology

THE WORLD is the house of the strong. I shall not know until the end what I have lost or won in this place, in this vast gambling den where I have spent more than sixty years, dicebox in hand, shaking the dice.

> *Felices quibus, ante annos, secura malorum*
> *Atque ignara sui, perludum elabitur aetas.*[1]

What do I perceive? Forms. And what else? Forms. I know nothing of things. We walk among shadows. And we are shadows too, both to ourselves and to others. . . .

There is only one virtue: justice; only one duty: to achieve happiness; only one corollary: not to expect too much of life and not to fear death.

---

[1] "Fortunate ones, whose life slips away prematurely,
   Careless of evils and, in its play, unaware of its own passing!"

25. D'Holbach, A System of Nature

WHAT IS man's purpose in the sphere he occupies? It is self-preservation and the happiness of his existence. It is, therefore, important
for him to know the true means, so that his prudence and reason
may teach him to use them surely and consistently to reach his
goal. . . . Experience and reason show him that the men with
whom he is associated are necessary to him, can contribute to his
happiness and pleasures, and can help him with their own faculties.
Experience teaches him in what way he can make them contribute
to his designs and determine them to wish and to act in his favor.
He sees the actions which they approve and those that are displeas-
ing to them; the behavior which attracts them and that which
repels them; the judgments they make and the advantages or harmful effects which result from different ways of being and acting.
All these experiences give him the idea of virtue and vice, of right
and wrong, of goodness and wickedness, of decency and indecency, or honesty and dishonesty, etc.—in a word, he learns to
judge men and their actions, to distinguish the feelings which are
necessarily aroused in them according to the various effects we
make on them.

It is on the necessary diversity of these effects that the distinction between good and evil, between vice and virtue is founded.
This distinction is not founded, as some thinkers have believed, on
conventions among men, and still less on the illusory will of a
supernatural being, but on the eternal and unvarying relationships
among human beings living in society, which will subsist as long as
man and society do. . . . The virtuous man is the one whose
actions tend constantly to the well-being of his fellows. The
vicious man is the one whose behavior tends to the unhappiness of
those with whom he lives, which usually results in his own unhappiness. Whatever contributes to our true and permanent happi-

SOURCE: D'Holbach, Système de la Nature (London, 1771). Translated by the editor.

ness is reasonable; whatever disturbs our own happiness or that of beings who are necessary to it is mad and unreasonable. . . .

Our duties are the means which reason and experience show us to be necessary in order to attain our goal. These duties are a necessary consequence of the relations among men with an equal desire for their happiness and self-preservation. When we say that these duties create obligations, we are saying that unless we use these means, we cannot reach the end which our nature proposes to us. Thus moral obligation is the necessity of using the means that will make the beings with whom we live happy, in order to determine them to make us happy too. . . .

If man is forced by his nature to desire his well-being, he is also forced to love the means to it. It would be useless and perhaps unjust to ask a man to be virtuous if he cannot be virtuous without making himself unhappy. As soon as vice makes him happy he should love vice. As soon as useless acts or crimes are honoured and rewarded, what interest can he find in concerning himself with the happiness of others or in restraining the tides of his passions? . . . Most of our institutions conspire to thwart nature, to hinder, to turn aside and to damp down the impulses nature gives us and to substitute for them others which are the source of our unhappiness. . . .

When we say that self-interest is the sole motive of human actions we mean that each man works in his own way toward his own happiness; and that he places it in some object, visible or hidden, real or imaginary, and that his whole mode of behaviour tends toward getting it. If this is so, no man can be called disinterested. We apply that word only to the person whose motives we do not know, or whose self-interest we approve. Thus we call a person generous, faithful, and disinterested when he is more affected by the pleasure of helping an unfortunate friend than by that of keeping useless wealth in his coffers. We call a man disinterested when the self-interest of his glory is more precious to him than that of his fortune. Finally, we call a man disinterested when he makes sacrifices which we consider to be difficult to the object on which his happiness depends, whereas we do not attach the same value to that object. . . .

Since we must judge men's actions according to their effects on us, we approve the self-interest which motivates them whenever an advantage for mankind results from it. Thus we admire valor, generosity, love of freedom, etc. . . . . But in this judgment we are not ourselves disinterested. Experience, reflection, habit, reason have given us a moral taste, and we find as much pleasure in being the witnesses of a great and generous act as a man of good taste experiences on seeing a beautiful painting of which he is not the owner. He who has made a habit of practicing virtue is a man who constantly keeps before his eyes the self-interest which he has in deserving the affection, the esteem and the help of others, as well as the need to love and to approve himself. Filled with these ideas to which he has been habituated, he even refrains from secret crimes which would lower him in his own esteem. He resembles a man who, having contracted the habit of cleanness from childhood, would be painfully affected at seeing himself soiled even if no one else were a witness. The virtuous man is one who has been taught by correct ideas that his self-interest or happiness lies in acting in a way that others are forced to love and to approve out of their own self-interest. . . .

Ethics would be a useless science if it did not prove to man that his greatest interest is to be virtuous. Any obligation can be founded only on the probability or the certainty of obtaining some good or of avoiding some evil.

Some will not fail to point out to us and even to prove that in the present constitution of things virtue, far from procuring well-being to those who practice it, often plunges them into misfortune and continually puts obstacles to their happiness. Everywhere we see virtue deprived of reward. Even more—a thousand examples may convince us that in almost every country it is hated, persecuted, forced to suffer from the ingratitude and the injustice of men. I reply by admitting that, as a necessary consequence of the errors of the human race, virtue rarely leads to those things in which the common people place their happiness. Most societies, too often governed by men who are made enemies to virtue by the concurrence of ignorance, flattery, prejudice, the abuse of power and impunity, commonly lavish their esteem and rewards only to unworthy subjects, reward only frivolous and harmful qualities, and do not render to merit the justice that is due to it. But a good man desires neither the rewards nor the approval of a society so badly constituted. Content with domestic happiness, he does not seek to multiply relationships which would only multiply his dangers. He knows that a vicious society is a whirlwind in which an honest man cannot find his place. Therefore, he stays on the side, outside the beaten path in which he would be inevitably crushed. He does all the good he can within his sphere; he leaves the field open for the wicked who wish to descend into the arena. . . .

When we say that virtue is its own reward, we mean only that in a society guided by truth, experience, and reason, each man would know his true self-interest and would realize the purpose of the association; he would find real advantages or motives for doing his duties. In a word, he would be convinced that to achieve solid happiness, he must concern himself with the well-being of his fellow men and deserve their esteem, love, and help. Finally, in a well-organized society, government, education, laws, and example should work together to prove to each citizen that the nation of which he is a part is a whole that cannot be happy and survive without virtue. . . .

Even if the entire universe were unjust to the good man, he retains the advantage of loving and esteeming himself, of looking with pleasure into his own heart, of contemplating his actions with the same eyes that others would have were they not blind.

26.   Voltaire, Treatise on Metaphysics and Just and Unjust

A.   Treatise on Metaphysics

ON VIRTUE AND VICE

IN ORDER that a society might survive, laws were necessary, as rules are necessary in any game. Most of these laws seem arbitrary. They depend on the interests, passions, and opinions of those who devised them, and on the kind of climate in which men formed a society. In a warm country, where wine would excite the passions,

SOURCE: H. Temple Patterson (ed.), Traité de métaphysique (Manchester: Manchester University Press, 1937). Translated by the editor.

it is considered proper to make it unlawful; in colder climates it is considered honorable to get drunk. In one place, a man must content himself with one woman; in another, he is allowed to have as many as he can feed. In another country parents beg strangers to have the kindness to go to bed with their daughters; everywhere else, a girl who has given herself to a man is dishonored. In Sparta adultery was encouraged, in Athens it was punished by death. Among the Romans parents had the right of life and death over their children. In Normandy, a father can't even take a penny of the most disobedient son's wealth. The name of king is sacred among many nations, and abominated in others.

But all these peoples who behave so differently agree on one point: what they call *virtuous* is that which is in conformity with the established laws and what they call *criminal* is that which is contrary to them. Thus a man who opposes arbitrary power in Holland is a very virtuous man; and he who seeks to establish a republican government in France will be condemned to the ultimate punishment. The same Jew who in Metz would be sent to the galleys for having two wives could have four in Constantinople, and be all the more esteemed by the Moslems.

Most laws are so evidently at variance that it matters little by which laws a state is governed; what does matter very much is that once the laws are established they should be carried out. Thus it is inconsequential whether these rules or those apply in dice and cards. But it would be impossible to play for even a moment if those arbitrary rules which have been agreed on are not followed precisely.

Virtue and vice, moral good and evil are therefore in any country what is useful or harmful to society. And in all times and climes he who makes the greatest sacrifices for the public weal will be deemed most virtuous. It seems, then, that good actions are only those which are advantageous to us, and crimes those which are harmful. Virtue is the habit of doing those things which are pleasing to men; vice is the habit of doing those things which displease them.

Although what is called virtue in one place is precisely what is called vice in another, and although most rules of good and evil differ just like languages and dress, nonetheless it appears certain to me that there are natural laws to which all men are obliged to agree throughout the universe, whether or not they wish to. Certainly

God has not said to men: these are laws which I am giving to you from my own mouth and by which I command you to govern yourself. But he has done in man what he has done in many other animals. He gave the bees a powerful instinct which causes them to work and to feed together; and he has given to man certain feelings which he can never throw off and which are the eternal bonds and first laws of society, in which he foresaw that men would live. Benevolence toward our fellow men, for instance, is born within us and continually acts in us unless it is combated by self-love, which always wins out over it. Thus a man is always impelled to help another man when he can do so at no cost to himself. The most barbarous savage returning from carnage and dripping the blood of the enemies he has eaten will melt at the sight of his comrade's suffering and give him all the help he can.

Adultery and homosexuality are allowed in many nations. But you will not find a single one in which it is permissible to break your promise, because society can survive with adultery and homosexuality, but not among people who would consider it an honor to deceive each other.

In Sparta, theft was honored because all property was communal. But as soon as you have established a *thine* and *mine*, it would be impossible for you not to consider theft as contrary to society, and consequently as unjust.

It is so true that the good of society is the only measure of moral good and evil that we are obliged to change our ideas about right and wrong according to our needs.

We look with horror upon a father who cohabits with his daughter and we vilify with the epithet "incestuous" the brother who abuses his sister. But in a new colony in which only a father with a son and two daughters remain alive, we should consider the care that family took in not allowing the species to perish to be a very good action.

A brother who kills his brother is a monster, but a brother who would have no other way of saving his country except by sacrificing his brother would be a divine man. . . .

But, you will object, will you maintain that there are no crime and virtue, moral good and evil except in relation to ourselves? Is there no right in itself and independent of man? I will ask those who pose this question whether there is cold and heat, sweet and bitter, pleasant and unpleasant odor except in relation to ourselves.

Is it not true that a man who would affirm that heat exists by itself would be an absurd reasoner? Why then does he who affirms that moral good exists independently of us reason any better? Our physical good and ill exist only in relation to us; why should our moral good and ill be any different? . . .

But as God has not deigned, so far as I know, to interfere with our behavior, we have to get along with the gifts we have from Him. These gifts are reason, self-love, benevolence for our species, needs, passions—all of these means by which we have established society.

Many people will be ready to argue against me in this way: If I find my well-being in upsetting your society, in killing, stealing, calumniating, nothing will hold me back and I shall be able to abandon myself without scruples to all my passions. All I can say to those people is that they will probably be hanged, just as I shall have the wolves who want to carry off my lambs killed. It is precisely for them that laws were made, as tiles were invented to protect from hail and rain. . . .

From all this it is easy to see that, in all probability, all this murdering and brigandage are fatal to society but do not concern the Divinity in the least. God has put men and animals on the earth; it is up to them to get along as best they can. Too bad for the flies who fall into the spider's web! Too bad for the bull who is attacked by a lion and for the lambs who are caught by wolves! If a lamb were to say to a wolf: "You are violating moral law, and God will punish you," the wolf would answer: "I am looking after my physical well-being, and it is fairly clear that God is not particularly concerned whether I eat you or not." The wisest thing for the lamb to have done was not to stray from the shepherd and the dog who could have defended him. . . .

If anyone infers from all this that he is free to give himself up to all the passions of his limitless desires and, since there is no absolute virtue or vice, that he can do anything with impunity, that man had better see to it that he has an army of a hundred thousand loyal soldiers at his service; even then he will take a great risk by declaring himself the enemy of mankind. But if this man is only an ordinary individual, if he has any sense at all, he will see that he has made a very bad decision and that he will inevitably be punished, either by the punishments which men have so wisely invented against the enemies of society, or else by the very fear of punishment which is a cruel torture itself. . . . God has wisely endowed us with a pride which can never bear other men hating or despising us; to be despised by those with whom one lives is something that nobody has ever been able, or ever will be able, to bear. It is perhaps the greatest brake that nature has invented for men's injustices; it is by this mutual fear that God has decided to link them. Thus any reasonable man will conclude that it is obviously in his interest to be a decent person. His knowledge of the human heart, a conviction that there is nothing that is in itself right or wrong will never prevent him from being a good citizen and from carrying out all the duties of life.

B.   Just and Unjust

WHO HAS given us the perception of just and unjust? God, who gave us a brain and a heart. But when does our reason inform us that there are such things as vice and virtue? Just at the same time it teaches us that two and two make four. There is no innate knowledge, for the same reason that there is no tree that bears leaves and fruit when it first starts above the earth. There is nothing innate, or fully developed in the first instance; but—we repeat here what we have often said—God causes us to be born with organs, which, as they grow and become unfolded, make us feel all that is necessary for our species to feel, for the conservation of that species.

How is this continual mystery performed? Tell me, ye yellow inhabitants of the Isles of Sunda, ye black Africans, ye beardless Indians; and you—Plato, Cicero, and Epictetus. You all equally feel that it is better to give the superfluity of your bread, your rice, or your manioc, to the poor man who meekly requests it, than to kill him or scoop his eyes out. It is evident to the whole world that a benefit is more honorable to the performer than an outrage, that gentleness is preferable to fury.

The only thing required, then, is to exercise our reason in discriminating the various shades of what is right and wrong. Good

SOURCE: Tobias Smollett (ed.), *The Works of Voltaire; a contemporary version with notes*, revised and modernized with new translations by William J. Fleming, introduction Oliver H. G. Leigh (New York: E. R. DuMont, 1901).

and evil are often neighbors; our passions confound them; who shall enlighten and direct us? Ourselves, when we are calm and undisturbed. Whoever has written on the subject of human duties, in all countries throughout the world, has written well, because he wrote with reason. All have said the same thing; Socrates and Epictetus, Confucius and Cicero, Marcus Antoninus and Amurath II had the same morality.

We would repeat every day to the whole of the human race: Morality is uniform and invariable; it comes from God: dogmas are different; they come from ourselves.

Jesus never taught any metaphysical dogmas; He wrote no theological courses; He never said: I am consubstantial; I have two wills and two natures with only one person. He left for the Cordeliers and the Jacobins,[1] who would appear twelve hundred years after Him, the delicate and difficult topic of argument, whether His mother was conceived in original sin. He never pronounced marriage to be the visible sign of a thing invisible; He never said a word about concomitant grace; He instituted neither monks nor inquisitors; He appointed nothing of what we see at the present day.

God had given the knowledge of just and unjust, right and wrong, throughout all the ages which preceded Christianity. God never changed nor can change. The constitution of our souls, our principles of reason and morality, will ever be the same. How is virtue promoted by theological distinctions, by dogmas founded on those distinctions, by persecutions founded on those dogmas? Nature, terrified and horror-struck at all these barbarous inventions, calls aloud to all men: Be just, and not persecuting sophists.

You read in the "Zend-Avesta," which is the summary of the laws of Zoroaster, this admirable maxim: "When it is doubtful whether the action you are about to perform is just or unjust, abstain from doing it." What legislator ever spoke better? We have not here the system of "probable opinions," invented by people who call themselves "the Society of Jesus."

---

[1] Two monastic orders, not to be confused with the political parties of the French Revolution.

27.   Kant, *Fundamental Principles of the Metaphysic of Morals*

IT FOLLOWS incontestably that, to whatever laws any rational being may be subject, he being an end in himself must be able to regard himself as also legislating universally in respect of these same laws, since it is just this fitness of is maxims for universal legislation that distinguishes him as an end in himself; also it follows that this implies his dignity (prerogative) above all mere physical beings, that he must always take his maxims from the point of view which regards himself, and likewise every other rational being, as lawgiving beings (on which account they are called persons). In this way a world of rational beings (*mundus intelligibilis*) is possible as a kingdom of ends, and this by virtue of the legislation proper to all persons as members. Therefore every rational being must so act as if he were by his maxims in every case a legislating member in the universal kingdom of ends. The formal principle of these maxims is: So act as if thy maxim were to serve likewise as the universal law (of all rational beings). A kingdom of ends is thus only possible on the analogy of a kingdom of nature, the former, however, only by maxims, that is self-imposed rules, the latter only by the laws of efficient causes acting under necessitation from without. . . .

Morality, then, is the relation of actions to the autonomy of the will, that is, to the potential universal legislation by its maxims. An action that is consistent with the autonomy of the will is *permitted;* one that does not agree therewith is *forbidden.* A will whose maxims necessarily coincide with the laws of autonomy is a holy will, good absolutely . . .

From what has just been said, it is easy to see how it happens that although the conception of duty implies subjection to the law, we

SOURCE: *Kant's Critique of Practical Reason and other works on the theory of ethics*, trans. T. K. Abbott (London: Longmans, Green & Co., Ltd., 1954), pp. 56–63.

yet ascribe a certain *dignity* and sublimity to the person who fulfils all his duties. There is not, indeed, any sublimity in him, so far as he is *subject* to the moral law; but inasmuch as in regard to that very law he is likewise a *legislator*, and on that account subject to it, he has sublimity. We have also shown above that neither fear nor inclination, but simply respect for the law, is the spring which can give actions a moral worth. Our own will, so far as we suppose it to act only under the condition that its maxims are potentially universal laws, this ideal will which is possible to us is the proper object of respect; and the dignity of humanity consists just in this capacity of being universally legislative, though with the condition that it is itself subject to this same legislation. . . .

[1]If the will seeks the law which is to determine it anywhere else than in the fitness of its maxims to be universal laws of its own dictation, consequently if it goes out of itself and seeks this law in the character of any of its objects, there always results heteronomy.[2] The will in that case does not give itself the law, but it is given by the object through its relation to the will. This relation, whether it rests on inclination or on conceptions of reason, only admits of hypothetical imperatives: I ought to do something *because I wish for something else*. On the contrary, the moral, and therefore categorical, imperative says: I ought to do so and so, even though I should not wish for anything else. *Ex. gr.*, the former says: I ought not to lie if I would retain my reputation; the latter says: I ought not to lie although it should not bring me the least discredit. The latter therefore must so far abstract from all objects that they shall have no influence on the will, in order that practical reason (will) may not be restricted to administering an interest not belonging to it, but may simply show its own commanding authority as the supreme legislation. Thus, *ex. gr.*, I ought to endeavour to promote the happiness of others, not as if its realization involved any concern of mine (whether by immediate inclination or by any satisfaction indirectly gained through reason), but simply because a maxim which excludes it cannot be comprehended as a universal law in one and the same volition.

---

[1] This paragraph and the following directly attack French materialist ethics, as in d'Holbach.
[2] The opposite of autonomy, i.e., determination by objects outside the autonomous moral will.

Classification

OF ALL PRINCIPLES OF MORALITY WHICH CAN BE FOUNDED ON THE CONCEPTION OF HETERONOMY

Here as elsewhere human reason in its pure use, so long as it was not critically examined, has first tried all possible wrong ways before it succeeded in finding the one true way.

All principles which can be taken from this point of view are either *empirical* or *rational*. The *former*, drawn from the principle of *happiness*, are built on physical or moral feelings; the latter, drawn from the principle of *perfection*, are built either on the rational conception of perfection as a possible effect, or on that of an independent perfection (the will of God) as the determining cause of our will.

Empirical principles are wholly incapable of serving as a foundation for moral laws. For the universality with which these should hold for all rational beings without distinction, the unconditional practical[3] necessity which is thereby imposed on them is lost when their foundation is taken from *the particular constitution of human nature*, or the accidental circumstances in which it is placed. The principle of *private happiness*, however, is the most objectionable, not merely because it is false, and experience contradicts the supposition that prosperity is always proportioned to good conduct, nor yet merely because it contributes nothing to the establishment of morality—since it is quite a different thing to make a prosperous man and a good man, or to make one prudent and sharp-sighted for his own interests, and to make him virtuous—but because the springs it provides for morality are such as rather undermine it and destroy its sublimity, since they put the motives to virtue and to vice in the same class, and only teach us to make a better calculation, the specific difference between virtue and vice being entirely extinguished. On the other hand, as to moral feeling, this supposed special sense, the appeal to it is indeed superficial when those who cannot *think* believe that *feeling* will help them out, even in what concerns general laws: and besides, feelings which naturally differ infinitely in degree cannot furnish a uniform standard of good and evil, nor has anyone a right to form judg-

---

[3] In Kant's terminology, concerned with voluntary decision and action.

ments for others by his own feelings: nevertheless this moral feeling is nearer to morality and its dignity in this respect, that it pays virtue the honour of ascribing to her *immediately* the satisfaction and esteem we have for her, and does not, as it were, tell her to her face that we are not attached to her by her beauty but by profit.

Amongst the *rational* principles of morality, the ontological conception of *perfection*, notwithstanding its defects, is better than the theological conception which derives morality from a Divine absolutely perfect will. The former is, no doubt, empty and indefinite, and consequently useless for finding in the boundless field of possible reality the greatest amount suitable for us; moreover, in attempting to distinguish specifically the reality of which we are now speaking from every other, it inevitably tends to turn in a circle, and cannot avoid tacitly presupposing the morality which it is to explain; it is nevertheless preferable to the theological view, first, because we have no intuition of the Divine perfection, and can only deduce it from our own conceptions, the most important of which is that of morality, and our explanation would thus be involved in a gross circle; and, in the next place, if we avoid this, the only notion of the Divine will remaining to us is a conception made up of the attributes of desire of glory and dominion, combined with the awful conceptions of might and vengeance, and any system of morals erected on this foundation would be directly opposed to morality. . . .

In every case where an object of the will has to be supposed, in order that the rule may be prescribed which is to determine the will, there the rule is simply heteronomy; the imperative is conditional, namely, *if* or *because* one wishes for this object, one should act so and so: hence it can never command morally, that is categorically. Whether the object determines the will by means of inclination, as in the principle of private happiness, or by means of reason directed to objects of our possible volition generally, as in the principle of perfection, in either case the will never determines itself *immediately* by the conception of the action, but only by the influence which the foreseen effect of the action has on the will; *I ought to do something, on this account, because I wish for something else;* and here there must be yet another law assumed in me as its subject, by which I necessarily will this other thing, and this law again requires an imperative to restrict this maxim. For the influence which the conception of an object within the reach of our faculties can exercise on the will of the subject in consequence of its natural properties, depends on the nature of the subject, either the sensibility (inclination and taste), or the understanding and reason, the employment of which is by the peculiar constitution of their nature attended with satisfaction. It follows that the law would be, properly speaking, given by nature, and as such, it must be known and proved by experience, and would consequently be contingent, and therefore incapable of being an apodictic[4] practical rule, such as the moral rule must be. Not only so, but it is inevitably only heteronomy; the will does not give itself the law, but it is given by a foreign impulse by means of a particular natural constitution of the subject adapted to receive it. An absolutely good will, then, the principle of which must be a categorical imperative, will be indeterminate as regards all objects, and will contain merely the *form of volition* generally, and that as autonomy, that is to say, the capability of the maxims of every good will to make themselves a universal law. This is itself the only law which the will of every rational being imposes on itself, without needing to assume any spring or interest as a foundation.

[4] Necessary in itself and incontestably true.

28. De Sade, Juliette, or the Prosperities of Vice

WHEN the laws were promulgated, when the weak consented to give up a part of their freedom in order to keep the other part, the first thing whose peaceful enjoyment they desired, the first object of the controls they demanded was, without question, the security of their possessions. The strong agreed to laws which they felt sure they would be able to evade, and they were passed. It was decreed that each man would have peaceful possession of his inheritance and that anyone who disturbed him and his possessions would be punished. But in all that there was nothing natural, nothing that

SOURCE: De Sade, *Histoire de Juliette* (Paris: Pauvert, 1954), Translated by the editor.

nature dictated, nothing that it inspired; everything was the work of men, henceforth divided into two classes. The first class yielded one quarter in order to obtain tranquil enjoyment of the rest. The second class absorbed this quarter and, seeing that it could have the other three quarters whenever it wanted to, agreed to prevent not themselves from despoiling the weak, but the weak from despoiling each other, so that they themselves could despoil them more easily. Thus theft, nature's sole institution, was banished from the earth; but it existed in different form—legal theft came into being. The judges stole by receiving payment for the justice they should have dispensed without charge. The priest stole by receiving payment for acting as mediator between man and his God. The merchant stole by monopolizing goods and by selling them for a third more than their real worth. Sovereigns stole by imposing arbitrary taxes on their subjects. All these thefts were allowed, all were authorized under the precious name of "rights." Only the most natural rights were punished now, for example the simple act of a man who, needing money, demanded it pistol in hand from those who he thought were richer than he. Nobody thought of the fact that the first thieves, who went unnoticed, were the sole cause of the crimes of the second thief, the sole cause which forced him to recover, by armed force, properties which the first usurper had so cruelly snatched away. For, if all these thefts were only usurpations which caused the poverty of the subordinate persons, the second thefts, perpetrated by these inferior beings, made necessary by the first, were no longer crimes; they were secondary effects brought about by the main causes, and, as soon as you authorized the main cause, it became legally impossible for you to punish its effects; you could no longer do it without injustice. If you push a valet against a precious vase and his fall breaks the vase, you no longer have a right to punish him for his clumsiness; you should blame only the cause which forced you to push him. When an unfortunate farmer, reduced to beggary by the burden of taxes which you imposed on him, abandons his plow, arms himself, and lays in wait for you on the highway, you are surely committing a great infamy if you punish him; for it is not he who wronged you, he is the valet whom you have pushed against the vase. Do not push him, and he will not break anything; and if you do push him, do not be surprised if he does break something. And so this unfortunate man commits no crime when he goes out to steal from you. He is trying to recover goods which you have previously usurped from him, you or others like you. He is doing only what is natural; he is trying to re-establish the balance which, in morals as in physics, is the first of nature's laws; he is doing only what is just.

But that is not what I wanted to prove. I need no proofs, I need no arguments to show that the weak man is doing only what he must when he tries to recover his usurped possessions. What I want to convince you of is that the strong is himself committing neither crime nor injustice when he tries to despoil the weak, because that is my own situation, that is the act in which I indulge every day. Now this demonstration is not difficult. And the act of theft in this case is surely more natural than in the other instance. It is not the reprisals of the weak against the strong which are truly within nature; they are so morally, but not physically, since in order to carry out these reprisals the weak man must use forces which he has not received, he must take on a character which was not given to him and so constrain nature in some fashion. But what is truly in accordance with the laws of that wise mother is the abuse of the weak by the strong, since such a procedure requires him to use only gifts which he has received. He does not, like the weak, take on a character different from his own; he merely puts into action the effects of the character he received from nature. Therefore whatever results is natural: his oppression, his violence, his cruelty, his tyranny, his injustices, all these diverse expressions of the character which was imprinted in him by the hand of the power which placed him in the world are therefore simple and pure like the hand which engraved them in him. When he uses all his rights to suppress the weak man and to despoil him, he is then doing only the most natural thing in the world. If our common mother had wished that equality which the weak tries to establish, if she had really desired that property were equitably distributed, why would she have created two classes, one of the strong, the other of the weak? Has she not given ample proof by this difference that her intention was that it should obtain in regard to property as in regard to corporal abilities? Does she not prove that her purpose is that everything should be on one side and nothing on the other precisely in order to reach the equilibrium which is the basis of all her laws? In order for equilibrium to exist in nature, it must not be men who establish it. Their equilibrium disturbs nature's; what seems in our eyes to be contrary to it is precisely what establishes it in her eyes, and that is so because we think that from this lack of equilibrium come the crimes by which she establishes her order. The strong seize everything; that is a lack of balance, according to man. The weak defend themselves and pillage the strong; those are crimes which establish the equilibrium necessary to nature. Let us then never have scruples about what we can steal from the weak, for it is not we who are committing a crime; it is the self-defense or the revenge of the weak which is criminal. By stealing from the poor, by despoiling the orphan, by usurping the widow's inheritance, man is only using rights which he received from nature. The crime would be in not profiting from them; the impoverished wretch whom she offers up to our blows is the prey that she offers to the vulture. If the strong man seems to be disturbing the order by robbing the one who is under him, the weak re-establish it by robbing those who are above them, and both are serving nature.

If we go back to the origins of the right of property, we inevitably go back to usurpation. Nevertheless, theft is punished only because it attacks the right of property; but this right is itself, in its origin, only a theft; therefore the law punishes theft for attacking theft, the weak for trying to recover his rights, and the strong for trying either to establish or increase his by taking advantage of what nature has given him. Can there exist in the whole world a more frightful consequence? As long as there is no legitimately established property (and there cannot be any), it would be most difficult to prove that theft is a crime, for what theft upsets on the one hand, it re-establishes on the other; and nature being no more concerned about the first than about the second, it is quite impossible to establish any offense to its laws when we favor one of these rather than the other. The weak man is right, then, when, in trying to recover his usurped possessions, he purposely attacks the strong and obliges him to make restitution. The only wrong he can do is to violate the character of weakness imprinted in him by nature; she created him to be poor and a slave and he does not want to submit—that is his wrong. The strong man cannot be charged with this wrong, since he stays within his character and acts according to it; therefore he is right, both when he tries to despoil the weak and to obtain pleasure at his expense. Now let each of them search for a moment within his heart. The weak man, when he decides to attack the strong, whatever his rights may be, will experience a slight struggle; this resistance to his satisfying himself comes from the fact that he has just violated nature's laws by adopting a character which is not his own. The strong man, on the contrary, when he despoils the weak, that is to say, when he enjoys all the rights which nature gave him, by exercising them as fully as possible, finds pleasure in direct ratio to the limits of this extension. The more atrocious the harm he does to the weak, the more voluptuously he is thrilled. He delights in injustice. He enjoys the tears which his cruelty wrings from his victim. The more he crushes him, the more he oppresses him, the happier he is, because then he is making a greater use of the gifts given him by nature, and because the use of those gifts becomes a need and, consequently, his source of voluptuousness. Besides, this necessary enjoyment which springs from the comparison which the fortunate man makes between himself and the unfortunate, this truly delectable enjoyment is never more solid for the fortunate man than when the unhappiness he inflicts is complete. The more he crushes his victim, the more he enhances the worth of the comparison and consequently, the more he stimulates his voluptuous thrill. There are, then, two quite real pleasures in the wrongs he does to the weak: the increase of his own material possessions, and the moral enjoyment of the comparisons which he makes all the more delectable in proportion as the injuries he inflicts weaken his victim. Let him pillage, then, let him burn, ravage, leave the wretch nothing more than enough breath to prolong a life which the oppressor needs in order to establish his laws of comparison. Whatever he does will be within nature; whatever he invents will be only the use of the active powers he received from her; the more use he makes of his powers, the more pleasure he will experience, the better he will use the faculties, and the better, consequently, he will serve nature.

V

Politics

ONE OF the major distinctions between the eighteenth century and its predecessor is its awareness of the need to remake the structures of government and even, in the minds of more radical thinkers, to remake society itself. Instead of "need," one should perhaps use the word "inevitability." Ideologies did not yet exist. Nevertheless, from the vantage point of a later age, one can see the developments that flowed out of the eighteenth century, the tendencies of which it was not itself clearly aware; to us those tendencies appear self-evidently "liberal," "collectivist," "totalitarian," and so on.

At widely separated points, the English moralist, Bernard Mandeville, and the French lawyer and publicist, Linguet (who was guillotined during the Terror), both present types of an avowedly exploitative society based on power. Mandeville's "Essay on Charity, and Charity Schools" was added to *The Fable of the Bees* in 1723. He rests his argument on the need for a depressed labor force, whence he concludes that society must cultivate a class of subhumans. Defense of slavery, exemplified in the first chapter from Linguet's *Théorie des lois civiles* (1772), was more common than is generally recognized, for it is the campaign against slavery that has mainly attracted the attention of historians. Paradoxically, Linguet's defense of an exploitative society explicitly contains the basis for a revolt against all society. If the natural heirs of such writers as Mandeville, Linguet, Sabatier de Castres, and Rivarol were the "social Darwinists" of the nineteenth century and the fascists of the twentieth, the anarchist movement in the late nineteenth and early twentieth centuries was the natural reaction to the type of society they defended. There were a few anarchists in the eighteenth century, too—Lahontan, Meslier (a priest), the monk Dom Deschamps, and Sade—but we have not been able to include them in these selections.

Three of our writers preferred collectivist societies—all with totalitarian implications. Morelly believed that property was the cause of all social evils, and his utopia is communistic. Overtly an optimist about human nature, his rigidly regimented planning reveals his true pessimism about men.

The latter point applies also to Rousseau. After denouncing property in the *Discours sur l'origine de l'inégalité* (1755), Rousseau decided it was enough to regulate it—and everything else, especially men's opinions and passions. He detests the societies of his time; all existing societies are exploitative and alienate men from each other. His purpose is to end the state of war among men, to create a true society, a true harmony. To do this, it is necessary to "remake" men, to "form citizens" by "capturing their wills" and "controlling their opinions," through techniques which include "education," censorship, constant surveillance, and a calculated use of deceit. The "human self" (vicious and ego-centered) must be replaced by the "communal self"; this can be done only by a complete transformation of attitudes and motivations. Rousseau is the true inventor of the technique modern behaviorists call "behavioral engineering," although it had already been adumbrated by La Mettrie and Helvétius. Rousseau insists on popular sovereignty and the rule of law as the only way to avoid dependence on persons or power groups, but only on the condition that wills are "captured" and an "inflexible yoke" imposed.

Restif de la Bretonne, an eccentric who wrote late in the century, also outlined a utopian communist state in his *Découverte australe, par un homme volant* (1781), a work dominated by fantasy that touches on the ridiculous. Here, too, freedom, the supposed aim, gives way to regimentation; as in Rousseau, the arts, for instance, are discouraged and limited to furthering the purposes of the state. All three writers propound egalitarianism, but their social systems, though open to men of talent, are of necessity hierarchically structured.

In some respects, Helvétius belongs with this group. He was the first to develop a theory of conditioning behavior by "education." Together with government and laws, education can, he believes, completely determine human conduct. Helvétius was not, however, a collectivist or an egalitarian. Like the preceding writers, he does give society and social control primacy over the individual: "The public good is the supreme law." Contrary to the others, he believes in sexual freedom, advancing the paradox that when the laws do not forbid acts, there are no vices.

The writers of the Age of Enlightenment are mostly famous for their formulation of the democratic theories of modern liberal societies. This reputation is well founded, although it is only one aspect of the political thought of the time. Montesquieu, in his great work, *De l'Esprit des lois* (1748), attempted a "scientific" or empirical inquiry into the laws of government. Laws, inherent in the nature of things, rule all political affairs. In the sense that they are beyond the reach of arbitrary will, such "natural" laws enable us to judge institutions, both abstractly and in their actual performance. No one form of government is best for all, but Montesquieu clearly prefers a monarchy, as exemplified by England, with its separation of powers and intermediary bodies as a protection for individual liberty. But Montesquieu goes beyond the nature of political institutions to the kind of society inherent in each form of government—monarchical, despotic, aristocratic, and democratic. When he writes of democracy, it is important to remember that he has in mind the ancient city-state, or *polis*, where citizens themselves made the laws. His description of this kind of state, which involves great control of private lives, influenced Rousseau. It was not the kind of society Montesquieu would have liked to live in.

The *Encyclopédie* of Diderot and d'Alembert, in its political articles, generally expressed the middle-class ideology—the desire for reform, for a voice in government, and for laissez faire under the monarchy. In several articles, such as Diderot's "Droit naturel," a more democratic view was expressed in a weak voice. The conservative viewpoint Diderot held during the years when he edited the *Encycyopédie* later underwent a profound transformation, especially during his visit to the Netherlands and Russia in 1773–74. In the various pieces he composed for Catherine the Great in 1774, he urged on her the separation of Church and State, representative government, civil liberties, inalienable rights, and economic laissez faire. Like others in his time, Diderot believed that morals depend on legislation and government. Despite considerable naïveté in his thinking (of which Catherine was well aware), his emphasis on the individual, and on his happiness, is laudable and provides a contrast to the theories of Rousseau.

Louis-Sébastien Mercier (1740–1814) was a man of letters best known in his time as the author of the vivid *Tableau de Paris* and of a number of *drames*. His most curious book is his disjointed and idiosyncratic utopia, *L'An Deux Mille Quatre Cent Quarante, rêve s'il en fût jamais* (*The Year 2440, Dream If There Ever Was One*, 1770). Although not all of his ideas were what we would now call liberal, he did outline the major factors that determine the character of such a society. He also reversed the accepted notion that the government makes the people what it is. The selection presented in document 36 forms a contrast to the views of Linguet.

D'Holbach is a good example of the admixture of various tendencies in an age when ideologies were not clear or fixed. His theories make morals a part of politics, and he is tempted to prefer a wise and benevolent despot; but he finally decides in favor of representative government and civil liberties. A pessimist about history and human nature, he was optimistic in his ideal plans for the future.

The selections from Madison and Jefferson—the last postdates our period but belongs to it in spirit—typify the American Enlightenment, which drew heavily on Locke and the British parliamentary and libertarian traditions but infused them with natural rights theories, Montesquieu's separation of powers, and other French ideas. The question of factions and the general welfare is treated by Madison in the tenth of *The Federalist* papers (1787–88) in a manner that contrasts sharply with that of Rousseau (*Du Contrat social*, II, 3). Factions are natural to man, society, and government; what is required is to analyze and solve the problem of factions, always remembering that liberty is more precious than coerced harmony. Other ideas of interest abound in this essay; among them are Montesquieu's checks and balances, the uselessness of moral and religious restraint on self-interest, the aversion to mob rule. Jefferson, on the other hand, expresses his faith in an enlightened citizenry—this despite his low opinion of men, who devour each other. His ideal would be an aristocracy of virtue and talent, chosen by all the people in free elections. His faith in progress and the future shines brightly.

29. Mandeville, "An Essay on Charity, and Charity Schools"

THE WHOLE Earth being Curs'd, and no Bread to be had but what we eat in the sweat of our Brows, vast Toil must be undergone before Man can provide himself with Necessaries for his Sustenance and the bare Support of his corrupt and defective Nature as he is a single Creature; but infinitely more to make Life comfortable in a Civil Society, where Men are become taught Animals, and great Numbers of them have by mutual compact framed themselves into a Body Politick; and the more Man's Knowledge increases in this State, the greater will be the variety of Labour required to make him easy. It is impossible that a Society can long subsist, and suffer many of its Members to live in Idleness, and enjoy all the Ease and Pleasure they can invent, without having at the same time great Multitudes of People that to make good this Defect will condescend to be quite the reverse, and by use and patience inure their Bodies to work for others and themselves besides.

The Plenty and Cheapness of Provisions depends in a great measure on the Price and Value that is set upon this Labour, and consequently the Welfare of all Societies, even before they are tainted with Foreign Luxury, requires that it should be perform'd by such of their Members as in the first Place are sturdy and robust and never used to Ease or Idleness, and in the second, soon contented as to the necessaries of Life; such as are glad to take up with the coarsest Manufacture in every thing they wear, and in their

SOURCE: F. B. Kaye (ed.), *The Fable of the Bees* (Oxford: The Clarendon Press, 1924), I, pp. 286–88.

Diet have no other aim than to feed their Bodies when their Stomachs prompt them to eat, and with little regard to Taste or Relish, refuse no wholesome Nourishment that can be swallow'd when Men are Hungry, or ask anything for their Thirst but to quench it.

As the greatest part of the Drudgery is to be done by Day-light, so it is by this only that they actually measure the time of their Labour without any thought of the Hours they are employ'd, or the weariness they feel; and the Hireling in the Country must get up in the Morning, not because he has rested enough, but because the Sun is going to rise. This last Article alone would be an intolerable Hardship to Grown People under Thirty, who during Nonage had been used to lie a-bed as long as they could sleep: but all three together make up such a Condition of Life as a Man more mildly Educated would hardly choose; tho' it should deliver him from a Gaol or a Shrew.

If such People there must be, as no great Nation can be happy without vast Numbers of them, would not a Wise Legislature cultivate the Breed of them with all imaginable Care, and provide against their Scarcity as he would prevent the Scarcity of Provision itself? No Man would be poor and fatigue himself for a Livelihood if he could help it: The absolute necessity all stand in for Victuals and Drink, and in cold Climates for Clothes and Lodging, makes them submit to any thing that can be bore with. If no body did Want no body would work; but the greatest Hardships are look'd upon as solid Pleasures, when they keep a Man from Starving.

From what has been said it is manifest, that in a free Nation where Slaves are not allow'd of, the surest Wealth consists in a Multitude of laborious Poor; for besides that they are the never-failing Nursery of Fleets and Armies, without them there could be no Enjoyment, and no Product of any Country could be valuable. To make the Society happy and People easy under the meanest Circumstances, it is requisite that great Numbers of them should be Ignorant as well as Poor. Knowledge both enlarges and multiplies our Desires, and the fewer things a Man wishes for, the more easily his Necessities may be supply'd.

The Welfare and Felicity therefore of every State and Kingdom, require that the Knowledge of the Working Poor should be confin'd within the Verge of their Occupations, and never extended (as to things visible) beyond what relates to their Calling. The more a Shepherd, a Plowman or any other Peasant knows of the World, and the things that are Foreign to his Labour or Employment, the less fit he'll be to go through the Fatigues and Hardships of it with Cheerfulness and Content.

Reading, Writing and Arithmetick, are very necessary to those, whose Business require such Qualifications, but where People's livelihood has no dependence on these Arts, they are very pernicious to the Poor, who are forc'd to get their Daily Bread by their Daily Labour. Few Children make any Progress at School, but at the same time they are capable of being employ'd in some Business or other, so that every Hour those of poor People spend at their Book is so much time lost to the Society. Going to School in comparison to Working is Idleness, and the longer Boys continue in this easy sort of Life, the more unfit they'll be when grown up for downright Labour, both as to Strength and Inclination. Men who are to remain and end their Days in a Laborious, Tiresome and Painful Station of Life, the sooner they are put upon it at first, the more patiently they'll submit to it for ever after.

30. Montesquieu, The Spirit of the Laws

Book I

CHAPTER I. OF THE RELATION OF LAWS TO DIFFERENT BEINGS

Laws, in their most general signification, are the necessary relations arising from the nature of things. In this sense all beings have their laws: the Deity his laws, the material world its laws, the intelligences superior to man their laws, the beasts their laws, man his laws.

They who assert that a blind fatality produced the various effects we behold in this world talk very absurdly; for can any-

SOURCE: Oliver Wendell Holmes (ed.), The Spirit of the Laws, trans. Thomas Nugent, rev. J. V. Prichard (New York: D. Appleton and Co., 1900).

thing be more unreasonable than to pretend that a blind fatality could be productive of intelligent beings?

There is, then, a prime reason; and laws are the relations subsisting between it and different beings, and the relations of these to one another.

God is related to the universe, as Creator and Preserver; the laws by which he created all things are those by which he preserves them. He acts according to these rules, because he knows them; he knows them, because he made them; and he made them because they are in relation to his wisdom and power.

Since we observe that the world, though formed by the motion of matter, and void of understanding, subsists through so long a succession of ages, its motions must certainly be directed by invariable laws; and could we imagine another world, it must also have constant rules, or it would inevitably perish.

Thus the creation, which seems an arbitrary act, supposes laws as invariable as those of the fatality of the atheists. It would be absurd to say that the Creator might govern the world without those rules, since without them it could not subsist.

These rules are a fixed and invariable relation. In bodies moved, the motion is received, increased, diminished, or lost, according to the relations of the quantity of matter and velocity; each diversity is uniformity, each change is constancy.

Particular intelligent beings may have laws of their own making, but they have some likewise which they never made. Before there were intelligent beings, they were possible; they had therefore possible relations, and consequently possible laws. Before laws were made, there were relations of possible justice. To say that there is nothing just or unjust but what is commanded or forbidden by positive laws, is the same as saying that before the describing of a circle all the radii were not equal.

We must therefore acknowledge relations of justice antecedent to the positive law by which they are established; as, for instance, if human societies existed, it would be right to conform to their laws; if there were intelligent beings that had received a benefit of another being, they ought to show their gratitude; if one intelligent being had created another intelligent being, the latter ought to continue in its original state of dependence; if one intelligent being injures another, it deserves a retaliation; and so on.

But the intelligent world is far from being so well governed as the physical. For though the former has also its laws, which of their own nature are invariable, it does not conform to them so exactly as the physical world. This is because, on the one hand, particular intelligent beings are of a finite nature, and consequently liable to error; and on the other, their nature requires them to be free agents. Hence they do not steadily conform to their primitive laws; and even those of their own instituting they frequently infringe.

Whether brutes be governed by the general laws of motion, or by a particular movement, we can not determine. Be that as it may, they have not a more intimate relation to God than the rest of the material world; and sensation is of no other use to them than in the relation they have either to other particular beings or to themselves.

By the allurement of pleasure they preserve the individual, and by the same allurement they preserve their species. They have natural laws, because they are united by sensation; positive laws they have none, because they are not connected by knowledge. And yet they do not invariably conform to their natural laws; these are better observed by vegetables, that have neither understanding nor sense.

Brutes are deprived of the high advantages which we have; but they have some which we have not. They have not our hopes, but they are without our fears; they are subject like us to death, but without knowing it; even most of them are more attentive than we to self-preservation, and do not make so bad a use of their passions.

Man, as a physical being, is like other bodies governed by invariable laws. As an intelligent being, he incessantly transgresses the laws established by God, and changes those of his own instituting. He is left to his private direction, though a limited being, and subject, like all finite intelligences, to ignorance and error: even his imperfect knowledge he loses; and as a sensible creature, he is hurried away by a thousand impetuous passions. Such a being might every instant forget his Creator; God has therefore reminded him of his duty by the laws of religion. Such a being is liable every moment to forget himself; philosophy has provided against this by the laws of morality. Formed to live in society, he might forget his fellow-creatures; legislators have therefore by political and civil laws confined him to his duty.

CHAPTER III. OF POSITIVE LAWS

As soon as man enters into a state of society he loses the sense of his weakness; equality ceases, and then commences the state of war.

Each particular society begins to feel its strength, whence arises a state of war between different nations. The individuals likewise of each society become sensible of their force; hence the principal advantages of this society they endeavour to convert to their own emolument, which constitutes a state of war between individuals.

These two different kinds of states give rise to human laws. Considered as inhabitants of so great a planet, which necessarily contains a variety of nations, they have laws relating to their mutual intercourse, which is what we call the law of nations. As members of a society that must be properly supported, they have laws relating to the governors and the governed, and this we distinguish by the name of political law. They have also another sort of laws, as they stand in relation to each other; by which is understood the civil law.

The law of nations is naturally founded on this principle, that different nations ought in time of peace to do one another all the good they can, and in time of war as little injury as possible, without prejudicing their real interests.

The object of war is victory; that of victory is conquest; and that of conquest preservation. From this and the preceding principle all those rules are derived which constitute the law of nations.

All countries have a law of nations, not excepting the Iroquois themselves, though they devour their prisoners: for they send and receive ambassadors, and understand the rights of war and peace. The mischief is that their law of nations is not founded on true principles.

Besides the law of nations relating to all societies, there is a polity or civil constitution for each particularly considered. No society can subsist without a form of government. "The united strength of individuals," as Gravina[1] well observes, "constitutes what we call the body politic."

---

[1] Gian Vincenzo Gravina, Italian jurisconsult (1632–94).

The general strength may be in the hands of a single person, or of many. Some think that Nature having established paternal authority, the most natural government was that of a single person. But the example of paternal authority proves nothing. For if the power of a father relates to a single government, that of brothers after the death of a father, and that of cousin-germans after the decease of brothers, refer to a government of many. The political power necessarily comprehends the union of several families.

Better is it to say that the government most conformable to Nature is that which best agrees with the humour and disposition of the people in whose favour it is established.

The strength of individuals can not be united without a conjunction of all their wills. "The conjunction of those wills," as Gravina again very justly observes, "is what we call the civil state."

Law in general is human reason, inasmuch as it governs all the inhabitants of the earth: the political and civil laws of each nation ought to be only the particular cases in which human reason is applied.

They should be adapted in such a manner to the people for whom they are framed that it should be a great chance if those of one nation suit another.

They should be in relation to the nature and principle of each government; whether they form it, as may be said of political laws; or whether they support it, as in the case of civil institutions.

They should be in relation to the climate of each country, to the quality of its soil, to its situation and extent, to the principal occupation of the natives, whether husbandmen, huntsmen, or shepherds: they should have relation to the degree of liberty which the constitution will bear; to the religion of the inhabitants, to their inclinations, riches, numbers, commerce, manners, and customs. In fine, they have relations to each other, as also to their origin, to the intent of the legislator, and to the order of things on which they are established; in all of which different lights they ought to be considered.

This is what I have undertaken to perform in the following work. These relations I shall examine, since all these together constitute what I call the "Spirit of the Laws."

I have not separated the political from the civil institutions, as I do not pretend to treat of laws, but of their spirit; and as this spirit consists in the various relations which the laws may bear to different objects, it is not so much my business to follow the natural order of laws as that of these relations and objects.

I shall first examine the relations which laws bear to the nature and principle of each government; and as this principle has a strong influence on laws, I shall make it my study to understand it thoroughly: and if I can but once establish it, the laws will soon appear to flow thence as from their source. I shall proceed afterward to other and more particular relations.

Book II

CHAPTER II. OF LAWS DIRECTLY DERIVED FROM THE NATURE OF GOVERNMENT

I. There are three species of government: republican, monarchical, and despotic. In order to discover their nature, it is sufficient to recollect the common notion, which supposes three definitions, or rather three facts: that a republican government is that in which the body, or only a part of the people, is possessed of the supreme power; monarchy, that in which a single person governs by fixed and established laws; a despotic government, that in which a single person directs everything by his own will and caprice.

This is what I call the nature of each government; we must now inquire into those laws which directly conform to this nature, and consequently are the fundamental institutions.

II. When the body of the people is possessed of the supreme power, it is called a democracy. When the supreme power is lodged in the hands of a part of the people, it is then an aristocracy.

In a democracy the people are in some respects the sovereign, and in others the subject.

There can be no exercise of sovereignty but by their suffrages, which are their own will; now the sovereign's will is the sovereign himself. The laws therefore which establish the right of suffrage are fundamental to this government. And indeed it is as important to regulate in a republic, in what manner, by whom, to whom, and concerning what, suffrages are to be given, as it is in a monarchy to know who is the prince, and after what manner he ought to govern.

Libanius says that at "Athens a stranger who intermeddled in the assemblies of the people was punished with death." This is because such a man usurped the rights of sovereignty.

It is an essential point to fix the number of citizens who are to form the public assemblies; otherwise it would be uncertain whether the whole, or only a part of the people, had given their votes. At Sparta the number was fixed at ten thousand. But Rome, designed by Providence to rise from the weakest beginnings to the highest pitch of grandeur; Rome, doomed to experience all the vicissitudes of fortune; Rome, who had sometimes all her inhabitants without her walls, and sometimes all Italy and a considerable part of the world within them; Rome, I say, never fixed the number, and this was one of the principal causes of her ruin.

The people, in whom the supreme power resides, ought to have the management of everything within their reach: that which exceeds their abilities must be conducted by their ministers.

But they can not properly be said to have their ministers, without the power of nominating them: it is, therefore, a fundamental maxim in this government, that the people should choose their ministers—that is, their magistrates.

They have occasion, as well as monarchs, and even more so, to be directed by a council or senate. But to have a proper confidence in these, they should have the choosing of the members; whether the election be made by themselves, as at Athens, or by some magistrate deputed for that purpose, as on certain occasions was customary at Rome.

The people are extremely well qualified for choosing those whom they are to intrust with part of their authority. They have only to be determined by things to which they can not be strangers, and by facts that are obvious to sense. They can tell when a person has fought many battles, and been crowned with success; they are, therefore, capable of electing a general. They can tell when a judge is assiduous in his office, gives general satisfaction, and has never been charged with bribery: this is sufficient for choosing a prætor. They are struck with the magnificence or riches of a fellow-citizen; no more is requisite for electing an ædile. These are facts of which they can have better information in a public forum than a monarch in his palace. But are they capable of conducting an intricate affair, of seizing and improving the opportunity and critical moment of action? No; this surpasses their abilities.

Should we doubt the people's natural capacity, in respect to the discernment of merit, we need only cast an eye on the series of surprising elections made by the Athenians and Romans; which no one surely will attribute to hazard.

We know that though the people of Rome assumed the right of raising plebeians to public offices, yet they never would exert this power; and though at Athens the magistrates were allowed, by the law of Aristides, to be elected from all the different classes of inhabitants, there never was a case, says Xenophon, when the common people petitioned for employments which could endanger either their security or their glory.

As most citizens have sufficient ability to choose, though unqualified to be chosen, so the people, though capable of calling others to an account for their administration, are incapable of conducting the administration themselves.

The public business must be carried on with a certain motion, neither too quick nor too slow. But the motion of the people is always either too remiss or too violent. Sometimes with a hundred thousand arms they overturn all before them; and sometimes with a hundred thousand feet they creep like insects.

In a popular state the inhabitants are divided into certain classes. It is in the manner of making this division that great legislators have signalized themselves; and it is on this that the duration and prosperity of democracy have ever depended.

Servius Tullius followed the spirit of aristocracy in the distribution of his classes. We find in Livy and in Dionysius Halicarnassus in what manner he lodged the right of suffrage in the hands of the principal citizens. He had divided the people of Rome into one hundred and ninety-three centuries, which formed six classes; and ranking the rich, who were in smaller numbers, in the first centuries, and those in middling circumstances, who were more numerous, in the next, he flung the indigent multitude into the last; and as each century had but one vote, it was property rather than numbers that decided the election.

Solon divided the people of Athens into four classes. In this he was directed by the spirit of democracy, his intention not being to fix those who were to choose, but such as were eligible: therefore, leaving to every citizen the right of election, he made the judges eligible from each of those four classes; but the magistrates he ordered to be chosen only out of the first three, consisting of persons of easy fortunes.

As the division of those who have a right of suffrage is a

fundamental law in republics, so the manner of giving this suffrage is another fundamental.

The suffrage by lot is natural to democracy; as that by choice is to aristocracy.

The suffrage by lot is a method of electing that offends no one, but animates each citizen with the pleasing hope of serving his country.

Yet as this method is in itself defective, it has been the endeavour of the most eminent legislators to regulate and amend it.

Solon made a law at Athens, that military employments should be conferred by choice; but that senators and judges should be elected by lot.

The same legislator ordained that civil magistracies, attended with great expense, should be given by choice; and the others by lot.

In order, however, to amend the suffrage by lot, he made a rule, that none but those who presented themselves should be elected; that the person elected should be examined by judges, and that every one should have a right to accuse him if he were unworthy of the office; this participated at the same time of the suffrage by lot, and of that by choice. When the time of their magistracy had expired, they were obliged to submit to another judgment in regard to their conduct. Persons utterly unqualified must have been extremely backward in giving in their names to be drawn by lot.

The law which determines the manner of giving suffrage is likewise fundamental in a democracy. It is a question of some importance whether the suffrages ought to be public or secret. Cicero observes that the laws which rendered them secret toward the close of the republic were the cause of its decline. But as this is differently practised in different republics, I shall offer here my thoughts concerning this subject.

The people's suffrages ought doubtless to be public; and this should be considered as a fundamental law of democracy. The lower class ought to be directed by those of higher rank, and restrained within bounds by the gravity of eminent personages. Hence, by rendering the suffrages secret in the Roman Republic, all was lost; it was no longer possible to direct a populace that sought its own destruction. But when the body of the nobles are to vote in an aristocracy, or in a democracy the senate, as the business is then only to prevent intrigues, the suffrages can not be too secret.

Intriguing in a senate is dangerous; it is dangerous also in a body of nobles; but not so among the people, whose nature is to act through passion. In countries where they have no share in the government, we often see them as much inflamed on account of an actor as ever they could be for the welfare of the state. The misfortune of a republic is when intrigues are at an end; which happens when the people are gained by bribery and corruption: in this case they grow indifferent to public affairs, and avarice becomes their predominant passion. Unconcerned about the government and everything belonging to it, they quietly wait for their hire.

It is likewise a fundamental law in democracies, that the people should have the sole power to enact laws. And yet there are a thousand occasions on which it is necessary the senate should have the power of decreeing; nay, it is frequently proper to make some trial of a law before it is established. The constitutions of Rome and Athens were excellent. The decrees of the senate had the force of laws for the space of a year, but did not become perpetual till they were ratified by the consent of the people.

III. In an aristocracy the supreme power is lodged in the hands of a certain number of persons. These are invested both with the legislative and executive authority; and the rest of the people are, in respect to them, the same as the subjects of a monarchy in regard to the sovereign.

They do not vote here by lot, for this would be productive of inconveniences only. And indeed, in a government where the most mortifying distinctions are already established, though they were to be chosen by lot, still they would not cease to be odious; it is the nobleman they envy, and not the magistrate.

When the nobility are numerous, there must be a senate to regulate the affairs which the body of the nobles are incapable of deciding, and to prepare others for their decision. In this case it may be said that the aristocracy is in some measure in the senate, the democracy in the body of the nobles, and the people are a cipher.

It would be a very happy thing in an aristocracy if the people, in some measure, could be raised from their state of annihilation. Thus at Genoa, the bank of St. George being administered by the people gives them a certain influence in the government, whence their whole prosperity is derived.

The senators ought by no means to have the right of naming their own members; for this would be the only way to perpetuate abuses. At Rome, which in its early years was a kind of aristocracy, the senate did not fill up the vacant places in their own body; the new members were nominated by the censors.

In a republic, the sudden rise of a private citizen to exorbitant power produces monarchy, or something more than monarchy. In the latter the laws have provided for, or in some measure adapted themselves to, the constitution; and the principle of government checks the monarch: but in a republic, where a private citizen has obtained an exorbitant power, the abuse of this power is much greater, because the laws foresaw it not, and consequently made no provision against it.

Book IV

CHAPTER V. OF EDUCATION IN A REPUBLICAN GOVERNMENT

It is in a republican government that the whole power of education is required. The fear of despotic governments naturally arises of itself amid threats and punishments; the honour of monarchies is favoured by the passions, and favours them in its turn; but virtue is a self-renunciation, which is ever arduous and painful.

This virtue may be defined as the love of the laws and of our country. As such love requires a constant preference of public to private interest, it is the source of all private virtues; for they are nothing more than this very preference itself.

This love is peculiar to democracies. In these alone the government is intrusted to private citizens. Now a government is like everything else: to preserve it we must love it.

Has it ever been known that kings were not fond of monarchy, or that despotic princes hated arbitrary power?

Everything therefore depends on establishing this love in a republic; and to inspire it ought to be the principal business of education; but the surest way of instilling it into children is for parents to set them an example.

People have it generally in their power to communicate their ideas to their children; but they are still better able to transfuse their passions.

If it happens otherwise, it is because the impressions made at home are effaced by those they have received abroad.

It is not the young people that degenerate; they are not spoiled till those of maturer age are already sunk into corruption.

Book V

Chapter II. What Is Meant by Virtue in a Political State

Virtue in a republic is a most simple thing; it is a love of the republic; it is a sensation, and not a consequence of acquired knowledge; a sensation that may be felt by the meanest as well as by the highest person in the state. When the common people adopt good maxims, they adhere to them more steadily than those whom we call gentlemen. It is very rarely that corruption commences with the former: nay, they frequently derive from their imperfect light a stronger attachment to the established laws and customs.

The love of our country is conducive to a purity of morals, and the latter is again conducive to the former. The less we are able to satisfy our private passions, the more we abandon ourselves to those of a general nature. How comes it that monks are so fond of their order? It is owing to the very cause that renders the order insupportable. Their rule debars them from all those things by which the ordinary passions are fed; there remains therefore only this passion for the very rule that torments them. The more austere it is—that is, the more it curbs their inclinations—the more force it gives to the only passion left them.

Chapter III. What Is Meant by a Love of the Republic in a Democracy

A love of the republic in a democracy is a love of the democracy; as the latter is that of equality.

A love of the democracy is likewise that of frugality. Since every individual ought here to enjoy the same happiness and the same advantages, they should consequently taste the same pleasures and form the same hopes, which can not be expected but from a general frugality.

The love of equality in a democracy limits ambition to the sole desire, to the sole happiness, of doing greater services to our country than the rest of our fellow-citizens. They can not all render her equal services, but they all ought to serve her with equal alacrity. At our coming into the world, we contract an immense debt to our country, which we can never discharge.

Hence distinctions here arise from the principle of equality, even when it seems to be removed by signal services or superior abilities.

The love of frugality limits the desire of possessing to the search for necessaries for our family, and superfluities go to our country. Riches give a power which a citizen can not use for himself, for then he would be no longer equal. They likewise procure pleasures which he ought not to enjoy, because these would be also repugnant to the equality.

Thus well-regulated democracies, by establishing domestic frugality, made way at the same time for public expenses, as was the case at Rome and Athens, when magnificence and profusion arose from the very fund of frugality. And as religion commands us to have pure and unspotted hands when we make our offerings to the gods, the laws required a frugality of life to enable them to be liberal to our country.

The good sense and happiness of individuals depend greatly upon the mediocrity of their abilities and fortunes. Therefore, as a republic, where the laws have placed many in a middling station, is composed of wise men, it will be wisely governed; as it is composed of happy men, it will be extremely happy.

Book VII

Chapter II. Of Sumptuary Laws in a Democracy

We have observed that in a republic, where riches are equally divided, there can be no such thing as luxury; and as we have shown in the fifth book, that this equal distribution constitutes the excellence of a republican government; hence it follows that the less luxury there is in a republic, the more it is perfect. There was none among the old Romans, none among the Lacedæmonians; and in republics where this equality is not quite lost, the spirit of commerce, industry, and virtue renders every man able and willing to live on his own property, and consequently prevents the growth of luxury.

The laws concerning the new division of lands, insisted upon so eagerly in some republics, were of the most salutary nature. They are dangerous only as they are sudden. By reducing instantly the wealth of some, and increasing that of others, they form a revolution in each family, and must produce a general one in the state.

In proportion as luxury gains ground in a republic, the minds of the people are turned toward their particular interests. Those who are allowed only what is necessary have nothing but their own reputation and their country's glory in view. But a soul depraved by luxury has many other desires, and soon becomes an enemy to the laws that confine it. The luxury in which the garrison of Rhegium began to live was the cause of their massacring the inhabitants.

No sooner were the Romans corrupted than their desires became boundless and immense. Of this we may judge by the price they set on things. A pitcher of Falernian wine was sold for a hundred Roman denarii; a barrel of salt meat from the kingdom of Pontus cost four hundred; a good cook four talents; and for boys, no price was reckoned too great. When the whole world, impelled by the force of corruption, is immersed in voluptuousness, what must then become of virtue?

CHAPTER VII. OF PUBLIC CONTINENCY

So many are the imperfections that attend the loss of virtue in women, and so greatly are their minds depraved when this principal guard is removed, that in a popular state public incontinency may be considered as the last of miseries, and as a certain forerunner of a change in the constitution.

Hence it is that the sage legislators of republican states have ever required of women a particular gravity of manners. They have proscribed not only vice, but the very appearance of it. They have banished even all commerce of gallantry—a commerce that produces idleness, that renders the women corrupters, even before they are corrupted, that gives a value to trifles, and debases things of importance; a commerce, in fine, that makes people act entirely by the maxims of ridicule, in which the women are so perfectly skilled.

Book XI

CHAPTER II. DIFFERENT SIGNIFICATIONS OF THE WORD LIBERTY

There is no word that admits of more various significations, and has made more varied impressions on the human mind, than that of Liberty. Some have taken it as a means of deposing a person on whom they had conferred a tyrannical authority; others for the power of choosing a superior whom they are obliged to obey;

others for the right of bearing arms, and of being thereby enabled to use violence; others, in fine, for the privilege of being governed by a native of their own country, or by their own laws. A certain nation for a long time thought liberty consisted in the privilege of wearing a long beard. Some have annexed this name to one form of government exclusive of others: those who liked a monarchical state gave it to monarchy. Thus they have all applied the name of liberty to the government most suitable to their own customs and inclinations; and as in republics the people have not so constant and so present a view of the causes of their misery, and as the magistrates seem to act only in conformity to the laws, hence liberty is generally said to reside in republics, and to be banished from monarchies. In fine, as in democracies, the people seem to act almost as they please, this sort of government has been deemed the most free, and the power of the people has been confounded with their liberty.

Chapter III. In What Liberty Consists

It is true that in democracies the people seem to act as they please; but political liberty does not consist in an unlimited freedom. In governments—that is, in societies directed by laws—liberty can consist only in the power of doing what we ought to will, and in not being constrained to do what we ought not to will.

We must have continually present to our minds the difference between independence and liberty. Liberty is a right of doing whatever the laws permit, and if a citizen could do what they forbid he would be no longer possessed of liberty, because all his fellow-citizens would have the same power.

Democratic and aristocratic states are not in their own nature free. Political liberty is to be found only in moderate governments; and even in these it is not always found. It is there only when there is no abuse of power. But constant experience shows us that every man invested with power is apt to abuse it, and to carry his authority as far as it will go. Is it not strange, though true, to say that virtue itself has need of limits?

To prevent this abuse, it is necessary from the very nature of things that power should be a check to power. A government may be so constituted as no man shall be compelled to do things to which the law does not oblige him, nor forced to abstain from things which the law permits.

CHAPTER IV. OF THE END OR VIEW OF DIFFERENT GOVERNMENTS

Though all governments have the same general end, which is that of preservation, yet each has another particular object. Increase of dominion was the object of Rome; war, that of Sparta; religion, that of the Jewish laws; commerce, that of Marseilles; public tranquillity, that of the laws of China; navigation, that of the laws of Rhodes; natural liberty, that of the policy of the savages; in general, the pleasures of the prince, that of despotic states; that of monarchies, the prince's and the kingdom's glory; the independence of individuals is the end aimed at by the laws of Poland, thence results the oppression of the whole.

One nation there is also in the world that has for the direct end of its constitution political liberty.[1] We shall presently examine the principles on which this liberty is founded; if they are sound, liberty will appear in its highest perfection.

To discover political liberty in a constitution, no great labour is requisite. If we are capable of seeing it where it exists, it is soon found, and we need not go far in search of it.

Book XV

CHAPTER II. ORIGIN OF THE RIGHT OF SLAVERY AMONG THE ROMAN JURISCONSULTS

One would never have imagined that slavery should owe its birth to pity, and that this should have been excited in three different ways.

The law of nations to prevent prisoners from being put to death has allowed them to be made slaves. The civil law of the Romans empowered debtors, who were subject to be ill-used by their creditors, to sell themselves. And the law of Nature requires that children whom a father in a state of servitude is no longer able to maintain should be reduced to the same state as the father.

These reasons of the jurisconsults are all false. It is false that killing in war is lawful, unless in a case of absolute necessity; but when a man has made another his slave, he can not be said to have been under a necessity of taking away his life, since he actually did not take it away. War gives no other right over prisoners than to disable them from doing any further harm by securing their

[1] Montesquieu refers to England.

persons. All nations concur in detesting the murdering of prisoners in cold blood.

Neither is it true that a freeman can sell himself. Sale implies a price; now, when a person sells himself, his whole substance immediately devolves to his master; the master, therefore, in that case, gives nothing, and the slave receives nothing. You will say he has a peculium.[2] But this peculium goes along with his person. If it is not lawful for a man to kill himself because he robs his country of his person, for the same reason he is not allowed to barter his freedom. The freedom of every citizen constitutes a part of the public liberty, and in a democratic state is even a part of the sovreignty. To sell one's freedom is so repugnant to all reason as can scarcely be supposed in any man. If liberty may be rated with respect to the buyer, it is beyond all price to the seller. The civil law, which authorizes a division of goods could not include in those goods a part of the men who were to make this division. The same law annuls all iniquitous contracts; surely then it affords redress in a contract where the grievance is most enormous.

The third way is birth, which falls with the two former; for if a man could not sell himself, much less could he sell an unborn infant. If a prisoner of war is not to be reduced to slavery, much less are his children.

The lawfulness of putting a malefactor to death arises from this circumstance: the law by which he is punished was made for his security. A murderer, for instance, has enjoyed the benefit of the very law which condemns him; it has been a continual protection to him; he can not, therefore, object to it. But it is not so with the slave. The law of slavery can never be beneficial to him; it is in all cases against him, without ever being for his advantage; and therefore this law is contrary to the fundamental principle of all societies.

If it be pretended that it has been beneficial to him, as his master has provided for his subsistence, slavery, at this rate, should be limited to those who are incapable of earning their livelihood. But who will desire such slaves? As to infants, Nature, who has supplied their mothers with milk, had provided for their sustenance; and the remainder of their childhood approaches so near the age in which they are most capable of being of service that he who

[2] Private property. Allowed to slaves under Roman law.

supports them can not be said to give them an equivalent which can entitle him to be their master.

Nor is slavery less opposed to the civil law than to that of Nature. What civil law can restrain a slave from running away, since he is not a member of society, and consequently has no interest in any civil institutions? He can be retained only by a family law—that is, by the master's authority.

CHAPTER IV. OF THE SLAVERY OF THE NEGROES

Were I to vindicate our right to make slaves of the Negroes, these should be my arguments:

The Europeans, having extirpated the Americans, were obliged to make slaves of the Africans, for clearing such vast tracts of land.

Sugar would be too dear if the plants which produce it were cultivated by any other than slaves.

These creatures are all over black, and with such a flat nose that they can scarcely be pitied.

It is hardly to be believed that God, who is a wise Being, should place a soul, especially a good soul, in such a black, ugly body.

It is so natural to look upon colour as the criterion of human nature, that the Asiatics, among whom eunuchs are employed, always deprive the blacks of their resemblance to us by a more opprobrious distinction.

The colour of the skin may be determined by that of the hair, which, among the Egyptians, the best philosophers in the world, was of such importance that they put to death all the red-haired men who fell into their hands. The Negroes prefer a glass necklace to that gold which polite nations so highly value. Can there be a greater proof of their wanting common sense?

It is impossible for us to suppose these creatures to be men, because, allowing them to be men, a suspicion would follow that we ourselves are not Christians.

Weak minds exaggerate too much the wrong done to the Africans. For were the case as they state it, would the European powers, who make so many needless conventions among themselves, have failed to enter into a general one, in behalf of humanity and compassion?

31.   Linguet, Theory of Civil Laws, or Fundamental Principles of Society

Book V—Chapter VIII. What We Should Think of the Declamations of the Philosophers Against Servitude in General

IT IS quite true that the authors of whom I have spoken, in their outbursts against hereditary servitude, also proscribe original servitude. They proclaim that the right of slavery is in general an unjust right. Still more, they prove it. In that regard I think as they do, as I have already said. Between them and me there is this difference: they think this injustice to be harmful, and I believe it to be necessary; they condemn it as the enemy of all rights, and I consider it their foundation; they pity mankind for having adopted it and regard its destruction as the first step toward the common happiness of society, whereas I, while pitying mankind too for having committed this imprudence, am entirely convinced that it is beyond our power to rectify it without destroying that same society which owes its existence to it.

They reason on the basis of a chimerical equilibrium which they stubbornly believe to be possible, and I on the basis of an obvious and indisputable fact. In order for the two trays of a scale to remain at an even height, it is necessary not to put a heavier weight on one than on the other. Now let us inquire whether society can maintain itself when its two extremities bear two equal weights. Society can only begin when one of its trays facilitates, by its lowering, the elevation of the other one. It subsists only because of this inequality. Slavery is the weight with which it is necessary to oppress the side that goes down. *"It is not true,"* says M. de Montesquieu, *"that a free man can sell himself."* I agree; but is it true that one cannot capture him? Why is it not true for him as for all other animals, whom force subjects and who receive nothing in

SOURCE: S. N. H. Linguet, *Théorie des lois civiles; ou, Principes fondamentaux de la société* (London, 1767). Translated by the editor.

exchange for the freedom of which they are deprived? *If it has a price for the person who buys it, it is priceless for the person who sells it.* I agree. But what value can it have for the one who takes it? Its value in regard to him consists in the use he makes of it, in the enjoyment he derives from it, and not in the equivalent that he gives for it.

The civil law, continues M. de Montesquieu, which has allowed men a share in property, has not been able to put among those properties that part of the men who were supposed to do the sharing, but the law, without doubt, was able to include among them the part that was not to have a share, and that is exactly what it has not failed to do. This operation it was even obliged to perform. I have proven that without it there would not have been any wealth to share. In the history of the world human freedom has been the first article of commerce, the first object of ownership. It is poverty which has produced wealth; but it is slavery that has made poverty. It is only as a result of this fateful filiation that civil law, which has made permanent the rather dubious legitimacy of its ancestors, appeared.

This civil law *makes restitution in contracts which contain a wrong; it cannot avoid making restitution against an agreement which contains the most enormous wrong of all.* This principle is true in special cases; but it is not true in the case in question, in which restitution would be even more impossible than the enormity of the wrong. If you make restitution to me for slavery, because it violates natural rights, then make restitution to me also for all kinds of property, which violate them no less. If my brother has the right to seize exclusive possession of a field which our common mother has given to us in association, why should he not also have the right to force me to work the field for his profit? In this matter, as in several others that are more difficult to conceive, it is only the first step that counts. Once it has been taken, it implies and legitimizes all the succeeding steps.

To what then do the *philosophes'* declamation on this matter come down to? To very little. They never account for more than one aspect of the question. They excoriate slavery and exalt society. But that is only to try to strengthen a statue by breaking its pedestal. Slavery is harsh for those who must bear it—who would deny that? But poverty is also harsh for the unfortunate wretches it depresses. How pleasant is the condition of a day worker who, after having made 10 *sous* for a hard day's work in winter time, goes back at night to his ice-covered hut to eat with trembling hand a crust of black bread near the straw mat on which he is to sleep?

As for you, well-to-do *philosophe*, who in your study, seated near a crackling fire, take pleasure in these dreams about freedom, why don't you help to make them come true by sharing some of your wealth with that poor wretch whose just share you have taken? Since you are so scrupulous, return to him what you have taken from him. Give us the practical example of such honorable restitution, whose justice you are so insistent on demonstrating. Or, if this idea frightens you, if in reality you are more attached to self-love than to the love of humanity that you display so magnificently in your books, then stop talking about restitution. Let the world go on as it is. Don't try to make the principles of your ancestors, from which you depart only with your pens, ridiculous and odious. Do not think of their justice or injustice, but only of their necessity.

I shall develop these reflections further. What I say here suffices to prove that slavery is just in its continuance, even if it is not in its beginning. It is quite legitimate for the wretches who are condemned to it to weep bitterly over their fate; but the legislator must not be moved by their tears. It is not insensitivity that should make him pitiless, but necessity. The immensity of the ills they suffer is no more reason to relieve them from those ills than the fatigue of a bad road is a reason to oblige a traveller to get off his horse and to journey on foot.

Conclusion of This Book

What can we conclude from this book and even in general from everything that has preceded? A cruel truth but one that it is necessary to tell men; an axiom as indisputable as those of geometry, in the eyes of whoever uses his reason; a principle which is beyond doubt, according to the observations I have just developed and according to those which anyone will be able to add to them. This axiom is that dependency, slavery, baseness are, as a great man of our time has put it on a less serious occasion, the lot of three fourths of human beings. It is because they are subjected to the pains of being downtrodden that the other quarter, who govern them, are able to enjoy a comfortable ease. Whatever name you give to those two springs of society; whatever mask you use to cover them; whether they be called domesticity or servitude,

empire or liberty, it always means for the one a total self-abnega-
tion, a complete sacrifice of the rights we consider a part of being a
man; and for the others a doubling, or if you prefer, an abuse of
these same rights.

Whether one is served by bought slaves or by hired workers, it
makes no difference, since one is still being served. The serf is not
in a harsher dependence on his master than is the day worker on his
need. Their chains woven from the same matter have only different colors. Here they are black and seem massive; there they seem
less sad and lighter. But weigh them with impartiality, and you
will find no difference; both are made by the same necessity. They
have exactly the same weight, or rather if there is a bit of disadvantage on one side, it is on the side which seems to be lighter. . . .

Do you not see that the opulence of the shepherds depends on
the obedience and, since we must say it, on the crushing of this
mass of the herd? If the sheep, which compose it, ever took it into
their heads to resist the dog who herds them together, would they
not soon be dispersed and destroyed, and their masters ruined?
Believe me: in his interest, in yours, and even in theirs, let them go
on thinking as they do now, that this dog who barks at them is, by
himself, stronger than all of them together.

Let them run, stupidly, just at the sight of his shadow. Everybody will be the better for it. You will find it easier to bring them
together, to shear their fleeces. They will be more easily protected
against devouring wolves; protected, it is true, only in order to be
eaten by men. But after all, that fate was assigned to them the
moment they entered a barn. Before talking about letting them out,
begin by overthrowing the barn, that is, society.

I know that this language is not the one ordinarily found in
books; but it is the language of reason and truth. I should undoubtedly win a lot more favor by arguing on the other side; it is much
easier to wax eloquent about it. It is more honorable, and even
much easier, to seem to take the side of humanity against its oppressors. It is so easy to declaim against the powerful and against
the masters! It is easy to find words and readers when presenting
only ideas about independence. The multitude is bound to be with
you when they rapturously contemplate these romantic pictures.
Sometimes you even win over the wise who are seduced when the
picture is effectively done. . . .

Either kill my tyrant or do not show me the horror of his
tyranny. Do not tell me that you can free me from his grasp since

nothing is more false. Let me believe that the torments I am enduring are just and inevitable. Perhaps I shall find in the impossibility of escaping resources to bear more patiently the anguish in which I am condemned to die.

What then is the purpose of your discourse? I am suffering, and according to you I could, and even should, not suffer. I am perishing in chains, and you cry that no one has the right to keep me in chains.[1] What is your purpose? Are you trying to force me to unite in my heart the feeling of injustice to that of slavery? Are you trying to double my regrets by increasing my misery, and to climax my despair by showing me the image of a happiness to which I can never aspire?

How much wiser would be the terrible but sincere voice that would say to me: "Suffer and die in chains; that is your destiny. Society lives on the destruction of freedom, just as carnivorous animals live on the murder of weak animals. Since you were not born a tiger do not murmur against providence which made you to be born a lamb. Be satisfied with your lot, since you cannot hope for another. And even when the monster whose food you are to be devours you, submit to your fate with resignation, since it is not possible to change it; since by putting off your torture you would not avoid it, and your resistance, by making your end slower, would only be making it more cruel.

If it is true that there are motives capable of consoling men who are reduced to slavery, or to some equivalent or worse abasement under another name, it is these. They may even be strengthened by the spectacle of hierarchy which we can observe in the world. In whatever rank we find ourselves placed, we can always flatter ourselves that there is some one lower. The vilest of Polish peasants, leading an ass that his master has entrusted to him, may think that without society this wretched animal would not be submitted to him. The rustic scepter with which he governs it may compensate for the humiliation he undergoes at the approach of the imperious rod which controls him. By exercising the right to strike without pity, he must feel that the same reason which gives it to him also imposes on him the necessity of receiving just as rude blows without complaint. It is above all of this necessity that he

[1] A common misinterpretation of the opening sentence of Chapter 1 of Rousseau's *Contrat social:* "Man was born free, and everywhere he is in chains."

must be convinced, since it is the base and link of society; and that is why the philosophy which urges patience is much more reasonable than the philosophy which provokes men to revolt.

32. Morelly, Code of Nature

Part I. What Kind of Education Would Prevent Vice

SINCE reason in man replaces a kind of blind feeling, he was made to be the most gentle and manageable of all animals. He would indeed have become that, if his stupid feelings had at first been mechanically used to familiarize him only with peaceful habits. Reason would then have perfected them. Reason's function is not (whatever our philosophers may say) to combat our violent passions, or to prevent disorders which would never have existed if man had been prepared and, so to speak, tamed by the mechanism of an education in conformity with our principles. He would not have needed to use his mental faculties, except to know and enjoy the advantages of his wisely regulated society. Accustomed from early childhood to bend to its laws, it would never have occurred to him to break them. No fear of lacking subsistence or necessary and useful things would have aroused excessive desires within him. If his parents had wisely prevented him from acquiring any idea of property, if all rivalry had been forestalled or forbidden in the use of the communal wealth, would it have been possible for man even to think of grabbing, either by force or by ruse, what no one would ever have contested?

MOST LEGISLATORS HAVE BROKEN THE LINKS OF SOCIABILITY AND CAUSED OR MAINTAINED THE HARMFUL EFFECTS OF THAT RUPTURE

. . . Let us now show that those supposedly wise men, which we like imbeciles admire, have, by depriving half of mankind of the

SOURCE: Morelly, Code de La Nature (Paris, 1755), translated by the editor.

goods of nature, abrogated its wise arrangements and opened the gates to all crimes.

These guides, as blind as those they have claimed to lead, have extinguished all the motives of affection which would necessarily have been the ties among all the forces of mankind. They have converted foresight and mutual help into timid worry, which is shared by the isolated members of the whole body. They have, by agitating these disunited parts in a thousand contrary ways, confused everything and lit the fires of burning greed. They have aroused the hunger, the voracity of insatiable avarice; their constitutions have exposed man to the continuous risks of utter want. Is it astonishing that, to ward off these dangers, passions have become enkindled to the point of fury? Could they have gone about it better in order to make this animal devour his own kind?

The Natural State of Savage Nations Which Are Susceptible to the Rules of a Wise Government

. . . [The Legislator] will be able to distribute work among the members of society; establish the time schedules for various general or special occupations; combine mutual assistance; calculate the various degrees of usefulness of the several professions; define what each must contribute to the Republic in order to provide for the needs of its members. Concerning all these matters and the numbers of agents, the Legislator will establish the allotment of work. He will propose the age most suitable for maintaining the public order and the economy, and the most robust will be charged with carrying this out. . . .

When things are arranged in this way, who will ever think of wanting to dominate others, when there is no property which can inspire the desire to subjugate others? There can be no tyrants in a society in which all authority consists precisely of assuming the painful duties, without participating in any of the necessities or luxuries of life except those which one has in common with the other citizens and without any advantages or rewards except the esteem and affection of one's fellow citizens.

True Causes of the Decadence and Revolutions of the Most Flourishing States

If you ask what governs men, from the scepter to the crook, from the tiara to the lowest frock, the answer is easy: self-interest, or an outside interest which we adopt out of vanity and which always depends on the former. But where do all the monsters come from? From property.

Therefore, oh sages of the earth, you look in vain for a perfect state of freedom wherever such tyrants reign. Discourse as much as you will about the best form of government; inquire into the ways of founding the wisest republic; make a populous nation find its happiness in observing your laws; if you have not cut out property by the roots, you have done nothing. Some day your Republic will fall into the most deplorable state. There is no use attributing those sad changes to *fortune*, to a *blind fate* which causes the instability of empires as well as that of individuals; those words are empty of meaning.

THE PRINCIPAL MOTIVE OF ALL HUMAN ACTION AND THE PRINCIPAL OF ALL SOCIAL HARMONY

There can be no question that the motive or aim of every human action is the desire to be happy. It is not less certain that this desire is the effect of an essential property of a being who is destined to know that he exists and to watch over his own self-preservation. In a word, this desire is an effect of our sensitivity. Now, in order to make us obey its laws promptly and efficaciously, sensitivity must make us refer everything to ourselves without reflection, and make us imagine that everything was made for us, and that without us everything that exists would be without point. It alone can allow a man to say, like Tiberius:

Me misceatur igne terra mortuo.[1]

However, it is from the force and vehemence of this feeling that providence draws the principle of all social harmony. I have already explained that this impulse, in a creature of feeling who we may suppose to be the only one of its kind, is analogous to a rocking motion impressed on matter, which soon loses its uniformity to give way to the variety of the most beautiful combinations among bodies. It is according to similar rules that God built and governs the moral world. But let us put aside comparisons which are not within reach of every reader.

Man always and inevitably decides to be happy. His powerlessness constantly warns him that he cannot be happy without help from others. He knows, too, that there are innumerable beings who

---

[1] "When I'm dead, let earth be mixed with fire."

possess the same desire. At each moment he is convinced that his happiness depends on that of others and that benevolence is the best and surest means to his present happiness. Everything seems to cry out to him: "You want to be happy, then be good to others. Without worrying at first about where your being came from, learn that you cannot enjoy it without benevolence. Do you want to elevate yourself to the knowledge of your Creator? Be benevolent."

Why is he deaf to this counsel and why does he listen to advice that is diametrically opposed to his happiness?

It is because popular morality, like politics, has overthrown and corrupted most ideas, as well as the order of ideas.

Let us therefore try to recognize and to follow the true path of nature. . . .

MODEL OF LEGISLATION IN
CONFORMITY WITH NATURE'S INTENTIONS

Nothing in society shall belong separately to anyone as individual property, except the things he is actually using either for his needs, his pleasures, or his daily work.

Every citizen will be publicly supported and employed.

Every citizen shall contribute his share to the public good according to his strength, his talent, and his age. His duties will be determined according to these factors in conformity with the distributive laws.

Nothing, according to the sacred laws, will be sold or exchanged among citizens, so that, for example, a person who needs some herbs, vegetables, or fruits will go to the public square, where those things will be brought by those who grow them, and take whatever he needs for a single day's supply. . . . If someone needs an article of clothing, he will take it from the man who makes it; the latter will take the cloth from the one who manufactures it; and the latter will take the raw materials from the storehouse where they will have been brought by those who gather them. And so with all other things that will be distributed to each father for his use and for his children.

Every citizen, without exception, from the age of twenty to twenty-five will be obliged to be an agricultural worker unless he is excused on the grounds of infirmity.

Around a regularly shaped square, public stores with all kinds of goods and public assembly halls will be erected in a uniform and pleasing style.

Outside of this center the living quarters of the city will be arranged in equal size and shape, divided in regular fashion into streets.

All the buildings of each city will be built, maintained, and repaired by that corps of workers who are allotted to architecture. In each trade guild there will be a master for each ten or twenty workers. He will have the job of teaching them, of inspecting their work, of accounting for their work and conduct to the chief of the guild, who will be appointed annually. Each master will enjoy a life appointment and will have a turn as chief.

At the age of ten, every citizen will begin to learn the trade to which he is inclined, or for which he shows ability, without being forced. Between fifteen and eighteen he will marry. From twenty to twenty-five he will work at agriculture. At twenty-six he will be a master in his first trade if he takes it up again. . . .

Every citizen at the age of thirty will dress according to his taste but without unusual luxury. He will eat with his family, temperately and without excess. A law will order the senators and the chiefs to repress such excesses severely and to give an example of moderation themselves.

Between the ages of ten and thirty, the young people in each trade will wear a uniform dress of the same cloth, clean but coarse and suitable to their occupation. Each guild will be distinguished by a color in conformity to the principal object of its work, or by some other mark.

Every citizen will have a work outfit and a holiday outfit which will be modestly adorned and attractive; all this according to the wealth of the Republic and without any ornament that might indicate preference or advantage for any person. All vanity will be suppressed by the leaders and the heads of families.

Every citizen, as soon as he has reached the age of puberty, will marry. Nobody will be excused unless nature or health is an obstacle. Nobody may live in an unmarried state until the age of forty.

At the beginning of each year the marriage ceremonies will be publicly celebrated. The young of both sexes will be assembled, and in the presence of the senate, each boy will choose the girl he likes and, having obtained her consent, will marry her.

A first marriage is indissoluble for ten years. After that, divorce will be allowed either with the consent of both parties or at the desire of one. Divorced women will not be allowed to remarry individuals younger than they or younger than the one they have left. Only widows will have this freedom. Persons of either sex who have been married will not be allowed to marry young people who have not been married. When the nation has reached a point of growth at which the number of citizens who are born is approximately equal to the number of those who die, the tribes and cities will be kept at a stable level.

Mothers will nurse their children if their health allows, and will be required to do so unless they can prove ill-health.

At the age of five, all the children in each tribe will be assembled and each sex separately lodged and fed in a house built for that purpose. Their food, clothing, and first instruction will be uniformly the same without any distinctions, according to the rules prescribed by the senate.

As the children's reason begins to develop they will be taught the laws of our country; they will be taught to respect them, to obey their parents, the leaders, and the elderly. They will be trained to be helpful to their equals, to cultivate their friendship, never to lie. . . .

At the age of ten every child will leave this common paternal home and go to the workshops, where he will be lodged, fed, clothed, and taught by the masters and leaders of each trade, whom he shall obey as his own parents; this all together in each guild and workshop, where each sex will be separately instructed in the occupations that are suitable for it.

The masters and mistresses, like the guild leaders, will join moral to mechanical instruction.

The number of persons who will work at the sciences and the arts, which demand more wisdom, intelligence, skill, and talents than bodily strength, will be determined for each kind of study and for each city. The citizens who show the greatest talent will be taught young, without this kind of study or work excusing them from agricultural labor when they reach the proper age. Nobody except the prescribed number of teachers and students selected for the arts and sciences will be allowed to apply himself to them before the age of thirty.

Any moral philosophy not built on the plan and system of the laws will be absolutely forbidden. The observations and precepts of that science will reinforce the usefulness and wisdom of those laws. . . .

There will be a public code for all sciences; nothing will ever be added to the metaphysical and moral parts of it beyond the limits prescribed by the laws. Only physical, mathematical, or mechanical discoveries, confirmed by experiment and reasoning, may be added.

Each chapter of the laws will be separately engraved on columns or pyramids in the public square of each city. Their intentions will always be followed literally according to the exact meaning of the text without the slightest change or alteration ever being allowed.

33. Helvétius, On the Mind and A Treatise on Man

A. On the Mind

SECOND DISCOURSE. ON THE MIND IN RELATION TO SOCIETY

CHAPTER XV. OF THE USE ACCRUING TO MORALITY, FROM THE
KNOWLEDGE OF THE PRINCIPLES LAID DOWN IN THE
PRECEDING CHAPTERS

IF MORALITY hitherto has little contributed to the happiness of mankind, it is not owing to any want of perspicuity or beauty of style, or propriety and loftiness of sentiment in the moralists: but amidst all their superior talents, it must be owned that they have not often enough considered the different vices of nations as necessarily resulting from the different form of their government; yet, it is only by considering morality in this point of light, that it can become of any real use to men. What have hitherto been the effects of all the splendid maxims of morality? If some individuals have been corrected by them of faults which perhaps they reproached themselves with, no change in the manners of nations

SOURCE: Helvétius, De L'Homme (London, 1776), an anonymous eighteenth-century translation.

have [sic] been produced. What is this to be imputed to? It is because the vices of a people, if I may presume to say so, always lie at the bottom of its legislation. There he must search, who would pluck up the root whence its vices arise. He who wants either penetration, or courage, for such an undertaking, is in this respect of little or no use to the universe. To attempt extinguishing the vices annexed to the legislation of a people, without making any change in this legislation, is no less than rejecting the just consequence after admitting the principles.

What can be hoped for from so many declamations against the falsity of women, if this vice be the necessary effect of an opposition betwixt the desires of nature, and the sentiments which by the law of decency women are forced to affect? In Malabar and Madagascar, all women are faithful, because they have gallants without number, and they never pitch on a husband till after repeated trials; it is the same with the savages of New Orleans, and of those people where the relations of the Great Sun, the princes of the blood may, on any disgust taken at their husbands, dismiss them and marry others. In such countries, no unfaithful wives are heard of, because they have no manner of interest to be so.

Very far am I from inferring that from these examples the same manners should be introduced among us; I only say, that women cannot reasonably be reproached with a breach of faith which decency and the laws, as it were, imposed on them as a necessity; and that whilst the causes are suffered to subsist, the effects will continue.

For a second instance, we shall take defamation. This is a vice, but a necessary vice, because in every country where the citizens have no share in the administration of public affairs, these citizens, being thus little concerned about mental improvement, must stagnate in a scandalous sloth. Now, if in this country it be the fashion to contract a numerous acquaintance, and to frequent public places, and loquacity is accounted the mark of breeding and spirit; he who is ignorant, and not able to discourse of things, must necessarily make persons the subject of his talk: and panegyric being insupportable, are obliged to talk scandal: thus this vice cannot be suppressed without abolishing the productive cause, without delivering the citizens from idleness, and consequently without altering the form of government. Why is the man of sense generally less a busybody in private companies than the man of fashion? It is because the former, taken up with greater objects, speaks of persons only as they have, like great men, an immediate relation with great things; likewise the man of sense, as he never defames but by way of revenge, it is very rarely he defames; whereas the man of the world must either defame or be mute.

What I say of defaming, I likewise say of debauchery, against which the moralists have always so violently inveighed: debauchery is so generally allowed to be a necessary consequence of luxury, that any farther proof of it would be superfluous. Now, if luxury, which I am very far from thinking, but which is commonly believed, be very useful to the state; if, as may be easily shewn, the taste for it cannot be extinguished, and citizens brought to the observance of sumptuary laws, without altering the form of government, then some alterations of this kind must take place, antecedently to any hopes of abolishing debauchery. Every harangue on this head is good divinity, but not policy; the object of policy and legislation is the opulency, power, and happiness of a people: now with regard to this, I say, that if luxury be really useful to France, it would be ridiculous to attempt to introduce there an austerity of manners incompatible with a taste for luxury. There is no proportion between the advantages which commerce and luxury procure to a state in its present constitution (advantages which to suppress debauchery it must forego) and the infinitely small evil occasioned by the love of women. This is to complain of finding in a rich mine some sparks of copper intermixed with veins of gold.

Wherever luxury is necessary, it is solecism in politics to account intriguing a moral vice; and if it must be called a moral vice, the consequence is that, in some countries and some ages, there are useful vices;[1] and that it is to the mud of the Nile Egypt owes its fertility. In effect, on a political examination of the behaviour of intriguing women, it will be found that, though in certain respects blamable, they are, in others, of great use to the public; that for instance, in the use they make of their money, they are more advantageous to the state than the most virtuous of their sex. By the desire of pleating, which sends an intriguing woman to the

[1] Helvétius echoes Mandeville's theory.

mercer and milliner, she not only saves an infinite number of workmen from the indigence into which sumptuary laws at once would plunge them, but the same desire puts her upon acts of the most judicious charity. If luxury be supposed useful to a nation, is it not the women of dress, who by exciting the industry of the artists of luxury, continually improve their usefulness to the state? Virtuous women therefore are not so well advised by their directors in bestowing on beggars and criminals, as intriguing women by the desire of pleasing. These support useful members of society: the others nuisances, even the enemies of mankind.

From what I have said it follows that no change in the ideas of a people is to be hoped for till after a change in its legislation; that the reformation of manners is to be begun by the reformation of laws; and declamations against a vice useful in the present form of government, would politically be detrimental, were they not found fruitless. But so they will always be, for it is only the force of the laws that can ever act on the bulk of a nation. Besides, let me be allowed cursorily to observe that among the moralists there are very few who, by setting our passions at variance, know how to avail themselves of them, so as to procure their opinions to be adopted. Most of their admonitions are too dogmatical, and imperious; yet they should be sensible, that invectives will never prevail against sentiments: that it is only a passion which can get the better of a passion; for instance, to bring a gay woman to more reserve and modesty in public, her vanity must be contrasted with her coquetry, and it must be urged to her, that modesty is an invention of love and of refined delight;[2] that it is to the gauze which covers

---

[2] It is by considering modesty in this light, that we may answer the arguments of the Stoics and Cynics, who affirmed that the virtuous man did nothing in private which he should not do in public, and who consequently believed that they might publicly act the pleasures of love. If most legislators have censured these Cynical principles, and classed modesty among the virtues, it is, will it be answered, because they apprehended that the frequent sight of enjoyment might cast some disgust on a pleasure, on which depends the conversation of the species, and the continuance of the world. They were likewise aware that dress, concealing some female charms, decked a woman with all the beauties which a lively imagination could suggest; that this dress inflamed curiosity; heightened the joys of female caresses; rendered their favours more extatic, and multiplied the delights of our afflictive state. If Lycurgus banished from Sparta a certain kind of modesty; and if the young women, in presence of a whole people, wrestled naked with the youth of the other sex; the legislator's intention herein was, that being made

a woman's beauties, that the world owes most of its pleasures; that at Malabar, where the young beauties appear in company half naked; that in certain parts of America, where the women wear no covering, the desires have nothing of that ardour and vivacity, which curiosity would impart to them; that in those countries, beauty serves only for the call of necessity; and that, on the contrary, among those nations where modesty has placed a veil between desires and nudities, this mysterious veil is the talisman which holds the lover at this charmer's feet; that in fine, modesty puts, into beauty's weak hands, the sceptre to which power submits. Besides, they will say to the woman of gallantry, You must know that the wretched are very numerous; that the unfortunate born enemies to the happy man make a crime of his happiness;[3] that they hate in him a felicity too independent of them; that the subject of your amusements is to be concealed from their sight; and that levity and indecency, by betraying the secrets of your pleasures, exposes you to all the strokes of their revenge.

By thus substituting the soft language of interest, instead of the peremptory clamour of invective, the moralists may establish their maxims. I shall not enlarge farther on this head: but return to my subject; and I say, that all men tend only towards their happiness; that it is a tendency from which they cannot be diverted; that the attempt would be fruitless, and even the success dangerous; consequently, it is only by incorporating personal and general interest, that they can be rendered virtuous. This being granted, morality is evidently no more than a frivolous science, unless blended with politics and legislation: whence I conclude that, if philosophers would be of use to the world, they should survey objects from the same point of view as the legislator. Though not invested with the same power they are to be actuated by the same principle. The moralist is to indicate the laws, of which the legislator insures the execution by stamping them with the seal of his authority.

---

stronger by such exercise, their children might be more robust and fitter for the constitution of that state, which was purely military. He knew that however the custom of seeing naked women might cool the desire of seeing their hidden beauties, the desire itself was unextinguishable, especially in a country where it was only in secret and by stealth, that husbands were admitted to the embraces of their wives. Besides, Lycurgus, as he made love one of the principal springs of his legislative system, intended it for the recompense, and not the occupation of the Spartan.—Original footnote.

[3] Helvétius is probably referring to the Church.

B. A Treatise on Man

Chapter II. Of the Importance of This Question[1]

If it be true that the talents and the virtues of a people determine their power and their happiness, no question can be more important than this, to wit,

If in each individual his talents and his virtues be the effect of his organisation,[2] or of the education he receives.

I am of the latter opinion, and propose to prove here what perhaps is only advanced in the treatise of *L'Esprit*. If I can demonstrate that man is, in fact, nothing more than the product of his education, I shall doubtless reveal an important truth to mankind. They will learn, that they have in their own hands the instrument of their greatness and their felicity, and that to be happy and powerful nothing more is requisite than to perfect the science of education.

But by what means shall we discover whether man be in fact the product of his education? By a thorough discussion of the question. If this examination should not give the solution, we ought still make it; for it will be useful, as it will compel us to the study of ourselves.

Mankind are, but too often, unknown to him that governs them; yet to guide the motions of the human puppet, it is necessary to know the wires by which he is moved. Without this knowledge, what wonder is it that his motions are frequently so contrary to those the legislature requires.

If some errors should creep into a work that treats on man, it will still be a valuable work.

What mass of light does the knowledge of mankind throw upon the several parts of government. The ability of the groom consists in knowing all that is to be done to the animal he is to manage; and the ability of a minister, in knowing all that is to be done in the management of the people he is to govern.

The science of man is a part of the science of government.

Source: Helvétius, *De L' Homme* (London, 1776), the eighteenth-century translation of W. Hooper.

---

[1] The question is the power of education to control behavior.
[2] Inherited make-up or disposition, corporal and mental.

(1) The minister should connect it with that of public affairs.

(2) It is then that he will establish just laws.

Let philosophers therefore penetrate continually more and more into the abyss of the human heart, let them there search out all the principles of its actions, and let the minister, profiting by their discoveries, make of them, according to time, place, and circumstances, a happy application.

If the knowledge of mankind be regarded as absolutely necessary to the legislature, nothing can be more important than the examination of a problem which implies that knowledge.

If they who are personally indifferent to this question, shall judge of it only as relative to public interest, they will perceive that of all the obstacles to the perfection of education, the greatest is to regard our talents and virtues as the effect of organisation. No opinion is more favourable to the idleness and negligence of instructors. If organisation make us almost entirely what we are, why do we reproach the master with the ignorance and stupidity of his pupils? Why, he will say, do you impute to education the faults of nature? What answer will you make him? When you admit a principle, how can you deny its immediate consequence?

On the contrary, if we prove that talents and virtues are acquisitions, we shall rouse the industry of the master, and prevent his negligence; we shall render him more assiduous in stifling the vices, and cultivating the virtues of his pupils.

The genius most ardent in carrying the instruments of education to perfection, will perceive perhaps in an infinity of those minute articles, now regarded as insignificant, the hidden seeds of our vices, our virtues, our talents, and imbecilities; and who can say to what point genius may then carry its discoveries? Of this we are certain, that we are as yet ignorant of the true principles of education, and that it is at the present day reduced almost entirely to certain false sciences, to which even ignorance is preferable.

CHAPTER III. OF THE ALTERATIONS THAT HAPPEN IN THE CHARACTERS OF INDIVIDUALS

That which occurs in a great and striking manner in nations, occurs in little, and in a manner less sensible, in individuals. Almost every change in their situation produces one in their characters.[3] A

---

[3] Manners with fortunes, humours turn with climes,
  Tenets with books, and principles with times.
  Asks men's opinions: Scoto now shall tell

man is severe, peevish, imperious; menaces and torments his slaves, his children and domestics. He loses himself by chance in a forest, and when night comes on, retires to a cavern, where he perceives a lion is couching. Does this man preserve his morose and quarrelsome temper? No: he creeps with the utmost caution into a corner of the den, lest by the smallest noise he should rouse the fury of the beast.

From the den of the natural lion let us transport him to the cavern of a moral lion: let us place him in the service of a cruel and despotic tyrant: mild and moderate in the presence of his master, perhaps this man will become the most mean and cringing of all his slaves. But it will be said, his character is constrained, not altered: it is a tree that is bent by force, and whose natural elasticity will soon restore it to its former figure. But can it be imagined, that after a tree has been for some years bent into a particular figure, it will ever return to its original form? Whoever says that men do not easily change their characters by constraint, only says that habits long established are not to be destroyed in an instant.

The man of ill humour preserves his character, because he has always some inferior on whom he can exercise his ill nature. But let him be kept a long time in the presence of a lion or a tyrant, and there is no doubt but a continued restraint, transformed into a habit, will soften his character. In general, as long as we are young enough to contract new habits, the sole incurable faults, and vices, are those we cannot correct without employing means of which morals, laws, or customs do not allow the practice. There is nothing impossible to education: it makes the bear dance.

If we reflect on this subject, we perceive that our first nature, as Pascal and experience prove, is nothing else than our first habit.

Man is born without ideas and without passions, but he is born an imitator and docile to example; consequently it is to instruction he owes his habits and his character. Now I ask, why habits contracted during a certain time, cannot at length be effaced by contrary habits. How many people do we see change their character with their rank, according to the different place they occupy at court, and in the ministry; in short, according to the change that happens in their situation. Why does the robber, when transported

---

How trade increases, and the world goes well;
Strike off his pension, by the setting sun,
And Britain, if not Europe, is undone.
                          POPE   (Original footnote.)

from England to America, frequently become honest? Because he becomes a man of property, and has land to cultivate; in short, because his situation is changed.

The officer in the camp is void of compassion; accustomed to the sight of blood, he beholds it unmoved. But when he returns to London, Paris, or Berlin, he returns to the feelings of humanity. Why should we regard each character as the effect of a particular organisation, when we cannot determine what that organisation is? Why search in occult qualities for the cause of a moral phenomenon, which the development of the passion of self-love so clearly and readily explains?

CHAPTER VII. OF THE MORAL EDUCATION OF MAN

It is evident from this sketch, to what a degree of perfection such a catechism might carry the education of a citizen; how much it would enlighten the subject and the monarch in their respective duties, and lastly, what just ideas it would give him of morality.

If the fundamental principle of the science of morals be reduced to the simple fact of corporeal sensibility, that science will become adapted to the capacity of men of all ages and all understandings: all may have the same idea of it.

From the moment we regard corporeal sensibility as the first principle of morality, its maxims cease to be contradictory, its axioms all linked together will bear the most rigorous demonstration; in short, its principles being freed from the darkness of speculative philosophy will become evident, and the more generally adopted as the people will be the more clearly convinced of the interest they have to be virtuous.

Whoever shall elevate himself to this first principle, will see, if I may so say, with the first glance of his eye, all the imperfections of a legislation: he will see if the bulwark opposed by the laws to such passions as are contrary to the public good, be sufficiently strong to support their efforts: if the law rewards and punishes in such just proportion as will necessitate men to virtue: lastly, he will perceive in that so much vaunted axiom of the present morality,

Do unto others as thou wouldst they should do unto thee,

only a secondary, domestic maxim, and one that is always insufficient to inform mankind of what they owe to their country. He will presently substitute for it that axiom which declares,

That the public good is the supreme law.

An axiom that includes, in a manner more general and more explicit, all that is useful in the former, and is applicable to all the different situations in which a citizen may find himself; that agrees equally well with the private man, the judge, the minister, etc. It is, if I may so say, from the sublimity of such a principle, that descending even to the local conventions, which form the customary law of each people, every one may instruct himself in the particular nature of his engagements, in the wisdom or folly of the laws and customs of his country, and form a more just judgment of them, as he will have more habitually present to his mind the grand principles by which are estimated the wisdom, and even the equity of the laws.

We may therefore furnish youth with sound and determinate ideas of morality. By the aid of a catechism of probity we may carry this part of education to the highest degree of perfection: but what obstacles are there to surmount!

34.   Rousseau, Political Economy; The Social Contract; A Constitution for Corsica; and On the Government of Poland

A.   Political Economy

. . . Let me be allowed to use for a moment a comparison which is commonplace and inexact in many respects, but useful to make myself clear.

The political body, taken as a unit, may be considered as an organized, living body, similar to that of man . . .

The life of both is the *self* common to the whole, the reciprocal sensitivity and the internal interconnectedness of all the parts . . .

The body politic, therefore, is also a moral being possessing a will; and this general will, which always tends to the preservation

SOURCE: Translated by Stephen J. Gendzier in *Denis Diderot's The Encyclopedia* (New York: Harper & Row, Inc., 1967), pp. 189–92 passim, with some additional portions translated by the editor (in brackets). Reprinted by permission of the publishers.

and welfare of the whole and of every part, is the source of the laws, constitutes for all the members of the state in their relations to one another and to it the rule of what is right and wrong; a truth that shows, by the way, how much sense there was to the indictment of so many writers who treated as theft the subtle rule prescribed to children at Sparta for obtaining their frugal meals, is if everything ordained by the law were not lawful.

I. The first and most important maxim of legitimate or popular government, that is to say, of government whose object is the good of the people, is, therefore, as I have said, to follow in everything the general will. But to follow this will it is necessary to know it and above all to distinguish it from the particular will, beginning with one's self; this distinction is always difficult to make, and only the most sublime virtue can provide us with sufficient enlightenment. As, in order to will, it is necessary to be free, another difficulty no less great than the former presents itself; namely, to secure at one and the same time the public liberty and the authority of the government. Look into the motives that have induced men, once united by their common needs in a general society, to unite themselves still more intimately through civil societies: you will find no other motive than that of securing the property, life, and liberty of each member by the protection of all. Now, how can men be forced to defend the liberty of any one among them without interfering with that of others? And how can they provide for the public needs without tampering with the individual property of those who are forced to contribute to them? With whatever sophistry all this may be covered over, it is certain that if my will can be constrained, I am no longer free, and that I am no longer master of my property if any one else can lay his hands on it. This difficulty, which must have seemed insurmountable, has been removed, with the first, by the most sublime of all institutions, or rather by a divine inspiration which teaches man to imitate here below the immutable degrees of the Deity. By what inconceivable art has a means been found of subjugating men in order to make them free; of using in the service of the state the properties, the persons, and even the lives of all its members without constraining and without consulting them; of confining their will by their own admission, of enforcing their consent over their own refusal and forcing them to punish themselves when they do something they have not willed? How is it possible that they all obey and yet nobody commands, that they all serve and yet have no masters but be even freer in fact than under apparent subjection, for each person loses no part of his liberty but what might be harmful to that of another? These wonders are the work of the law. It is to law alone that men owe justice and liberty. It is this salutary organ of the will of all that re-establishes in civil right the natural equality between men. It is this celestial voice that dictates to each citizen the precepts of public reason and teaches him to act according to the maxims of his own judgment and not to be in a state of contradiction with himself. It is with this voice alone that heads of state should speak when they command; for as soon as a man casts aside the laws and claims to subject another to his private will, he immediately departs from the civil society and meets him face to face in the pure state of nature in which obedience is prescribed only by necessity . . .

[But although the government is not the master of the law, it is a great deal to be its guarantor and to have a thousand ways of making it loved. The art of ruling consists only in that. When you have power, there is no skill in making everyone tremble, and not even very much in winning hearts; for experience has ever taught the people to be grateful to its leaders for all the harm they do not do, and to worship them when the people are not hated by them. An imbecile who is obeyed may punish crimes like anyone else. The true stateman knows how to forestall them; it is over wills even more than over actions that he extends his respectable empire. If he could manage to make everyone act properly, he would have nothing more to do, and his masterpiece would be to remain idle. It is certain, at any rate, that the greatest talent of leaders is to disguise their power so as to make it less odious, and to manage the state so quietly that it seems not to need managers. . . .

How, you will ask me, can we know the general will in those instances in which it has not been declared? Will it be necessary to assemble the whole nation on the occasion of each unforeseen event? No, and all the less because it is not sure that its decision will be the expression of the general will; because this means is impractical with a large population, and because it is rarely necessary when the government is well intentioned. For the leaders know quite well that the general will is always in favor of the decision which is most conducive to the public interest, that is to say, the most equitable; so that it is necessary only to be just in order to be sure that one is following the general will . . .

It is a great deal to have established order and peace throughout the republic; it is a great deal that the state is tranquil and the law respected. But if one does nothing more, all that will be more appearance than reality; the government will find it difficult to secure obedience if it limits itself to obedience. If it is good to know how to use men such as they are, it is much better yet to make them into men such as you need them to be. The most absolute authority is that which penetrates within man and is wielded over wills no less than over actions. It is certain that a people is in the long run what the government makes it: warriors, citizens, men, when it wants to; rabble and scum, when it wants to. . . . Form men, then, if you want to command men. If you want the laws to be obeyed see to it that they are loved and that, for men to do what they should, it is enough for it to occur to them that they should do it. That was the great art of ancient governments. . . . But our modern governments, which think they have done everything when they collect money, do not even imagine that it is necessary or possible to go that far.]

II. The second essential rule of public *economy* is not less important than the first. If you wish to have the general will accomplish its purpose, make all the particular wills agree with it; and as virtue is nothing more than this conformity of the particular wills with the general will, we could say the same thing in a few words: establish the reign of virtue.

If our politicians were less blinded by their ambition, they would see how impossible it is for any establishment whatever to function in the spirit of its institution unless it is guided in accordance with the law of duty; they would feel that the greatest support of public authority lies in the heart of the citizens and that nothing can take the place of morality in the maintenance of government. It is not only upright men who know how to administer the laws, but at bottom only good honest people know how to obey them. A man who has finally mastered his remorse will not be intimidated by punishments that are less severe and less lasting and from which there is at least the hope of escaping: whatever precautions are taken, those who only await impunity in order to do wrong will hardly fail to find means of eluding the law and avoiding its penalties. Then as all the particular interests unite against the general interest, which is no longer that of any individual, public vices have more power in enervating the laws than the laws have in repressing vice: so that the corruption of the people and their rules will finally spread to the government, however wise it may be. The worst of all abuses is to give the appearance of obeying the laws only in order actually to break them with security. The best laws soon became the most pernicious; and it would be a hundred times better that they should not exist; for laws would then be a final expedient that people would still have available after they had tried everything else. In such a situation it is vain to add edicts to edicts and regulations to regulations. Everything serves only to introduce new abuses without correcting the old ones. The more laws are multiplied, the more they are scorned, and all the officials appointed to oversee them are only so many more people destined to break them either by sharing the plunder with their precursors or by pillaging new sources on their own. The reward of virtue soon becomes that of robbery: the most vile men have the greatest credit in society; the greater they are, the more despicable they become; their infamy shatters their high repute, and they are dishonored by their honors. If they buy the approval of the leaders or the protection of women, it is only so that they may sell justice, duty, and the state in their turn: in the meantime the people, who do not see that their vices are the primary causes of their misfortunes, moan and complain that "all our misfortunes come solely from those whom we pay to protect us from such things."

B.   The Social Contract

BOOK I—CHAPTER VI. THE SOCIAL PACT

I ASSUME that men have reached a point at which the obstacles that endanger their preservation in the state of nature overcome by their resistance the forces which each individual can exert with a view to maintaining himself in that state. Then this primitive condition can no longer subsist, and the human race would perish unless it changed its mode of existence.

Now, as men cannot create any new forces, but only combine and direct those that exist, they have no other means of self-preservation than to form by aggregation a sum of forces which

SOURCE: L. G. Crocker (ed.), *The Social Contract*, trans. Henry J. Tozer (New York: Washington Square Press, 1967), pp. 17–19, 21–22, 30–32, 38–46, 58, 134–35, 144–47.

may overcome the resistance, to put them in action by a single motive power, and to make them work in concert.

This sum of forces can be produced only by the combination of many; but the strength and freedom of each man being the chief instruments of his preservation, how can he pledge them without injuring himself, and without neglecting the cares which he owes to himself? This difficulty, applied to my subject, may be expressed in these terms: —

"To find a form of association which may defend and protect with the whole force of the community the person and property of every associate, and by means of which each, coalescing with all, may nevertheless obey only himself, and remain as free as before." Such is the fundamental problem of which the social contract furnishes the solution.

The clauses of this contract are so determined by the nature of the act that the slightest modification would render them vain and ineffectual; so that, although they have never perhaps been formally enunciated, they are everywhere the same, everywhere tacitly admitted and recognized, until, the social pact being violated, each man regains his original rights and recovers his natural liberty, while losing the conventional liberty for which he renounced it.

These clauses, rightly understood, are reducible to one only, viz., the total alienation to the whole community of each associate with all his rights; for, in the first place, since each gives himself up entirely, the conditions are equal for all; and, the conditions being equal for all, no one has any interest in making them burdensome to others.

Further, the alienation being made without reserve, the union is as perfect as it can be, and an individual associate can no longer claim anything; for, if any rights were left to individuals, since there would be no common superior who could judge between them and the public, each, being on some point his own judge, would soon claim to be so on all; the state of nature would still subsist, and the association would necessarily become tyrannical or useless.

In short, each giving himself to all, gives himself to nobody; and as there is not one associate over whom we do not acquire the same rights which we concede to him over ourselves, we gain the equivalent of all that we lose, and more power to preserve what we have.

If, then, we set aside what is not of the essence of the social contract, we shall find that it is reducible to the following terms: "Each of us puts in common his person and his whole power under the supreme direction of the general will; and in return we receive every member as an indivisible part of the whole."

Forthwith, instead of the individual personalities of all the contracting parties, this act of association produces a moral and collective body, which is composed of as many members as the assembly has voices, and which receives from this same act its unity, its common self (*moi*), its life, and its will. This public person, which is thus formed by the union of all the individual members, formerly took the name of city, and now takes that of republic or body politic, which is called by its members State when it is passive, sovereign when it is active, power when it is compared to similar bodies. With regard to the associates, they take collectively the name of people, and are called individually citizens, as participating in the sovereign power, and subjects, as subjected to the laws of the State. But these terms are often confused and are mistaken one for another; it is sufficient to know how to distinguish them when they are used with complete precision.

Book I—Chapter VII. The Sovereign

. . . Now, the sovereign, being formed only of the individuals that compose it, neither has nor can have any interest contrary to theirs; consequently the sovereign power needs no guarantee towards its subjects, because it is impossible that the body should wish to injure all its members; and we shall see hereafter that it can injure no one as an individual. The sovereign, for the simple reason that it is so, is always everything that it ought to be.

But this is not the case as regards the relation of subjects to the sovereign, which, notwithstanding the common interest, would have no security for the performance of their engagements, unless it found means to ensure their fidelity.

Indeed, every individual may, as a man, have a particular will contrary to, or divergent from, the general will which he has as a citizen; his private interest may prompt him quite differently from the common interest; his absolute and naturally independent existence may make him regard what he owes to the common cause as a gratuitous contribution, the loss of which will be less harmful to others than the payment of it will be burdensome to him; and, regarding the moral person that constitutes the State as an imaginary being because it is not a man, he would be willing to enjoy the rights of a citizen without being willing to fulfil the duties of a subject. The progress of such injustice would bring about the ruin of the body politic.

In order, then, that the social pact may not be a vain formulary, it tacitly includes this engagement, which can alone give force to the others—that whoever refuses to obey the general will shall be constrained to do so by the whole body; which means nothing else than that he shall be forced to be free; for such is the condition which, uniting every citizen to his native land, guarantees him from all personal dependence a condition that ensures the control and working of the political machine, and alone renders legitimate civil engagements, which without it, would be absurd and tyrannical, and subject to the most enormous abuses.

Book II—Chapter III. Whether the General Will Can Err

It follows from what precedes that the general will is always right and always tends to the public advantage; but it does not follow that the resolutions of the people have always the same rectitude. Men always desire their own good, but do not always discern it; the people are never corrupted, though often deceived, and it is only then that they seem to will what is evil.

There is often a great deal of difference between the will of all and the general will; the latter regards only the common interest, while the former has regard to private interests, and is merely a sum of particular wills; but take away from these same wills the pluses and minuses which cancel one another, and the general will remains as the sum of the differences.

If the people came to a resolution when adequately informed and without any communication among the citizens, the general will would always result from the great number of slight differences, and the resolution would always be good. But when factions, partial associations, are formed to the detriment of the whole society, the will of each of these associations becomes general with reference to its members, and particular with reference to the State; it may then be said that there are no longer as many voters as there are men, but only as many voters as there are associations. The differences become less numerous and yield a less general result. Lastly, when one of these associations becomes so great that it predominates over all the rest, you no longer have as the result a sum of small differences, but a single difference; there is then no longer a general will, and the opinion which prevails is only a particular opinion.

It is important, then, in order to have a clear declaration of the general will, that there should be no partial association in the State, and that every citizen should express only his own opinion. Such was the unique and sublime institution of the great Lycurgus. But if there are partial associations, it is necessary to multiply their number and prevent inequality, as Solon, Numa, and Servius did. These are the only proper precautions for ensuring that the general will may always be enlightened, and that the people may not be deceived.

Book II—Chapter VI. The Law

By the social compact we have given existence and life to the body politic; the question now is to endow it with movement and will by legislation. For the original act by which this body is formed and consolidated determines nothing in addition as to what it must do for its own preservation.

What is right and conformable to order is such by the nature of things, and independently of human conventions. All justice comes from God, He alone is the source of it; but could we receive it direct from so lofty a source, we should need neither government nor laws. Without doubt there is a universal justice emanating from reason alone; but this justice, in order to be admitted among us, should be reciprocal. Regarding things from a human standpoint, the laws of justice are inoperative among men for want of a natural sanction; they only bring good to the wicked and evil to the just when the latter observe them with every one, and no one observes them in return. Conventions and laws, then, are necessary to couple rights with duties and apply justice to its object. In the state of nature, where everything is in common, I owe nothing to those to whom I have promised nothing; I recognize as belonging to others only what is useless to me. This is not the case in the civil state, in which all rights are determined by law.

But then, finally, what is a law? So long as men are content to attach to this word only metaphysical ideas, they will continue to

argue without being understood; and when they have stated what a
law of nature is, they will know no better what a law of the State
is.

I have already said that there is no general will with reference to
a particular object. In fact, this particular object is either in the
State or outside of it. If it is outside the State, a will which is
foreign to it is not general in relation to it; and if it is within the
State, it forms part of it; then there is formed between the whole
and its part a relation which makes of it two separate beings, of
which the part is one, and the whole, less this same part, is the
other. But the whole less one part is not the whole, and so long as
the relation subsists, there is no longer any whole, but two unequal
parts; whence it follows that the will of the one is no longer
general in relation to the other.

But when the whole people decree concerning the whole people,
they consider themselves alone; and if a relation is then constituted,
it is between the whole object under one point of view and the
whole object under another point of view, without any division at
all. Then the matter respecting which they decree is general like
the will that decrees. It is this act that I call a law.

When I say that the object of the laws is always general, I mean
that the law considers subjects collectively, and actions as abstract,
never a man as an individual nor a particular action. Thus the law
may indeed decree that there shall be privileges, but cannot confer
them on any person by name; the law can create several classes of
citizens, and even assign the qualifications which shall entitle them
to rank in these classes, but it cannot nominate such and such
persons to be admitted to them; it can establish a royal government
and a hereditary succession, but cannot elect a king or appoint a
royal family; in a word, no function which has reference to an
individual object appertains to the legislative power.

From this standpoint we see immediately that it is no longer
necessary to ask whose office it is to make laws, since they are acts
of the general will; nor whether the prince is above the laws, since
he is a member of the State; nor whether the law can be unjust,
since no one is unjust to himself; nor how we are free and yet
subject to the laws, since the laws are only registers of our wills.

We see, further, that since the law combines the universality of
the will with the universality of the object, whatever any man

prescribes on his own authority is not a law; and whatever the sovereign itself prescribes respecting a particular object is not a law, but a decree, not an act of sovereignty, but of magistracy.

I therefore call any State a republic which is governed by laws, under whatever form of administration it may be; for then only does the public interest predominate and the commonwealth count for something. Every legitimate government is republican;[1] I will explain hereafter what government is.

Laws are properly only the conditions of civil associations. The people, being subjected to the laws, should be the authors of them; it concerns only the associates to determine the conditions of association. But how will they be determined? Will it be by a common agreement, by a sudden inspiration? Has the body politic an organ for expressing its will? Who will give it the foresight necessary to frame its acts and publish them at the outset? Or how shall it declare them in the hour of need? How would a blind multitude, which often knows not what it wishes because it rarely knows what is good for it, execute of itself an enterprise so great, so difficult, as a system of legislation? Of themselves, the people always desire what is good, but do not always discern it. The general will is always right, but the judgment which guides it is not always enlightened. It must be made to see objects as they are, sometimes as they ought to appear; it must be shown the good path that it is seeking, and guarded from the seduction of private interests; it must be made to observe closely times and places, and to balance the attraction of immediate and palpable advantages against the danger of remote and concealed evils. Individuals see the good which they reject; the public desire the good which they do not see. All alike have need of guides. The former must be compelled to conform their wills to their reason; the people must be taught to know what they require. Then from the public enlightenment results the union of the understanding and the will in the social body; and from that the close cooperation of the parts, and, lastly, the maximum power of the whole. Hence arises the need of a legislator.

[1] I do not mean by this word an aristocracy or democracy only, but in general any government directed by the general will, which is the law. To be legitimate, the government must not be combined with the sovereign power, but must be its minister; then monarchy itself is a republic. This will be made clear in the next book—Rousseau's footnote.

Book II—Chapter VII. The Legislator

In order to discover the rules of association that are most suitable to nations, a superior intelligence would be necessary who could see all the passions of men without experiencing any of them; who would have no affinity with our nature and yet know it thoroughly; whose happiness would not depend on us, and who would nevertheless be quite willing to interest himself in ours; and, lastly, one who, storing up for himself with the progress of time a far-off glory in the future, could labor in one age and enjoy in another.[2] Gods would be necessary to give laws to men.

The same argument that Caligula adduced as to fact, Plato put forward with regard to right, in order to give an idea of the civil or royal man whom he is in quest of in his work the *Statesman*. But if it is true that a great prince is a rare man, what will a great legislator be? The first has only to follow the model which the other has to frame. The latter is the mechanician who invents the machine, the former is only the workman who puts it in readiness and works it. "In the birth of societies," says Montesquieu, "it is the chiefs of the republics who frame the institutions, and afterwards it is the institutions which mold the chiefs of the republics."

He who dares undertake to give institutions to a nation ought to feel himself capable, as it were, of changing human nature; of transforming every individual, who in himself is a complete and independent whole, into part of a greater whole, from which he receives in some manner his life and his being; of altering man's constitution in order to strengthen it; of substituting a social and moral existence for the independent and physical existence which we have all received from nature. In a word, it is necessary to deprive man of his native powers in order to endow him with some which are alien to him, and of which he cannot make use without the aid of other people. The more thoroughly those natural powers are deadened and destroyed, the greater and more durable are the acquired powers, the more solid and perfect also are the institutions; so that if every citizen is nothing, and can be nothing, except in combination with all the rest, and if the force acquired by the

[2] A nation becomes famous only when its legislation is beginning to decline. We are ignorant during how many centuries the institutions of Lycurgus conferred happiness on the Spartans before they were known in the rest of Greece—Rousseau's footnote.

whole be equal or superior to the sum of the natural forces of all the individuals, we may say that legislation is at the highest point of perfection which it can attain.

The legislator is in all respects an extraordinary man in the State. If he ought to be so by his genius, he is not less so by his office. It is not magistracy nor sovereignty. This office, which constitutes the republic, does not enter into its constitution; it is a special and superior office, having nothing in common with human government; for, if he who rules men ought not to control legislation, he who controls legislation ought not to rule men; otherwise his laws, being ministers of his passions, would often serve only to perpetuate his acts of injustice; he would never be able to prevent private interests from corrupting the sacredness of his work.

When Lycurgus gave laws to his country, he began by abdicating his royalty. It was the practice of the majority of the Greek towns to entrust to foreigners the framing of their laws. The modern republics of Italy often imitated this usage; that of Geneva did the same and found it advantageous.[3] Rome, at her most glorious epoch, saw all the crimes of tyranny spring up in her bosom, and saw herself on the verge of destruction, through uniting in the same hands legislative authority and sovereign power.

Yet the Decemvirs themselves never arrogated the right to pass any law on their sole authority. Nothing that we propose to you, they said to the people, can pass into law without your consent. Romans, be yourselves the authors of the laws which are to secure your happiness.

He who frames laws, then, has, or ought to have, no legislative right, and the people themselves cannot, even if they wished, divest themselves of this incommunicable right, because, according to the fundamental compact, it is only the general will that binds individuals, and we can never be sure that a particular will is conformable to the general will until it has been submitted to the free votes of the people. I have said this already, but it is not useless to repeat it.

---

[3] Those who consider Calvin only as a theologian are but little acquainted with the extent of his genius. The preparation of our wise edicts, in which he had a large share, does him as much credit as his *Institutes*. Whatever revolution time may bring about in our religion, so long as love of country and of liberty is not extinct among us, the memory of that great man will not cease to be revered—Rousseau's footnote.

Thus we find simultaneously in the work of legislation two things that seem incompatible—an enterprise surpassing human powers, and, to execute it, an authority that is a mere nothing.

Another difficulty deserves attention. Wise men who want to speak to the vulgar in their own language instead of in a popular way will not be understood. Now, there are a thousand kinds of ideas which it is impossible to translate into the language of the people. Views very general and objects very remote are alike beyond its reach; and each individual, approving of no other plan of government than that which promotes his own interests, does not readily perceive the benefits that he is to derive from the continual deprivations which good laws impose. In order that a newly formed nation might approve sound maxims of politics and observe the fundamental rules of state-policy, it would be necessary that the effect should become the cause; that the social spirit, which should be the work of the institution, should preside over the institution itself, and that men should be, prior to the laws, what they ought to become by means of them. Since, then, the legislator cannot employ either force or reasoning, he must needs have recourse to an authority of a different order, which can compel without violence and persuade without convincing.

It is this which in all ages has constrained the founders of nations to resort to the intervention of heaven, and to give the gods the credit for their own wisdom, in order that the nations, subjected to the laws of the State as to those of nature, and recognizing the same power in the formation of man and in that of the State, might obey willingly, and bear submissively the yoke of the public welfare.

The legislator puts into the mouths of the immortals that sublime reason which soars beyond the reach of common men, in order that he may win over by divine authority those whom human prudence could not move.[4] But it does not belong to every man to make the gods his oracles, nor to be believed when he proclaims himself their interpreter. The great soul of the legislator is the real miracle which must give proof of his mission. Any man can engrave tables of stone, or bribe an oracle, or pretend secret intercourse with some divinity, or train a bird to speak in his ear, or find some other

---

[4] "It is true," says Machiavelli, "there never was in a nation any promulgator of extraordinary laws who had not recourse to God, because otherwise they would not have been accepted; for there are many advantages recognized by a wise man which are not so self-evident that they can convince others" (*Discourses on Titus Livius*, Book I, chapter II)—Rousseau's footnote.

clumsy means to impose on the people. He who is acquainted with such means only will perchance be able to assemble a crowd of foolish persons; but he will never found an empire, and his extravagant work will speedily perish with him. Empty deceptions form but a transient bond; it is only wisdom that makes it lasting. The Jewish law, which still endures, and that of the child of Ishmael, which for ten centuries has ruled half the world, still bear witness today to the great men who dictated them; and while proud philosophy or blind party spirit sees in them nothing but fortunate impostors, the true statesman admires in their systems the great and powerful genius which directs durable institutions.

It is not necessary from all this to infer with Warburton that politics and religion have among us a common aim, but only that, in the origin of nations, one serves as an instrument of the other.

Book II—Chapter XII. Division of the Laws

. . . To these three kinds of laws[5] is added a fourth, the most important of all, which is graven neither on marble nor on brass, but in the hearts of the citizens; a law which creates the real constitution of the State, which acquires new strength daily, which, when other laws grow obsolete or pass away, revives them or supplies their place, preserves a people in the spirit of their institutions, and imperceptibly substitutes the force of habit for that of authority. I speak of manners, customs, and above all of opinion—a province unknown to our politicians, but one on which the success of all the rest depends; a province with which the great legislator is occupied in private, while he appears to confine himself to particular regulations, that are merely the arching of the cult, of which manners, slow to develop, form at length the immovable keystone.

Of these different classes, political laws, which constitute the form of government, alone relate to my subject.

Book IV—Chapter VII. The Censorship

Just as the declaration of the general will is made by the law, the declaration of public opinion is made by the censorship. Public opinion is a kind of law of which the censor is minister, and which he only applies to particular cases in the manner of the Prince.

The censorial tribunal, then, far from being the arbiter of the

[5] Political, civil, and criminal—Ed.

opinion of the people, only declares it, and so soon as it departs from this position, its decisions are fruitless and ineffectual.

It is useless to distinguish the character of a nation from the objects of its esteem, for all these things depend on the same principle and are necessarily intermixed. In all the nations of the world it is not nature but opinion which decides the choice of their pleasures. Reform men's opinions and their manners will be purified of themselves. People always like what is becoming or what they judge to be so; but it is in this judgment that they make mistakes; the question, then, is to guide their judgment. He who judges of manners judges of honor; and he who judges of honor takes his law from opinion.

The opinions of a nation spring from its constitution. Although the law does not regulate morality, it is legislation that gives it birth, and when legislation becomes impaired, morality degenerates; but then the judgment of the censors will not do what the power of the laws has failed to do.

It follows from this that the censorship may be useful to preserve morality, never to restore it. Institute censors while the laws are vigorous; so soon as they have lost their power all is over. Nothing that is lawful has any force when the laws cease to have any.

The censorship supports morality by preventing opinions from being corrupted, by preserving their integrity through wise applications, sometimes even by fixing them when they are still uncertain. The use of seconds in duels, carried to a mad extreme in the kingdom of France, was abolished by these simple words in an edict of the king: "As for those who have the cowardice of appoint seconds." This judgment, anticipating that of the public, immediately decided it. But when the same edicts wanted to declare that it was also cowardice to fight a duel, which is very true, but contrary to common opinion, the public ridiculed this decision, on which its judgment was already formed.

I have said elsewhere[6] that as public opinion is not subject to constraint, there should be no vestige of this in the tribunal established to represent it. We cannot admire too much the art with which this force, wholly lost among the moderns, was set in operation among the Romans and still better among the Lacedæmonians.

[6] I merely indicate in this chapter what I have treated at greater length in the *Letter to M. d'Alembert*—Rousseau's footnote.

A man of bad character having brought forward a good measure in the Council of Sparta, the ephors, without regarding him, caused the same measure to be proposed by a virtuous citizen. What an honor for the one, what a stigma for the other, without praise or blame being given to either! Certain drunkards from Samos defiled the tribunal of the ephors; on the morrow a public edict granted permission to the Samians to be filthy. A real punishment would have been less severe than such impunity. When Sparta pronounced what was or was not honorable, Greece made no appeal from her decisions.

Book IV—Chapter VIII. Civil Religion

But, setting aside political considerations, let us return to the subject of right and determine principles on this important point. The right which the social pact gives to the sovereign over its subjects does not, as I have said, pass the limits of public utility. Subjects, then, owe no account of their opinions to the sovereign except so far as those opinions are of moment to the community. Now it is very important for the State that every citizen should have a religion which may make him delight in his duties; but the dogmas of this religion concern neither the State nor its members, except so far as they affect morality and the duties which he who professes it is bound to perform towards others. Each may have, in addition, such opinions as he pleases, without its being the business of the sovereign to know them; for, as he has no jurisdiction in the other world, the destiny of his subjects in the life to come, whatever it may be, is not his affair, provided they are good citizens in this life.

There is, however, a purely civil profession of faith, the articles of which it is the duty of the sovereign to determine, not exactly as dogmas of religion, but as sentiments of sociability, without which it is impossible to be a good citizen or a faithful subject. Without having power to compel any one to believe them, the sovereign may banish from the State whoever does not believe them; it may banish him not as impious, but as unsocial, as incapable of sincerely loving law and justice and of sacrificing at need his life to his duty. But if any one, after publicly acknowledging these dogmas, behaves like an unbeliever in them, he should be punished with death; he has committed the greatest of crimes, he has lied before the laws.

The dogmas of civil religion ought to be simple, few in number, stated with precision, and without explanations or commentaries. The existence of the Deity, powerful, wise, beneficent, prescient, and bountiful, the life to come, the happiness of the just, the punishment of the wicked, the sanctity of the social contract and of the laws; these are the positive dogmas. As for the negative dogmas, I limit them to one only, that is, intolerance; it belongs to the creeds which we have excluded.

Those who distinguish civil intolerance from theological intolerance are, in my opinion, mistaken. These two kinds of intolerance are inseparable. It is impossible to live at peace with people whom we believe to be damned; to love them would be to hate God who punishes them. It is absolutely necessary to reclaim them or to punish them. Wherever theological intolerance is allowed, it cannot but have some effect in civil life; and as soon as it has any, the sovereign is no longer sovereign even in secular affairs; from that time the priests are the real masters; the kings are only their officers.

Now that there is, and can be, no longer any exclusive national religion, we should tolerate all those which tolerate others, so far as their dogmas have nothing contrary to the duties of a citizen. But whosoever dares to say: "Outside the Church no salvation," ought to be driven from the State, unless the State be the Church and the Prince be the pontiff. Such a dogma is proper only in a theocratic government; in any other it is pernicious. The reason for which Henry IV is said to have embraced the Romish religion ought to have made any honorable man renounce it, and especially any prince who knew how to reason.

C. Project of a Constitution for Corsica (1765)

PART II

ANY CORSICAN who by the age of 40 is not married, or has not been married, will be deprived of the rights of citizenship for the rest of his life.

Any individual who changes his residence from one district to

SOURCE: C. E. Vaughan (ed.), *The Political Writings of Rousseau* (2 vols.; Cambridge: The University Press, 1915), vol. 1. Translated by the editor.

another will lose his citizenship for three years, and at the end of that time, will be registered in the new district by paying a fee; failing which, he will continue to be excluded from citizenship until he has paid.

No unmarried man will be allowed to make a will. All his property will go to the community.

Corsicans, be silent! I am going to speak in the name of all. Let those who do not consent move away, and let those who do consent raise their hands.

This act shall be preceded by a general proclamation ordering everyone to go to his home for a prescribed time, under pain of losing his birthright or his citizenship.

The people will be turned away from superstition by keeping them constantly busy with their duties as citizens, by national holidays with magnificent display, by taking away their time from ecclesiastical ceremonies and transferring it to civil ceremonies; and that can be done with a bit of cleverness, without getting the clergy angry, by arranging for them always to have some share in it; but let that share be so small that no one will pay much attention to it.

There will be no carriages on the island. Clergy and women may use two-wheeled buggies; but the laity, no matter what their rank, shall travel only on foot or on horseback, unless they are crippled or gravely ill.

The laws concerning inheritances should tend to reduce things to a state of equality so that everyone has something and nobody has too much.

Any boy who marries before the age of 20, or who waits past the age of 30, or who marries a girl less than 15, or an unmarried woman or widow whose age is more than 20 years different from his, will remain excluded from citizenship, unless he attains it as a public reward for services to the state.

In view of the unequal distribution of the island's products, communications must not be cut off; it is necessary in some matters to take into consideration the prejudices and short-sightedness of the common people.

The nation will not be illustrious but it will be happy. It will not be spoken of; it will be little esteemed by the outside world; but it will have plenty, peace and freedom in its midst.

I will not preach morality to them [the people], I will not order them to have virtues. But I will put them in such a position that they will have those virtues without even knowing the word; and that they will be good and just, without really knowing what justice and goodness are.

Private property being so reduced and so dependent, and government needs but little force, and leads the people, so to speak, by moving its finger.

The Corsicans are still almost in the healthy state of nature. But it requires much artifice to keep them in that state because their prejudices tend to move them away from it. They have precisely what is good for them but they do not want what is good for them.

Noble people, I do not wish to give you artificial and systematic laws invented by men, but to bring you back under the rule of the sole laws of nature and of order, which rule over the heart and do not tyrannize wills.

D. Considerations on the Government of Poland (1772)

CHAPTER I. STATE OF THE QUESTION

ALTHOUGH it is easy, if one wishes, to make better laws, it is impossible to make any that will not be thwarted by men's passions, just as they have done to earlier laws.

The most astute statesman cannot foresee and weigh possible future abuses. Putting the Law above man is in politics a problem which I compare to the squaring of the circle in geometry. Solve this problem and the government which is founded on that solution will be good and without abuses. But until you have done that you may be sure that wherever you think you have made laws rule, it will be men who rule.

There will never be a good and solid constitution except one in which the law rules over the hearts of the citizens. As long as the power of legislation does not reach that point, laws will always be evaded. But how do you reach hearts? That is what our teachers, who never see anything but force and punishment, scarcely think about; and it is something which material rewards would perhaps accomplish no better. Even the most perfect justice does not lead to it; because justice, like good health, is a benefit which we enjoy

SOURCE: *Ibid.* Translated by the editor.

without feeling it, which inspires no enthusiasm, and whose worth we realize only after it is lost.

How then shall we stir hearts and make the fatherland and its laws loved? Shall I dare to say it? By children's games; by practices which seem idle to superficial men but which form cherished habits and invincible bonds.

CHAPTER II. THE SPIRIT OF ANCIENT INSTITUTIONS

[Rousseau has designated Moses, Lycurgus, and Numa Pompilius as the great lawgivers and molders of a people. He speaks first of Moses]

In order to prevent his people from being integrated among foreign peoples, he gave them manners and customs that could not be merged with those of other nations. He loaded them with rights, with special ceremonies. He confined them in a thousand ways, to keep them constantly going and to make them always strangers amongst other men . . . so that their ways, their laws, their rites have lasted and will last as long as the world, despite the hatred and the persecution of the rest of mankind.

Lycurgus undertook to establish a nation [Sparta] that was already degraded by servitude and the vices which result from it. He imposed upon the people an iron yoke, of a kind that no other people has ever borne. But he attached them to this yoke, he identified them, so to speak, with it, by keeping it constantly present in their minds. Constantly, he showed them their country in their laws, in their games, in their houses, in their loves, in their celebrations. He never gave them a moment of release so that they could think of themselves alone. And from this continual constraint, ennobled by its object, was born in them that ardent love of country which was always the strongest, or rather the unique passion of the Spartans and which made of them superhuman beings . . .

The same spirit guided all the ancient lawgivers in their institutions. All sought for links which would attach the citizens to their country and to each other. They found them in peculiar customs, in religious ceremonies which by their nature were always national and exclusive, in games which often kept the citizens assembled, in physical exercises which increased their pride and self-esteem together with their strength; in public spectacles which, recalling to them the history of their forebears, their misfortunes, their virtues,

their victories, affected hearts, inflamed them with a keen emulation, and attached them powerfully to that fatherland which was
kept constantly in their minds.

CHAPTER III. APPLICATION

It is national institutions which form the genius, the character,
the tastes and manners of a people, which make them what they are
and not something else, which inspire in them that ardent love of
country founded on habits that cannot be uprooted, which make
them die of boredom among other peoples, even in the midst of
pleasures which they are not allowed to have in their own country . . .

[If the Poles are formed in this fashion, they will have] a vigour
which will replace the deceptive play of vain precepts, and which
will make them do by taste and by passion what is never done well
enough when it is done only by duty or self-interest. It is on souls
such as those that good legislation will have a grip. They will obey
the laws and will not evade them because the laws will suit them
and will have the internal compliance of their wills. Loving their
country, they will serve it with zeal and with all their heart. With
this feeling alone even bad legislation would make good citizens. . . .

Let there be many public games at which the good mother
country enjoys watching her children play! Let her often be preoccupied with them so that they should be always preoccupied
with her. It is necessary to abolish even at court, for the sake of
example, the ordinary amusements of courts—gaming, theater,
comedy, opera; everything that makes men effeminate; everything
that distracts them, isolates them, makes them forget their country
and their duty; everything which makes them feel happy everywhere, as long as they are having a good time. . . .

Do not neglect a certain pomp and ceremony. Let it be noble,
imposing, and let the magnificence be in the men rather than the
things. It is hard to realize how much the hearts of the common
people follow their eyes and how much the majesty of ceremonial
imposes on them. It gives to authority a certain appearance of order
and of rule which inspires confidence, and which banishes the ideas
of caprice and whim that are attached to arbitrary power. . . .

Besides it is not by sumptuary laws that one succeeds in extirpat-
ing luxury; it is necessary to uproot it from men's hearts, by im-

printing more healthful and noble tastes. To forbid the things that are not to be done is an inept and vain expedient, if one does not begin by making them hated and despised. The disapproval of law is not efficacious except when it reinforces that of judgment. Whoever takes it upon himself to establish a people must know how to control the opinions, and through them, to govern the passions of men.

Chapter IV. Education

This is the important article. It is education which must give souls the national form, and so direct their opinions and their tastes that they are patriots by inclination, by passion, by necessity. A child, on opening his eyes, should see his country, and until he dies he should see nothing but his country. Every true republican sucks with his mother's milk the love of his country, that is to say, of laws and liberty. That love comprises his whole existence; he sees only his country, he lives only for it; as soon as he is alone he is nothing; as soon as he has no more country, he is no more; and if he is not dead he is worse than dead . . .

Children must not be allowed to play separately according to their fantasy but all together and in public, in such a way that there is always a common goal to which all aspire, and which excites competition and emulation. . . .

Without these precautions, expect nothing of your laws.

Chapter VI. The Question of the Three Orders

Proud and holy liberty! If those poor people[1] could know you, if they knew the price it takes to acquire you and to keep you; if they knew how your laws are more austere than the harsh yoke of tyrants, their weak souls, slaves of passion, that should be stifled, would fear you a hundred times more than slavery. They would fly from you with fright as from a burden about to crush them.

---

[1] Rousseau speaks of the oppressed who let themselves be agitated by demagogues and "dare to speak of liberty without having any idea of what it is."

35.   The Encyclopedia

A.   Property

PROPERTY (Natural and Political Right) is the right that each one of the individuals comprising a society has to enjoy the wealth that he legitimately acquired.

One of the principal views of men in forming societies was to secure the undisturbed possession of the advantages that they had acquired or were able to acquire. They wanted no one to be in a position to hinder them in the enjoyment of their wealth. It is for that reason that each one consented to sacrifice a portion of it which they called taxes for the preservation and maintenance of the entire society. They wanted to furnish the chosen heads of state with the means of making every private individual secure in the enjoyment of the portion of wealth he had reserved for himself. However strong the affection and enthusiasm of men might have been for the sovereigns to whom they submitted, they never intended to give them absolute and unlimited power over all their wealth. They never expected to be compelled to work solely for them. The flattery of courtiers, who do not have to pay anything for the most absurd principles, tried to convince some princes that they had an absolute right over the wealth of their subjects. Only despots and tyrants have adopted these preposterous maxims. The king of Siam claims he is the proprietor of all the wealth of his subjects. The result of such a barbarous right is that the first fortunate rebel makes himself the proprietor of the wealth possessed by the king of Siam. Any power based only on force destroys itself by the same means. In the states where the rules of reason are followed, the property of private individuals is under the protection of the laws; the head of a family is assured of enjoying for himself and of handing down to his descendants the wealth that he

SOURCE: Translated by Stephen J. Gendzier in *Denis Diderot's The Encyclopedia* (New York: Harper & Row, Inc., 1967), pp. 202–03. Reprinted by permission of the publishers.

has amassed by his work. Good kings have always respected the possessions of their subjects. They have regarded the public funds that have been committed to them only as a trust that may not be misappropriated to satisfy their frivolous passions, the greed of their favorites, or the rapacity of their courtiers.

ANONYMOUS

B.   Government, m. n. (Nat. and Polit. Right)

IT IS certain that a society has the freedom to form a government in the manner which pleases it, to blend and to arrange its constituent elements in different ways. If the legislative power has been given by a nation to one person or to several for life or for a limited time, when this time comes to an end the sovereign power returns to the society from which it emanates. As soon as it has returned there, society can dispose of it again at will, placing it in the hands of those they find suitable in the manner they judge appropriate, and thus erect a new form of government. Let Pufendorf[1] qualify as much as he wishes all sorts of mixed governments with the label of irregularity, true regularity will always be that which best conforms to the good of civil societies.

Some political writers claim that all men who have been born under one government do not have the liberty to institute another one. Each person, they say, is born the subject of his father or of his prince, and consequently each person is under a perpetual obligation of subjection or fidelity. This reasoning is more specious than solid. Men have never regarded any natural subjection in which they are born, in regard to their father or to their prince, as a bond that obliges them without their own consent to submit to such authority. Sacred and profane history furnish us with frequent examples of a multitude of people who have revoked the allegiance and the jurisdiction in which they are born, of the family and the community in which they had been nourished, to establish elsewhere new societies and new governments. . . .

It is not enough to abrogate laws that are flaws in a state, the good of the people must be the great purpose of the government.

SOURCE: *Ibid.*, pp. 124–25. Reprinted by permission of the publishers.

[1] Samuel Pufendorf, German jurisconsult (1632–94).

The governors are appointed to fulfill it; and the civil constitution that invests them with this power is bound therein by the laws of nature and by the law of reason, which has determined that purpose in any form of government as the cause of its welfare. The greatest good of the people is its liberty. Liberty is to the body of the state what health is to each individual; without health man cannot enjoy pleasure; without liberty the state of welfare is excluded from nations. A patriotic governor will therefore see that the right to defend and to maintain liberty is the most sacred of his duties. . . .

If it happens that those who hold the reins of government find some resistance when they use their power for the destruction and not the conservation of things that rightfully belong to the people, they must blame themselves, because the public good and the advantage of society are the purposes of establishing a government. Hence it necessarily follows that power cannot be arbitrary and that it must be exercised according to the established laws so that the people may know its duty and be secure within the shelter of laws, and so that governors at the same time should be held within just limits and not be tempted to employ the power they have in hand to do harmful things to the body politic.

DE JAUCOURT

36. Mercier, The Year 2440—Dream If There Ever Was One

Chapter LVII. The Professor of Government

The purpose of all governments is tranquility; but in politics this word requires an explanation: the slave is tranquil under the despot's hand, but it is a tranquility under duress. Rebellion is very close to such passive obedience. In moderate governments minds keep their energy and souls their elevation. Men would be visibly

SOURCE: L. S. Mercier, *L'An deux mille quatre cent quarante, Rêve s'il en fût jamais* (London, 1772), from an eighteenth-century translation.

degraded if there were not a continuous internal struggle between liberty and authority. That is what has preserved the admirable constitution of England which is a fortunate mixture of republican institutions.

Every well-constituted government generates a continual action and reaction, without which it degenerates.

Civil government is a restriction on natural liberty. Every individual must sacrifice a portion of his strength to protect the liberty of all. But the extent of this sacrifice is so delicate and complicated a calculation for most men that they will always be more impressed by the dangers of authority than by the abuses of excessive liberty. This is the source of opposition to government, which will be the sharper in proportion as passions are stronger. The government is therefore obliged to abandon domestic passions to the subject.

It takes very wise men to endure patiently the yoke of government when it is not too harsh; but the pleasures of authority generally corrupt those who govern, and they gradually go beyond the limits which they have prescribed to themselves.

It is in the nature of things for there to be opposing groups in governments. As long as these bodies only observe or balance each other reciprocally, the attention that is necessary to maintain equilibrium also maintains the rule of laws.

There is, then, no reason to be concerned about moderate internal agitation. Absolute silence is only the lot of a herd of slaves in the presence of a haughty master. Citizens will always make their voices heard, and the quarrels aroused by subaltern groups are the best way to avoid the violent factions of civil war.

Those who constantly demand equality and the introduction of the state of nature into civil government are badly instructed. What seems to separate citizens, that is, what represses force and audacity, is precisely what united them.

It is therefore necessary to make inequality a part of political constitutions. The ideal would be to admit only that inequality which is necessary to the movement and maintenance of society. . . .

It is the people who make the government and not the government which makes the people. For a long time the cause has been mistaken. It is absurd to believe that laws will modify a people which will not know them, which will not love them, or which will adopt them only under duress.

When a people is advanced enough to receive good laws, they

form and propagate themselves. *The majesty of the people*—that is the most beautiful phrase that can exist in any language; it is *the people* who do everything.

Chapter LXXI. The Professor of Government (Continued)

Those who have wanted to base human equality on the equal division of land have committed a serious error, since one acre of land resembles another no more than one man resembles another. Equality is the necessary consequence of the establishment of society, since society needs farmers, farm hands, workers, artisans, to supply the needs of the soldier, the magistrate, and the priest. Extreme equality would necessarily be extreme confusion.

That is why republics have found it so difficult to rest on a secure basis. With their supposed and illusory equality they clashed with the order established by nature. It is necessary to have a single and constant spring which tends to enhance the national life. Remove the energetic principle of political life, and you remove all action toward the good which that spring is supposed to produce.

Why has Plato's republic been so justly mocked? It is because the whole, after you have admired some details or charming maxims, offers nothing that satisfies the mind, and you feel vaguely that the political machine lacks a moving principle.

Pride, natural rebelliousness, momentary passions, all rebel against this primitive spring. When societies become larger, more governed, and more numerous, this unique and prompt spring becomes more necessary. It has not been realized that politics would go astray within a maze without exit, if authority were not fixed in a central point which is considered the most essential to social happiness.

If contradiction rules among laws, principles, customs, it is for the lack of a simple spring that would act on all individuals; for who does not see that between two passionate beings the help of a third is needed to protect them against injustice and violence.

Too often equality has been confused with natural freedom. Man is not naturally equal to his fellow men, because one individual's faculties are naturally unequal to another's. . . .

Chapter LXXII. Freedom of the Press

Of all the possessions of man, thought is indisputably the most essentially undeniable. It is thought which distinguishes him emi-

nently from the other beings who share the earth with him. How is
it possible for despotism to have conceived the project of stripping
man of this faculty which constitutes his unique greatness? How
can we deprive him of this noble attribute? Is it not a faculty
which belongs to man and with which nature endows him when he
is born? It is therefore the height of outrage to wish to deprive him
of a quality inherent to his being. If man can have no other possession that is dearer to him than his thought, then there is none which
the law of nations should preserve with greater care. All other
possessions are nothing compared to this one. To deny man the
freedom of thought, or even the abuse of thought, is really to order
him to live in a state of degradation and to put him together with
crawling or vegetating beings. What is false, evil, and unreasonable
soon becomes despised; and the laws may not despoil man of the
use of his thought, because that would be to annihilate in him what
is most personal and most defining. . . .

Who will quiet factions? Who will submit all individuals to the
law? The enlightenment of the people. It will always be the source
of moderation. It is ignorance that drives people to extremist
parties; the security of governments is in direct ratio to the extent
and universality of knowledge. Do not citizens have to know the
laws of their country to love them? And when these laws, clarified
by so many enlightened men, are known, do they not become
imperceptibly favorable to the freedom of thought and the political rights of the citizens? The more the people reflect on the reciprocal links of society the better able they will be to resist dangerous ideas that some will try to give them.

Look at England. Universal enlightenment insures the tranquility of its church and government. . . . The strength of that republic is in the powerful spring which, after having enlightened the
citizens about the advantages of the constitution, makes them act
together for its happiness. Deprive this people of their enlightenment, and they will lose their greatness. It is men who are reduced
to having neither will nor opinions who should be deprived of
knowledge. But then let us no longer look for citizens; there are
only degraded men.

37. D'Holbach, Ethocracy, or Government Founded on Morals

The Union of Morals and Politics

THE GREAT Sully said that good morals and good laws form each other. Politics can never be separated from morals, nor lose it one moment from view, without equal danger to sovereigns and subjects. Whatever form of government a nation may adopt, those who exercise the public authority are, by that very fact, obliged to guide it toward happiness. But happiness is not compatible with vice or disorder and is found only in the practice of the duties of social life, in constant observance of justice, in respect for virtue. . . .

If, as everything demonstrates, the opposition of interests between the sovereign and the subject has produced the fatal divorce we so often find in both politics and morals, reason, guided by long and constant experience, should bring them together. United, then, with the people they govern, the rulers of nations should powerfully urge all the citizens to contribute according to their abilities to the general welfare.

This desirable reunion of Politics and Morality cannot alone effectuate a reform of morals, which philosophy deprived of power would attempt in vain. After all, what effect could the sterile counsels of reason, which always annoy hardened, corrupted, self-indulgent people, have? What effect can idle exhortations be against riotous passions and harmful inclinations strengthened by habit? As one enlightened magistrate has said, we need a practical morality, published by a legitimate authority and codified in law. . . . The unfavorable reception that the most useful truths encounter in a frivolous or perverse world should not discourage citizens who are strongly animated by a passion for the public

SOURCE: Paul Henri Thiry, Baron d' Holbach, *Ethocratie; ou, le gouvernement fondé sur la morale* (Amsterdam: M. M. Rey, 1776). Translated by the editor.

welfare. Time, Seneca said, is very wise, for it discovers everything. Truths that are important for men will never be lost; often
useless to the present generation, they will make the happiness of
future generations. What would be the condition of the human
mind if the wise, contradicted and persecuted by their contemporaries, had not sown for posterity, which is always more equitable
and less prejudiced than its ancestors and which enjoys advantages
they foolishly disdained!

Do we not have examples, present to our eyes, sufficient to prove
that we must not despair of the human race? May not a Prince,
who is a friend of justice and order, become in a short time the
restorer of a vast empire? Wisdom and equity, armed with great
power, are capable of changing the face of a State rapidly. Absolute power is very useful when it is directed to wiping out abuses
and injustices, to correcting vice and reforming morals. Despotism
would be the best government if we could be sure that it was
always in the hands of a Titus, a Trajan, a Marcus Aurelius; but
usually it falls into hands incapable of using it wisely. . . .

Virtue creates prosperous, happy, and powerful nations. Tyranny regrets prosperity and prefers to see them weak and under-
nourished. Good laws make the safety of a State, but tyranny does
not want to be hindered. . . .

If virtue and good morals are incompatible with bad government, they are the foundation of a reasonable government. In it,
the sovereign knows the duties which tie him to his people, and
which become the guarantees of their common security. . . .

Consequently, only honorable governments can command good
citizens. Only a legislator who is enlightened by reason and equity
can form collaborators in his political work. The sovereign must be
good and just himself if he wishes to rule over virtuous subjects.

Brief Idea of the Fundamental Laws of a Good Government

In order for the sovereign who is on the watch for the lies and
the flatteries of the courtiers who surround him to hear distinctly
the free voice of the citizens, the fundamental laws should set up in
a stable way a body of representatives, chosen from the most
honest and enlightened citizens and those who are most devoted to
the public welfare. They will be charged with defining the interests that they have in common with their fellow citizens.

To prevent betrayal by these representatives, the fundamental laws should see to it that elections are not carried on by factions, intrigues, bribery, or in the midst of public tumult. Any man who is convicted of having obtained his job through these reprehensible means deserves to be forever excluded from the right of defining the interests of his country. A secret ballot seems the surest way to assure tranquil elections.

The fundamental law should give the representatives the immutable right to assemble, without awaiting the ruler's convocation, since ministers and flatterers may prevent him from hearing the most just and pressing complaints of his people.

It is in the body of representatives of the nation that all laws should be made, discussed, corrected, abrogated. When this is done, the whole nation takes part in forming the rules it must follow, the taxes it must pay, the wars it is to undertake, or terminate, the sacrifices it must make for its own safety, the debts it may contract. But it would perhaps be useful for there to be rigorous laws to prevent a State from borrowing. Would not temporary taxes, as heavy as they may be, be more advantageous than accumulated debts with which the nation will be forever saddled? Too much borrowing often ruins a people just as surely as an individual. . . .

The law should always subordinate the national deputies or representatives to their constituents. The latter should have the right to punish or to recall with ignominy when their government has been betrayed. In a well-organized government, no man, whatever his rank, should be exempt from the fear of being punished for crimes. . . .

Since any government should have for its unvarying aim only the happiness of the nation it governs, the fundamental laws should ensure, in the most solemn way: (I) *freedom*, which is the right to do for one's own happiness, or one's own interest, all that is not contrary to the happiness or the interests of others; (II) the laws should irrevocably ensure *property*; that is to say, the secure and tranquil possession of things which the citizen may have justly acquired; (III) the same laws should ensure to every citizen the *security* of his person as long as he is just or doesn't harm society. A nation is under the most frightful tyranny when it depends on the passion or the caprice of any man powerful enough to imprison or dispose of the citizen who displeases him.

Thus, without justice, there can be in a State neither liberty, nor property, nor security. Liberty is only the power of exercising one's faculties in a way that hurts no one. Property is the right to possess justly or without harm to others. Personal security is the right to fear nothing from anyone as long as one is not hurting anyone. . . .

Good morals make good citizens, that is to say, men who are capable of using freedom properly and incapable of abusing it. Only an education which is moral and national can form for the State honest subjects who are worthy of freedom. Thus public education, so shamefully neglected, should be one of the principal concerns of a good government; itself just, it should form citizens who resemble it. . . .

The fundamental laws should determine the rights of an established religion, the fate of its ministers, the external conduct they should observe. But these laws should never intrude into dogma or seek to ferret out the opinions of peaceful citizens. They will forever proscribe the intolerance, religious disputes, the harangues of fanaticism, and above all the fury of persecution. Tyranny of thought is the most cruel, revolting, and useless violation of human liberty. . . .

Under a just and wise government laws should ensure the freedom of expression of one's thoughts. Freedom of the press is redoubtable only to tyranny, which is always worried and suspicious. A good government fears neither satire or criticism. It profits with pleasure from the knowledge and ideas that the lowest of citizens can sometimes give it. The laws should condemn only libelous writings and licentious works, which are alone harmful to society. Metaphysical discussions are interesting to very few people. Political rights may contain ideas which those who govern are free to judge, to adopt, or to reject. Extravagant systems are sufficiently punished by scorn, ridicule, and oblivion.

38.   Restif de la Bretonne, *The Australasian Discovery, by a Flying-Man, or the French Daedalus*

THE BASIS of all our morals is order. We say that the moral order must resemble the physical. In our country no one ever violates it, nor is he able to violate it. We are all equal. There is one simple, short, clear law which alone speaks; and never does man replace it. This law can be expressed in few words:

(1) Be just toward your brother; that is to say, do not require anything of him, do nothing to him that you would not do yourself or that you would not want others to do to you.

(2) Be just toward animals, as you would want an animal superior to man to be just to you.

(3) Let everything be held in common among equals.

(4) Let each one work for the general good.

(5) Let each one participate equally in it.

With this single law we take care of everything. We think that no people needs to have any other, unless it is a people of oppressors and slaves. In that case, although I have never seen such a people, I feel that there will be numerous laws and hindrances, such as are needed to legitimize injustice, inequality, and the tyranny of a few over the whole body. These unfortunate peoples think that in this way they are at least creating the happiness of the dominant. They are mistaken. There is no happiness except in fraternity, in this sweet feeling: "Nobody envies me, my happiness takes nothing away from anyone; all my brothers are equal in enjoyment." Ah! How can those who are supposedly happy in an unequal nation, if they are men, gorge themselves while other men are lacking the necessities of life! How can they seek pleasure while others suffer! How can they take delight in anything while others are crushed with labor! If they can withstand all that, their hearts are too

SOURCE: Nicolas Edme Restif de la Bretonne, *La Découverte australe* (Leipzig, 1781). Translated by the editor.

hardened for them to enjoy pleasure. They do not know it, they have no humanity; the feeling of compassion is extinguished in their hearts. . . .

"Do you have spectacles," asked Hermantin, "dramatic performances, illustrious Megapatagon?"

"Those kinds of pleasures are petty things, worthy of a nation of children," replied the wise Teugnil. "We want only reality, and we have only just enough time to enjoy true pleasures, without inventing artificial ones."

"Do you not have the fine arts like painting, sculpture, music, poetry?"

"We despise painting. Our paintings are our beautiful men and women whom we see daily. If the human race were wiped out and only one individual remained, condemned to live eternally alone on earth, we would find it excusable for him to apply himself to the two arts of painting and sculpture in order to beguile his solitude by a deceitful image. Perhaps, too, if we had your way of living and left our country to travel for years at a time, we might desire to paint those we love. But here, with our morals, painting and sculpture would be only a puerility. We have much greater esteem for the useful crafts than for those useless arts! Nevertheless, we have a few painters, a small group representing the fine actions of our most virtuous citizens. These paintings are destined to ornament the dwelling places of the old men who performed these deeds. As for music, I have told you that we have it. It is one of the charms of life to hear the trained sounds of the human voice, to sing the praise of great men, and our pleasures and loves. Poetry is the sister of music; it is a more animated and harmonious way of saying things. But we use it only for pleasing subjects. It is ridiculous in dramatic subjects, and harmful in didactic subjects. In a word, we have only three kinds of poetic forms, those which celebrate the actions of heroes, mankind's benefactors, of whom we can speak only with enthusiasm, and those we call *ode* and *song*. It is forbidden to put into verse any other production of the mind.
. . . There is even a limit in our enjoyments; we never carry them to the point of satiety. But what strengthens good morals among us is the fact that they are not abandoned, as you have told me they are in Europe, to individual caprice. By means of our equality and

our community, our moral life is uniform and public. We practice virtue in a body; we reject vice in a body; laziness, useless acts, overeating, debauchery—all that is made impossible.

39. Diderot, Observations on the Drawing Up of Laws

Observations on the Instructions of the Empress of Russia to the Deputies for the Drawing Up of Laws

THERE IS no true sovereign but the nation; there can be no true legislator but the people. It is only rarely that a people will submit itself sincerely to laws imposed on it; but it will respect, obey, and defend as its own work laws that it has created itself. . . . Laws are useless if there is a single member of society who may infringe them with impunity. . . .

The first line of a well-conceived code of law ought to bind the sovereign. It should begin thus: "We the people and we the Sovereign of this people conjointly swear to uphold these laws, by which we are both to be judged; and if it should happen that we the Sovereign change or break these laws, thus becoming the enemy of our people, it is just that our people should become our enemy also, that it should be freed from its oath of fidelity, that should the case require it. Such is the first law of our code: woe to the people that suffers the law to be treated with contempt.". . .

The distance between altar and throne can never be too great. Experience in all places and all ages has proved the danger of proximity between the altar and the throne. . . .

There is no place in the world where it has proved possible to reduce priests to the status of citizens pure and simple without the use of violence. . . . They have everywhere claimed the right to a special jurisdiction. . . . A wise and enlightened policy would prescribe very strictly what they are permitted to say [to the

SOURCE: Translated by Derek Coltman in *Diderot's Selected Writings* (New York: The Macmillan Company, 1966), pp. 299–306 *passim*. Reprinted by permission of the publishers.

people], and any transgression of those limits would be punished by severe penalties. For disturbances in society are never more fearful than when those who are stirring up the trouble can use the pretext of religion to mask their true designs.

Because they intercede for them with God, who alone has the power to exact vengeance for the oppression of kings, subject peoples, if too much oppressed, grow accustomed to regarding priests as their protectors . . .

The priest, whose philosophic system is a tissue of absurdities, secretly tends to maintain ignorance; reason is the enemy of faith, and faith is the foundation of the priest's position, his fortune, and his prestige. . . .

The philosopher speaks very ill of the priest; the priest speaks very ill of the philosopher. But the philosopher has never killed any priests, whereas the priest has killed a great many philosophers. Nor has the philosopher ever killed any kings, whereas the priest has killed a great many. . . .

Morals are in all countries the result of legislation and government; they are not African or Asian or European: they are good or bad. . . . Whatever Peter the Great brought to Russia, if it was good in Europe, then it was good everywhere. . . .

It is against this master [the ruler], potentially the most dangerous evildoer of all, that the laws ought principally to be directed. Other evildoers may disturb the social order; he alone has the power to overthrow it. . . .

Three excellent and successive despots would accustom a nation to blind obedience. Under such a rule, the people would forget their inalienable rights; they would be lulled into apathy and a fatal sense of security; they would no longer feel the continual sense of alarm that is the necessary guardian of their liberty. . . .

In any country whatsoever, the sovereign authority must therefore always be limited, and the limits imposed must be lasting ones. The difficult problem that faces us is not, therefore, how to give a people laws or even how to give it good ones; it is how to protect those laws from any attempt at infringement that might be made upon them by the ruler. . . .

Since it is the law of nature that there should be twenty madmen for each wise man, a good government will be one under which the liberty of individuals is as great as possible and the liberty of the sovereign as restricted as possible. . . .

It seems to me that the source of all political and civil power can only be the consent of the nation, a consent expressed either by the nation itself in assembly or by its deputies. . . .

If the depository [of the legislative power] is subordinated to and dependent upon the supreme power, then all legislation is useless. . . .

Nevertheless, one should enlighten and instruct [the people], though without expecting too much from this means.

The rights of the intermediary powers between sovereign and people ought to be fixed, and fixed in such a way that they cannot be revoked either by the legislator himself or by his successors: if the intermediary powers are dependent upon the supreme power, then they are nothing. A free people differs from a nation of slaves only by the inalienability of certain privileges that belong to man as man, to each class of citizens as a branch of the social order, and to each citizen as a member of society. . . . For a sovereign to bind himself and also to bind his successor, that is the height of heroism, humanity, and love for his subjects—but it is also one of the most difficult things to achieve by legislation. I know only three or four ways of doing it: public awareness or instruction, brevity of the code and the laws, education, a national oath and periodic assembly of the Estates-General, and, above all, confirmation of rights by the enjoyment of them over a long period of time.

The equality of citizens consists in their all being subjected to the same laws. The sentence should read "equally subjected."

This paragraph must necessarily lead to the abolition of all the privileges of the nobility, the clergy, and the magistracy. But I should like to know what precautions will be taken to ensure that citizens who are unequal in power, in influence, in means of all kinds will still be all equal in the courts of law. It should be so, it has always been supposed that it is so, but it never has been so, and perhaps it has never been possible for it to be so. It is a goal well worth our consideration. . . .

Patriotism is an ephemeral motive that scarcely ever outlasts the particular threat to society that aroused it.

Shame and the fear of disapproval, which act as checks to a small number of decent people, will never be sufficient to form the spirit and morals of a large nation. These means must be replaced by freedom, by security of persons and property, and by happiness.

The punishment for a bad action ought not to be legal conviction, yet no bad action ought often to go unpunished—that is to say, it ought to punish itself, which will always happen if any good or ill that befalls society is always indissolubly linked with the good or ill that befalls those who compose it.

There are no constant and universal morals except those founded upon laws.

The decisions of law courts should never be printed: in the long run, they form a counter authority to the law. Commentators on the Scriptures have committed a thousand heresies; commentators on the laws have buried those laws beneath their glosses. Let there be no other authority or means of defense in courts of law than law itself, reason, and natural justice. Once a sentence has been pronounced or executed, the court's decision must be obliterated: it should be illegal to cite it. If the court was in error, then citing that erroneous judgment is simply asking it to commit the same injustice again. All citing of precedents must be forbidden.

Before everything else, a society must be happy. It will be happy if the freedom and property of individuals are secure, if trade is unrestricted, if all classes of citizens are equal before the law, if taxes are levied in proportion to the ability to pay and do not exceed the needs of the State, if virtue and talent are assured of a just reward. . . .

If man was made only to plow and reap, to eat and sell, then it is no great matter. But it seems to me that a being capable of feeling was intended to achieve happiness through all his thoughts. Is there any reason for setting a limit to the mind and senses and for saying to man: You shall think only thus far; you shall feel only thus far? I believe that this kind of philosophy tends to keep man in a state of brutishness and to restrict his pleasures and happiness in a way quite contrary to his nature. Any philosophy that goes against human nature is absurd, as is all legislation that continually forces the citizen to sacrifice his own tastes and happiness to the good of society. I want society to be happy, but I also wish to be happy myself, and there are as many ways of being happy as there are individuals.

All true duties must have our own happiness as their foundation. . . .

40. Madison, The Federalist

To THE PEOPLE of the state of New York: Among the numerous advantages promised by a well-constructed Union, none deserves to be more accurately developed than its tendency to break and control the violence of faction. The friend of popular governments never finds himself so much alarmed for their character and fate, as when he contemplates their propensity to this dangerous vice. He will not fail, therefore, to set a due value on any plan which, without violating the principles to which he is attached, provides a proper cure for it. The instability, injustice, and confusion introduced into the public councils have, in truth, been the mortal diseases under which popular governments have everywhere perished; as they continue to be the favorite and fruitful topics from which the adversaries to liberty derive their most specious declamations. The valuable improvements made by the American constitutions on the popular models, both ancient and modern, cannot certainly be too much admired; but it would be an unwarrantable partiality, to contend that they have as effectually obviated the danger on this side, as was wished and expected. Complaints are everywhere heard from our most considerate and virtuous citizens, equally the friends of public and private faith, and of public and personal liberty, that our governments are too unstable, that the public good is disregarded in the conflicts of rival parties, and that measures are too often decided, not according to the rules of justice and the rights of the minor party, but by the superior force of an interested and overbearing majority. However anxiously we may wish that these complaints had no foundation, the evidence of known facts will not permit us to deny that they are in some degree true. It will be found, indeed, on a candid review of our situation, that some of the distresses under which we labor have been erroneously charged on the operation of our governments;

SOURCE: *The Federalist* (New York: The Heritage Press, 1945), pp. 54–62.

but it will be found, at the same time, that other causes will not alone account for many of our heaviest misfortunes; and, particularly, for that prevailing and increasing distrust of public engagements, and alarm for private rights, which are echoed from one end of the continent to the other. These must be chiefly, if not wholly, effects of the unsteadiness and injustice with which a factious spirit has tainted our public administrations.

By a faction, I understand a number of citizens, whether amounting to a majority or minority of the whole, who are united and actuated by some common impulse of passion, or of interest, adverse to the rights of other citizens, or to the permanent and aggregate interests of the community.

There are two methods of curing the mischiefs of faction: the one, by removing its causes; the other, by controlling its effects.

There are again two methods of removing the causes of faction: the one, by destroying the liberty which is essential to its existence; the other, by giving to every citizen the same opinions, the same passions, and the same interests.

It could never be more truly said than of the first remedy, that it was worse than the disease. Liberty is to faction what air is to fire, an ailment without which it instantly expires. But it could not be less folly to abolish liberty, which is essential to political life, because it nourishes faction, than it would be to wish the annihilation of air, which is essential to animal life, because it imparts to fire its destructive agency.

The second expedient is as impracticable as the first would be unwise. As long as the reason of man continues fallible, and he is at liberty to exercise it, different opinions will be formed. As long as the connection subsists between his reason and his self-love, his opinions and his passions will have a reciprocal influence on each other; and the former will be objects to which the latter will attach themselves. The diversity in the faculties of men, from which the rights of property originate, is not less an insuperable obstacle to a uniformity of interests. The protection of these faculties is the first object of government. From the protection of different and unequal faculties of acquiring property, the possession of different degrees and kinds of property immediately results; and from the influence of these on the sentiments and views of the respective proprietors, ensues a division of the society into different interests and parties.

The latent causes of faction are thus sown in the nature of man; and we see them everywhere brought into different degrees of activity, according to the different circumstances of civil society. A zeal for different opinions concerning religion, concerning government, and many other points, as well of speculation as of practice; an attachment to different leaders ambitiously contending for pre-eminence and power; or to persons of other descriptions whose fortunes have been interesting to the human passions, have, in turn, divided mankind into parties, inflamed them with mutual animosity, and rendered them much more disposed to vex and oppress each other than to co-operate for their common good. So strong is this propensity of mankind to fall into mutual animosities, that where no substantial occasion presents itself, the most frivolous and fanciful distinctions have been sufficient to kindle their unfriendly passions and excite their most violent conflicts. But the most common and durable source of factions has been the various and unequal distribution of property. Those who hold and those who are without property have ever formed distinct interests in society. Those who are creditors, and those who are debtors, fall under a like discrimination. A landed interest, a manufacturing interest, a mercantile interest, a moneyed interest, with many lesser interests, grow up of necessity in civilized nations, and divide them into different classes, actuated by different sentiments and views. The regulation of these various and interfering interests forms the principal task of modern legislation, and involves the spirit of party and faction in the necessary and ordinary operations of the government.

No man is allowed to be a judge in his own cause, because his interest would certainly bias his judgment, and, not improbably, corrupt his integrity. With equal, nay with greater reason, a body of men are unfit to be both judges and parties at the same time; yet what are many of the most important acts of legislation, but so many judicial determinations, not indeed concerning the rights of single persons, but concerning the rights of large bodies of citizens? And what are the different classes of legislators but advocates and parties to the causes which they determine? Is a law proposed concerning private debts? It is a question to which the creditors are parties on one side and the debtors on the other. Justice ought to hold the balance between them. Yet the parties are, and must be, themselves the judges; and the most numerous party, or, in other words, the most powerful faction must be expected to prevail. Shall domestic manufactures be encouraged, and in what degree, by restrictions on foreign manufactures? are questions which would be differently decided by the landed and the manufacturing classes, and probably by neither with a sole regard to justice and the public good. The apportionment of taxes on the various descriptions of property is an act which seems to require the most exact impartiality; yet there is, perhaps, no legislative act in which greater opportunity and temptation are given to a predominant party to trample on the rules of justice. Every shilling with which they overburden the inferior number, is a shilling saved to their own pockets.

It is in vain to say that enlightened statesmen will be able to adjust these clashing interests, and render them all subservient to the public good. Enlightened statesmen will not always be at the helm. Nor, in many cases, can such an adjustment be made at all without taking into view indirect and remote considerations, which will rarely prevail over the immediate interest which one party may find in disregarding the rights of another or the good of the whole.

The inference to which we are brought is, that the *causes* of faction cannot be removed, and that relief is only to be sought in the means of controlling its *effects*.

If a faction consists of less than a majority, relief is supplied by the republican principle, which enables the majority to defeat its sinister views by regular vote. It may clog the administration, it may convulse the society; but it will be unable to execute and mask its violence under the forms of the Constitution. When a majority is included in a faction, the form of popular government, on the other hand, enables it to sacrifice to its ruling passion or interest both the public good and the rights of other citizens. To secure the public good and private rights against the danger of such a faction, and at the same time to preserve the spirit and the form of popular government, is then the great object to which our inquiries are directed. Let me add that it is the great desideratum by which this form of government can be rescued from the opprobrium under which it has so long labored, and be recommended to the esteem and adoption of mankind.

By what means is this object attainable? Evidently by one of two only. Either the existence of the same passion or interest in a majority at the same time must be prevented, or the majority, having such co-existent passion or interest, must be rendered, by their number and local situation, unable to concert and carry into effect schemes of oppression. If the impulse and the opportunity be suffered to coincide, we well know that neither moral nor religious motives can be relied on as an adequate control. They are not found to be such on the injustice and violence of individuals, and lose their efficacy in proportion to the number combined together, that is, in proportion as their efficacy becomes needful.

From this view of the subject it may be concluded that a pure democracy, by which I mean a society consisting of a small number of citizens, who assemble and administer the government in person, can admit of no cure for the mischiefs of faction. A common passion or interest will, in almost every case, be felt by a majority of the whole; a communication and concert result from the form of government itself; and there is nothing to check the inducements to sacrifice the weaker party or an obnoxious individual. Hence it is that such democracies have ever been spectacles of turbulence and contention; have ever been found incompatible with personal security or the rights of property; and have in general been as short in their lives as they have been violent in their deaths. Theoretic politicians, who have patronized this species of government, have erroneously supposed that by reducing mankind to a perfect equality in their political rights, they would, at the same time, be perfectly equalized and assimilated in their possessions, their opinions, and their passions.

A republic, by which I mean a government in which the scheme of representation takes place, opens a different prospect, and promises the cure for which we are seeking. Let us examine the points in which it varies from pure democracy, and we shall comprehend both the nature of the cure and the efficacy which it must derive from the Union.

The two great points of difference between a democracy and a republic are; first, the delegation of the government, in the latter, to a small number of citizens elected by the rest; secondly, the greater number of citizens, and greater sphere of country, over which the latter may be extended.

The effect of the first difference is, on the one hand, to refine and enlarge the public views, by passing them through the medium of a chosen body of citizens, whose wisdom may best discern the true interest of their country, and whose patriotism and love of justice will be least likely to sacrifice it to temporary or partial considerations. Under such a regulation, it may well happen that the public voice, pronounced by the representatives of the people, will be more consonant to the public good than if pronounced by the people themselves, convened for the purpose. On the other hand, the effect may be inverted. Men of factious tempers, of local prejudices, or of sinister designs, may, by intrigue, by corruption, or by other means, first obtain the suffrages, and then betray the interests, of the people. The question resulting is, whether small or extensive republics are more favorable to the election of proper guardians of the public weal; and it is clearly decided in favor of the latter by two obvious considerations:

In the first place, it is to be remarked that, however small the republic may be, the representatives must be raised to a certain number, in order to guard against the cabals of a few; and that, however large it may be, they must be limited to a certain number, in order to guard against the confusion of a multitude. Hence, the number of representatives in the two cases not being in proportion to that of the two constituents, and being proportionally greater in the small republic, it follows that, if the proportion of fit characters be not less in the large than in the small republic, the former will present a greater option, and consequently a greater probability of a fit choice.

In the next place, as each representative will be chosen by a greater number of citizens in the large than in the small republic, it will be more difficult for unworthy candidates to practice with success the vicious arts by which elections are too often carried; and the suffrages of the people being more free, will be more likely to center in men who possess the most attractive merit and the most diffusive and established characters.

It must be confessed that in this, as in most other cases, there is a mean, on both sides of which inconveniences will be found to lie. By enlarging too much the number of electors, who render the representative too little acquainted with all their local circumstances and lesser interests; as by reducing it too much, you render him unduly attached to these, and too little fit to comprehend and pursue great and national objects. The federal Constitution forms a happy combination in this respect; the great and aggregate interests being referred to the national, the local and particular to the State legislatures.

The other point of difference is, the greater number of citizens and extent of territory which may be brought within the compass of republican than of democratic government; and it is this circumstance principally which renders factious combinations less to be dreaded in the former than in the latter. The smaller the society, the fewer probably will be the distinct parties and interests composing it; the fewer the distinct parties and interests, the more frequently will a majority be found of the same party; and the smaller the number of individuals composing a majority, and the smaller the compass within which they are placed, the more easily will they convert and execute their plans of oppression. Extend the sphere, and you take in a greater variety of parties and interests; you make it less probable that a majority of the whole will have a common motive to invade the rights of other citizens; or if such a common motive exists, it will be more difficult for all who feel it to discover their own strength, and to act in unison with each other. Besides other impediments, it may be remarked that, where there is a consciousness of unjust or dishonorable purposes, communication is always checked by distrust in proportion to the number whose concurrence is necessary.

Hence, it clearly appears, that the same advantage which a republic has over a democracy, in controlling the effects of faction, is enjoyed by a large over a small republic,—is enjoyed by the Union over the States composing it. Does the advantage consist in the substitution of representatives whose enlightened views and virtuous sentiments render them superior to local prejudices and to schemes of injustice? It will not be denied that the representation of the Union will be most likely to possess these requisite endowments. Does it consist in the greater security afforded by a greater variety of parties, against the event of any one party being able to outnumber and oppress the rest? In an equal degree does the increased variety of parties comprised within the Union, increase this security? Does it, in fine, consist in the greater obstacles opposed to the concert and accomplishment of the secret wishes of an unjust and interested majority? Here, again, the extent of the Union gives it the most palpable advantage.

The influence of factious leaders may kindle a flame within their particular States, but will be unable to spread a general conflagration through the other States. A religious sect may degenerate into a political faction in a part of the Confederacy; but the variety of sects dispersed over the entire face of it must secure the national councils against any danger from that source. A rage for paper money, for an abolition of debts, for an equal division of property, or for any other improper or wicked project, will be less apt to pervade the whole body of the Union than a particular member of it; in the same proportion as such a malady is more likely to taint a particular county or district, than an entire State.

In the extent and proper structure of the Union, therefore, we behold a republican remedy for the diseases most incident to republican government. And according to the degree of pleasure and pride we feel in being republicans, ought to be our zeal in cherishing the spirit and supporting the character of Federalists.

PUBLIUS

41. Jefferson, Letters to Colonel Edward Carrington and John Adams

---

A.   To Colonel Edward Carrington

Paris, January 16, 1787

THE TUMULTS in America I expected would have produced in Europe an unfavorable opinion of our political state. But it has not. On the contrary, the small effect of these tumults seems to have given more confidence in the firmness of our governments. The interposition of the people themselves on the side of government has had a great effect on the opinion here. I am persuaded myself that the good sense of the people will always be found to be the best army. They may be led astray for a moment, but will soon correct themselves. The people are the only censors of their governors; and even their errors will tend to keep these to the true

SOURCE: Andrew A. Lipscomb (ed.), *The Writings of Thomas Jefferson* (Washington, D.C.: The Thomas Jefferson Memorial Association of the United States), VI, 55–59.

principles of their institution. To punish these errors too severely would be to suppress the only safeguard of the public liberty. The way to prevent these irregular interpositions of the people, is to give them full information of their affairs through the channel of the public papers, and to contrive that those papers should penetrate the whole mass of the people. The basis of our governments being the opinion of the people, the very first object should be to keep that right; and were it left to me to decide whether we should have a government without newspapers, or newspapers without a government, I should not hesitate a moment to prefer the latter. But I should mean that every man should receive those papers, and be capable of reading them. I am convinced that those societies (as the Indians) which live without government, enjoy in their general mass an infinitely greater degree of happiness than those who live under the European governments. Among the former, public opinion is in the place of law, and restrains morals as powerfully as laws ever did anywhere. Among the latter, under pretence of governing, they have divided their nations into two classes, wolves and sheep. I do not exaggerate. This is a true picture of Europe. Cherish, therefore, the spirit of our people, and keep alive their attention. Do not be too severe upon their errors, but reclaim them by enlightening them. If once they become inattentive to the public affairs, you and I, and Congress and Assemblies, Judges and Governors, shall all become wolves. It seems to be the law of our general nature, in spite of individual exceptions; and experience declares that man is the only animal which devours his own kind; for I can apply no milder term to the governments of Europe, and to the general prey of the rich on the poor. The want of news has led me into disquisition instead of narration, forgetting you have every day enough of that. I shall be happy to hear from you sometimes, only observing that whatever passes through the post is read, and that when you write what should be read by myself only, you must be so good as to confide your letter to some passenger, or officer of the packet. I will ask your permission to write to you sometimes, and to assure you of the esteem and respect with which I have honor to be, dear Sir, your most obedient, and most humble servant.

THOMAS JEFFERSON

B. Jefferson to Adams

Monticello Oct. 28. [18] 13

Dear Sir

According to the reservation between us, of taking up one of the subjects of our correspondence at a time, I turn to your letters of Aug. 16. and Sep. 2.

The passage you quote from Theognis,[1] I think has an Ethical, rather than a political object. The whole piece is a moral *exhortation*, παραίνεσις, and this passage particularly seems to be a reproof to man, who, while with his domestic animals he is curious to improve the race by employing always the finest male, pays no attention to the improvement of his own race, but intermarries with the vicious, the ugly, or the old, for considerations of wealth or ambition. It is in conformity with the principle adopted afterwards by the Pythagoreans, and expressed by Ocellus in another form. Περι δε τῆς ἐκ τῶν αλληλων ανθρωπων γενεσεως etc.—ουχ ἡδονης ἑνεκα ἡ μιζις. Which, as literally as intelligibility will admit, may be thus translated. "Concerning the interprocreation of men, how, and of whom it shall be, in a perfect manner, and according to the laws of modesty and sanctity, conjointly, this is what I think right. First to lay it down that we do not commix for the sake of pleasure, but of the procreation of children. For the powers, the organs and desires for coition have not been given by god to man for the sake of pleasure, but for the procreation of the race. For as it were incongruous for a mortal born to partake of divine life, the immortality of the race being taken away, god fulfilled the purpose by making the generations uninterrupted and continuous. This therefore we are especially to lay down as a principle, that coition is not for the sake of pleasure." But Nature, not trusting to this moral and abstract motive, seems to have provided more securely for the perpetuation of the species by making it the effect of the oestrum

Source: Lester J. Cappon (ed.), *The Adams-Jefferson Letters* (Chapel Hill, N.C.: University of North Carolina Press, 1959), pp. 387–92.

[1] Theognis of Megara, Greek poet (Sixth Century b.c.)—Ed.

implanted in the constitution of both sexes. And not only has the commerce of love been indulged on this unhallowed impulse, but made subservient also to wealth and ambition by marriages without regard to the beauty, the healthiness, the understanding, or virtue of the subject from which we are to breed. The selecting the best male for a Haram of well chosen females also, which Theognis seems to recommend from the example of our sheep and asses, would doubtless improve the human, as it does the brute animal, and produce a race of veritable αριστοι ["aristocrats"]. For experience proves that the moral and physical qualities of man, whether good or evil, are transmissible in a certain degree from father to son. But I suspect that the equal rights of men will rise up against this privileged Solomon, and oblige us to continue acquiescence under the Ἀμαυρωοις γενεος ἀστων ["the degeneration of the race of men"] which Theognis complains of, and to content ourselves with the accidental aristoi produced by the fortuitous concourse of breeders. For I agree with you that there is a natural aristocracy among men. The grounds of this are virtue and talents. Formerly bodily powers gave place among the aristoi. But since the invention of gunpowder has armed the weak as well as the strong with missile death, bodily strength, like beauty, good humor, politeness and other accomplishments, has become but an auxiliary ground of distinction. There is also an artificial aristocracy founded on wealth and birth, without either virtue or talents; for with these it would belong to the first class. The natural aristocracy I consider as the most precious gift of nature for the instruction, the trusts, and government of society. And indeed it would have been inconsistent in creation to have formed man for the social state, and not to have provided virtue and wisdom enough to manage the concerns of the society. May we not even say that that form of government is the best which provides the most effectually for a pure selection of these natural aristoi into the offices of government? The artificial aristocracy is a mischievous ingredient in government, and provision should be made to prevent its ascendancy. On the question, What is the best provision, you and I differ; but we differ as rational friends, using the free exercise of our own reason, and mutually indulging its errors. *You* think it best to put the Pseudo-aristoi into a separate chamber of legislation where they may be hindered from doing mischief by their coordinate branches, and where also they may be a protection to wealth against the Agrarian and plundering enterprises of the Majority of the people. I think that to give them power in order to prevent them from doing mischief, is arming them for it, and increasing instead of remedying the evil. For if the coordinate branches can arrest their action, so may they that of the coordinates. Mischief may be done negatively as well as positively. Of this a cabal in the Senate of the U. S. has furnished many proofs. Nor do I believe them necessary to protect the wealthy; because enough of these will find their way into every branch of the legislation to protect themselves. From 15. to 20. legislatures of our own, in action for 30. years past, have proved that no fears of an equalisation of property are to be apprehended from them.

I think the best remedy is exactly that provided by all our constitutions, to leave to the citizens the free election and separation of the aristoi from the pseudo-aristoi, of the wheat from the chaff. In general they will elect the real good and wise. In some instances, wealth may corrupt, and birth blind them; but not in sufficient degree to endanger the society.

It is probable that our difference of opinion may in some measure be produced by a difference of character in those among whom we live. From what I have seen of Massachusetts and Connecticut myself, and still more from what I have heard, and the character given of the former by yourself, who know them so much better, there seems to be in those two states a traditionary reverence for certain families, which has rendered the offices of the government nearly hereditary in those families. I presume that from an early period of your history, members of these families happening to possess virtue and talents, have honestly exercised them for the good of the people, and by their services have endeared their names to them.

In coupling Connecticut with you, I mean it politically only, not morally. For having made the Bible the Common law of their land they seem to have modelled their morality on the story of Jacob and Laban. But altho' this hereditary succession to office with you may in some degree be founded in real family merit, yet in a much higher degree it has proceeded from your strict alliance of church and state. These families are canonised in the eyes of the people on the common principle "you tickle me, and I will tickle you." In Virginia we have nothing of this. Our clergy, before the revolution, having been secured against rivalship by fixed salaries, did not give themselves the trouble of acquiring influence over the people. Of wealth, there were great accumulations in particular families, handed down from generation to generation under the English law of entails. But the only object of ambition for the wealthy was a seat in the king's council. All their court then was paid to the crown and it's creatures; and they Philipised in all collisions between the king and people. Hence they were unpopular; and that unpopularity continues attached to their names. A Randolph, a Carter, or a Burwell must have great personal superiority over a common competitor to be elected by the people, even at this day.

At the first session of our legislature after the Declaration of Independance [sic], we passed a law abolishing entails. And this was followed by one abolishing the privilege of Primogeniture, and dividing the lands of intestates equally among all their children, or other representatives. These laws, drawn by myself, laid the axe to the root of Pseudo-aristocracy. And had another which I prepared been adopted by the legislature, our work would have been compleat. It was a Bill for the more general diffusion of learning. This proposed to divide every county into wards of 5. or 6. miles square, like your townships; to establish in each ward a free school for reading, writing and common arithmetic; to provide for the annual selection of the best subjects from these schools who might receive at the public expence a higher degree of education at a district school; and from these district schools to select a certain number of the most promising subjects to be compleated at an University, where all the useful sciences should be taught. Worth and genius would thus have been sought out from every condition of life, and compleatly prepared by education for defeating the competition of wealth and birth for public trusts.

My proposition had for a further object to impart to these wards those portions of self-government for which they are best qualified, by confiding to them the care of their poor, their roads, police, elections, the nomination of jurors, administration of justice in small cases, elementary exercises of militia, in short, to have made them little republics, with a Warden at the head of each, for all those concerns which, being under their eye, they would better manage than the larger republics of the county or state. A general call of ward-meetings by their Wardens on the same day thro' the state would at any time produce the genuine sense of the people on any required point, and would enable the state to act in mass, as your people have so often done, and with so much effect, by their town meetings. The law for religious freedom, which made a part of this system, having put down the aristocracy of the clergy, and restored to the citizen the freedom of the mind, and those of entails and descents nurturing an equality of condition among them, this on Education would have raised the mass of the people to the high ground of moral respectability necessary to their own safety, and to orderly government; and would have compleated the great object of qualifying them to select the veritable aristoi, for the trusts of government, to the exclusion of the Pseudalists: and the same Theognis who has furnished the epigraphs of your two letters assures us that "ουδεμιαν πω, Κυρν' ἀγαϑοι πολιν ὤλεσαν ἀνδρες [Curnis, good men have never harmed any city]." Altho' this law has not yet been acted on but in a small and inefficient degree, it is still considered as before the legislature, with other bills of the revised code, not yet taken up, and I have great hope that some patriotic spirit will, at a favorable moment, call it up, and make it the key-stone of the arch of our government.

With respect to Aristocracy, we should further consider that, before the establishment of the American states, nothing was known to History but the Man of the old world, crouded within limits either small or over-charged, and steeped in the vices which that situation generates. A government adapted to such men would be one thing; but a very different one that for the Man of these states. Here every one may have land to labor for himself if he chuses; or, preferring the exercise of any other industry, may exact for it such compensation as not only to afford a comfortable subsistence, but wherewith to provide for a cessation from labor in old age. Every one, by his property, or by his satisfactory situation, is interested in the support of law and order. And such men may safely and advantageously reserve to themselves a wholsome controul over their public affairs, and a degree of freedom, which in the hands of the Canaille of the cities of Europe, would be instantly perverted to the demolition and destruction of every thing public and private. The history of the last 25. years of France, and of the last 40. years in America, nay of it's last 200. years, proves the truth of both parts of this observation.

But even in Europe a change has sensibly taken place in the mind of Man. Science had liberated the ideas of those who read and reflect, and the American example had kindled feelings of right in the people. An insurrection has consequently begun, of science, talents and courage against rank and birth, which have fallen into contempt. It has failed in it's first effort, because the mobs of the cities, the instrument used for it's accomplishment, debased by ignorance, poverty and vice, could not be restrained to rational action. But the world will recover from the panic of this first catastrophe. Science is progressive, and talents and enterprize on the alert. Resort may be had to the people of the country, a more governable power from their principles and subordination; and rank, and birth, and tinsel-aristocracy will finally shrink into insignificance, even there. This however we have no right to meddle with. It suffices for us, if the moral and physical condition of our own citizens qualifies them to select the able and good for the direction of their government, with a recurrence of elections at such short periods as will enable them to displace an unfaithful servant before the mischief he meditates may be irremediable.

I have thus stated my opinion on a point on which we differ, not with a view to controversy, for we are both too old to change opinions which are the result of a long life of inquiry and reflection; but on the suggestion of a former letter of yours, that we ought not to die before we have explained ourselves to each other. We acted in perfect harmony thro' a long and perilous contest for our liberty and independance. A constitution has been acquired which, tho neither of us think perfect, yet both consider as competent to render our fellow-citizens the happiest and the securest on whom the sun has ever shone. If we do not think exactly alike as to it's imperfections, it matters little to our country which, after devoting to it long lives of disinterested labor, we have delivered over to our successors in life, who will be able to take care of it, and of themselves.

Of the pamphlet on aristocracy which has been sent to you, or who may be it's author, I have heard nothing but thro' your letter. If the person you suspect[1] it may be known from the quaint, mystical and hyperbolical ideas, involved in affected, new-fangled and pedantic terms, which stamp his writings. Whatever it be, I hope your quiet is not to be affected at this day by the rudeness of

---

[1] John Taylor of Caroline.

intemperance of scribblers; but that you may continue in tranquility to live and to rejoice in the prosperity of our country until it shall be your own wish to take your seat among the Aristoi who have gone before you. Ever and affectionately yours.

Th: Jefferson

VI

Humanitarianism

In the seventeenth century and the early decades of the eighteenth, humanitarianism was not a vital element of the *milieu,* though charity was of course preached in the churches and practiced by some. The moral outlook was egocentric, and while "secular morality" (*la morale laïque*) was not selfish, it was a tempered hedonism. Then the moral climate shifted more and more to social utilitarianism (through enlightened self-interest) and to the love of virtue, conceived of as the true path to happiness. The word *bienfaisance* had been coined by the abbé de Saint-Pierre before the middle years of the century and popularized by Voltaire. The campaigns for tolerance and against Negro slavery became part of an intellectual trend that, fusing with bourgeois sentimentality, acquired emotional values. The very idea of "humanity," which had developed in the wake of natural law doctrine, became a war cry, a composite of sympathy and benevolence, preached with enthusiasm by Diderot, Bernardin de Saint-Pierre, and others.

In a pre-industrial age, the practical aspects of humanitarianism were, as have been mentioned, the campaigns against slavery and religious persecution and the effort to secure a less barbarous penal code. Toleration had found its first strong preacher, and its best logician, in Pierre Bayle. He was followed by many others, but by none so persistent or so effective as Voltaire. Waging a long battle to rehabilitate the Protestant martyr Jean Calas, he wrote his eloquent *Traité sur la tolérance* (1763). His widely read *Dictionnaire philosophique* (1764) contained the article reproduced here (Document–42). Beneath its sardonic irony lies a feeling of bitterness and pessimism.

Although Montesquieu, Voltaire, and others had proposed a more humane penal code, it was the *Essay on Crimes and Punishments* of the Italian economist and criminologist, Cesare di Beccaria (1738–1794), which aroused men throughout the world. Written in 1764, it was translated into English in 1767. It will be apparent that Beccaria's theory is grounded on a view of human nature and behavior that was typical of the Enlightenment.

42. Voltaire, Philosophical Dictionary

Toleration

WHAT is toleration? It is the appurtenance of humanity. We are all full of weakness and errors; let us mutually pardon each other our follies—it is the first law of nature.

When, on the exchange of Amsterdam, of London, of Surat, or of Bassora, the Gueber, the Banian, the Jew, the Mahometan, the Chinese Deist, the Brahmin, the Christian of the Greek Church, the Roman Catholic Christian, the Protestant Christian, and the Quaker Christian, traffic together, they do not lift the poniard against each other, in order to gain souls for their religion. Why then have we been cutting one another's throats almost without interruption since the first Council of Nicaea?

Constantine began by issuing an edict which allowed all religions, and ended by persecuting. Before him, tumults were excited against the Christians, only because they began to make a party in the state. The Romans permitted all kinds of worship, even those of the Jews, and of the Egyptians, for whom they had so much contempt. Why did Rome tolerate these religions? Because neither the Egyptians, nor even the Jews, aimed at exterminating the ancient religion of the empire, or ranged through land and sea for proselytes; they thought only of money-getting; but it is undeniable, that the Christians wished their own religion to be the dominant one. The Jews would not suffer the statue of Jupiter at Jerusalem, but the Christians wished it not to be in the capitol. St. Thomas had the candor to avow, that if the Christians did not dethrone the emperors, it was because they could not. Their opinion was, that the whole earth ought to be Christian. They

SOURCE: Tobias Smollett (ed.), *The Works of Voltaire; a contemporary version with notes*, revised and modernized with new translations by William F. Fleming, introduction Oliver M. G. Leigh (New York: E. R. DuMont, 1901).

were therefore necessarily enemies to the whole earth, until it was converted.

Among themselves, they were the enemies of each other on all their points of controversy. Was it first of all necessary to regard Jesus Christ as God? Those who denied it were anathematized under the name of Ebionites, who themselves anathematized the adorers of Jesus.

Did some among them wish all things to be in common, as it is pretended they were in the time of the apostles? Their adversaries called them Nicolaites, and accused them of the most infamous crimes. Did others profess a mystical devotion? They were termed Gnostics, and attacked with fury. Did Marcion dispute on the Trinity? He was treated as an idolater.

Tertullian, Praxeas, Origen, Novatus, Novatian, Sabellius, Donatus, were all persecuted by their brethren, before Constantine; and scarcely had Constantine made the Christian religion the ruling one, when the Athanasians and the Eusebians tore each other to pieces and from that time to our own days, the Christian Church has been deluged with blood.

The Jewish people were, I confess, a very barbarous nation. They mercilessly cut the throats of all the inhabitants of an unfortunate little country upon which they had no more claim than they had upon Paris or London. However, when Naaman was cured of the leprosy by being plunged seven times in the Jordan—when, in order to testify his gratitude to Elisha, who had taught him the secret, he told him he would adore the god of the Jews from gratitude, he reserved to himself the liberty to adore also the god of his own king; he asked Elisha's permission to do so, and the prophet did not hesitate to grant it. The Jews adored their god, but they were never astonished that every nation had its own. They approved of Chemos having given a certain district to the Moabites, provided their god would give them one also. Jacob did not hesitate to marry the daughters of an idolater. Laban had his god, as Jacob had his. Such are the examples of toleration among the most intolerant and cruel people of antiquity. We have imitated them in their asburd passions, and not in their indulgence.

It is clear that every private individual who persecutes a man, his brother, because he is not of the same opinion, is a monster. This admits of no difficulty. But the government, the magistrates, the princes!—how do they conduct themselves towards those who have a faith different from their own? If they are powerful foreigners, it is certain that a prince will form an alliance with them. The Most Christian Francis I. will league himself with the Musulmans against the Most Catholic Charles V. Francis I. will give money to the Lutherans in Germany, to support them in their rebellion against their emperor; but he will commence, as usual, by having the Lutherans in his own country burned. He pays them in Saxony from policy; he burns them in Paris from policy. But what follows? Persecutions make proselytes. France will soon be filled with new Protestants. At first they will submit to be hanged; afterwards they will hang in their turn. There will be civil wars; then Saint Bartholomew will come; and this corner of the world will be worse than all that the ancients and moderns have ever said of hell.

Blockheads, who have never been able to render a pure worship to the God who made you! Wretches, whom the example of the Noachides, the Chinese literati, the Parsees, and of all the wise, has not availed to guide! Monsters, who need superstitions, just as the gizzard of a raven needs carrion! We have already told you—and we have nothing else to say—if you have two religions among you, they will massacre each other; if you have thirty, they will live in peace. Look at the Grand Turk: he governs Guebers, Banians, Christians of the Greek Church, Nestorians, and Roman Catholics. The first who would excite a tumult is empaled; and all is tranquil.

SECTION II

Of all religions, the Christian ought doubtless to inspire the most toleration, although hitherto the Christians have been the most intolerant of all men. Jesus, having deigned to be born in poverty and lowliness like his brethren, never condescended to practise the art of writing. The Jews had a law written with the greatest minuteness, and we have not a single line from the hand of Jesus. The apostles were divided on many points. St. Peter and St. Barnabas ate forbidden meats with the new stranger Christians, and abstained from them with the Jewish Christians. St. Paul reproached them with this conduct; and this same St. Paul, the Pharisee, the disciple of the Pharisee Gamaliel—this same St. Paul, who had persecuted the Christians with fury, and who after breaking with Gamaliel became a Christian himself—nevertheless, went afterwards to sacrifice in the temple of Jerusalem, during his apostolic vacation. For eight days he observed publicly all the ceremonies of the Jewish law which he had renounced; he even added devotions and purifications which were superabundant; he completely Judaized. The greatest apostle of the Christians did, for eight days, the very things for which men are condemned to the stake among a large portion of Christian nations.

43. Beccaria, An Essay on Crimes and Punishments

Chapter VI. Of the Proportion Between Crimes and Punishments

IT IS not only the common interest of mankind that crimes should not be committed, but that crimes of every kind should be less frequent, in proportion to the evil they produce to society. Therefore, the means made use of by the legislature to prevent crimes should be more powerful, in proportion as they are destructive of the public safety and happiness, and as the inducements to commit them are stronger. Therefore there ought to be a fixed proportion between crimes and punishments.

It is impossible to prevent entirely all the disorders which the passions of mankind cause in society. These disorders increase in proportion to the number of people, and the opposition of private interests. If we consult history, we shall find them increasing, in every state, with the extent of dominion. In political arithmetic, it is necessary to substitute a calculation of probabilities to mathematical exactness. That force which continually impels us to our own private interest, like gravity, acts incessantly, unless it meets with an obstacle to oppose it. The effects of this force are the confused series of human actions. Punishments, which I would call political obstacles, prevent the fatal effects of private interest, without destroying the impelling cause, which is that sensibility inseparable from man. The legislator acts, in this case, like a skilful

SOURCE: C. B. Beccaria, *An Essay on Crimes and Punishments*, with a commentary by M. de Voltaire (Albany, New York: Little, 1872), an anonymous nineteenth-century translation.

architect, who endeavours to counteract the force of gravity by combining the circumstances which may contribute to the strength of his edifice.

The necessity of uniting in society being granted, together with the conventions, which the opposite interests of individuals must necessarily require, a scale of crimes may be formed, of which the first degree should consist of those which immediately tend to the dissolution of society, and the last, of the smallest possible injustice done to a private member of that society. Between these extremes will be comprehended all actions contrary to the public good, which are called criminal, and which descend by insensible degrees, decreasing from the highest to the lowest. If mathematical calculation could be applied to the obscure and infinite combinations of human actions, there might be a corresponding scale of punishments, descending from the greatest to the least; but it will be sufficient that the wise legislator mark the principal divisions, without disturbing the order, lest to crimes of the *first* degree, be assigned punishments of the *last*. If there were an exact and universal scale of crimes and punishments, we should then have a common measure of the degree of liberty and slavery, humanity and cruelty, of different nations.

Any action, which is not comprehended in the above mentioned scale, will not be called a crime, or punished as such, except by those who have an interest in the denomination. The uncertainty of the extreme points of this scale has produced a system of morality which contradicts the laws; a multitude of laws that contradict each other; and many which expose the best men to the severest punishments, rendering the ideas of *vice* and *virtue* vague and fluctuating, and even their existence doubtful. Hence that fatal lethargy of political bodies, which terminates in their destruction.

Whoever reads, with a philosophic eye, the history of nations, and their laws, will generally find that the ideas of virtue and vice, of a good or a bad citizen, change with the revolution of ages; not in proportion to the alteration of circumstances, and consequently conformable to the common good; but in proportion to the passions and errors by which the different lawgivers were successively influenced. He will frequently observe that the passions and vices of one age are the foundation of the morality of the following; that violent passion, the offspring of fanaticism and enthusiasm, being weakened by time, which reduces all the phenomena of the natural and moral world to an equality, become, by degrees, the prudence of the age, and an useful instrument in the hands of the powerful or artful politician. Hence the uncertainty of our notions of honour and virtue; an uncertainty which will ever remain, because they change with the revolutions of time, and names survive the things they originally signified; they change with the boundaries of states, which are often the same both in physical and moral geography.

Pleasure and pain are the only springs of action in beings endowed with sensibility. Even among the motives which incite men to acts of religion, the invisible Legislator has ordained rewards and punishments. From a partial distribution of these will arise that contradiction, so little observed, because so common; I mean, that of punishing by the laws the crimes which the laws have occasioned. If an equal punishment be ordained for two crimes that injure society in different degrees, there is nothing to deter men from committing the greater, as often as it is attended with greater advantage.

Chapter XVI. Of Torture

The torture of a criminal, during the course of his trial, is a cruelty, consecrated by custom in most nations. It is used with an intent either to make him confess his crime, or explain some contradictions, into which he had been led during his examination; or to discover his accomplices; or for some kind of metaphysical and incomprehensible purgation of infamy; or, finally, in order to discover other crimes, of which he is not accused, but of which he may be guilty.

No man can be judged a criminal until he be found guilty; nor can society take from him the public protection, until it have been proved that he has violated the conditions on which it was granted. What right, then, but that of power, can authorize the punishment of a citizen, so long as there remains any doubt of his guilt? The dilemma is frequent. Either he is guilty, or not guilty. If guilty, he should only suffer the punishment ordained by the laws, and torture becomes useless, as his confession is unnecessary. If he be not guilty, you torture the innocent; for, in the eye of the law, every man is innocent, whose crime has not been proved. Besides, it is confounding all relations, to expect that a man should be both the accuser and accused; and that pain should be the test of truth, as if truth resided in the muscles and fibres of a wretch in torture. By this method, the robust will escape, and the feeble be condemned. These are the inconveniences of this pretended test of truth, worthy only of a cannibal; and which the Romans, in many respects barbarous, and whose savage virtue has been too much admired, reserved for the slaves alone.

What is the political intention of punishments? To terrify, and to be an example to others. Is this intention answered, by thus privately torturing the guilty and the innocent? It is doubtless of importance, that no crime should remain unpunished; but it is useless to make a public example of the author of a crime hid in darkness. A crime already committed, and for which there can be no remedy, can only be punished by a political society with an intention that no hopes of impunity should induce others to commit the same. If it be true that the number of those, who, from fear or virtue, respect the laws, is greater than of those by whom they are violated, the risk of torturing an innocent person is greater, as there is a greater probability that, *cæ teris paribus*, an individual has observed, than that he has infringed the laws. . . .

Another intention of torture is to oblige the supposed criminal to reconcile the contradictions into which he may have fallen during his examination; as if the dread of punishment, the uncertainty of his fate, the solemnity of the court, the majesty of the judge, and the ignorance of the accused, were not abundantly sufficient to account for contradictions, which are so common to men even in a state of tranquillity; and which must necessarily be multiplied by the perturbation of the mind of a man, entirely engaged in the thought of saving himself from imminent danger.

This infamous test of truth is a remaining monument of that ancient and savage legislation, in which trials by fire, by boiling water, or the uncertainty of combats, were called judgments of God; as if the links of that eternal chain, whose beginning is in the breast of the first cause of all things, could never be disunited by the intuitions of men. The only difference between torture and trials by fire and boiling water is that the event of the first depends on the will of the accused; and of the second, on a fact entirely physical and external: but this difference is apparent only, not real. A man on the rack, in the convulsions of torture, has it as little in his power to declare the truth, as, in former times, to prevent, without fraud, the effect of fire or of boiling water.

Every act of the will is invariably in proportion to the force of the impression on our senses. The impression of pain, then, may increase to such a degree, that, occupying the mind entirely, it will compel the sufferer to use the shortest method of freeing himself from torment. His answer, therefore, will be an effect as necessary as that of fire or boiling water; and he will accuse himself of crimes of which he is innocent. So that the very means employed to distinguish the innocent from the guilty, will most effectually destroy all difference between them.

It would be superfluous to confirm these reflections by examples of innocent persons, who from the agony of torture have confessed themselves guilty: innumerable instances may be found in all nations, and in every age. How amazing, that mankind have always neglected to draw the natural conclusion! Lives there a man who, if he have carried his thoughts ever so little beyond the necessities of life, when he reflects on such cruelty, is not tempted to fly from society, and return to his natural state of independence?

A very strange but necessary consequence of the use of torture is that the case of the innocent is worse than that of the guilty. With regard to the first, either he confesses the crime, which he has not committed, and is condemned; or he is acquitted, and has suffered a punishment he did not deserve. On the contrary, the person who is really guilty has the most favourable side of the question; for if he supports the torture with firmness and resolution, he is acquitted, and has gained, having exchanged a greater punishment for a less.

The law by which torture is authorized says, Man, be insensible to pain. Nature has indeed given you an irresistible self-love, and an unalienable right to self-preservation, but I create in you a contrary sentiment, an heroical hatred of yourselves. I command you to accuse yourselves, and to declare the truth, midst the tearing of your flesh and the dislocation of your bones.

Torture is used to discover whether the criminal be guilty of other crimes besides those of which he is accused: which is equivalent to the following reasoning: Thou art guilty of one crime, therefore it is possible that thou mayst have committed a thousand other: but the affair being doubtful, I must try it by my criterion of truth. The laws order thee to be tormented, because thou art guilty, because thou mayst be guilty, and because I choose thou shouldst be guilty.

Torture is used to make the criminal discover his accomplices; but if it has been demonstrated that it is not a proper means of discovering truth, how can it serve to discover the accomplices, which is one of the truths required? Will not the man who accuses himself yet more readily accuse other? Besides, is it just to torment one man for the crime of another? May not the accomplices be found out by the examination of the witnesses, or of the criminal; from the evidence, or from the nature of the crime itself; in short, by all the means that have been used to prove the guilt of a prisoner? The accomplices commonly fly when their comrade is taken. The uncertainty of their fate condemns them to perpetual exile, and frees society from the danger of further injury; whilst the punishment of the criminal, by deterring other, answers the purpose for which it was ordained.

Chapter XXVIII. Of the Punishment of Death

The useless profusion of punishments, which has never made men better, induces me to inquire whether the punishment of death be really just or useful in a well governed state? What right, I ask, have men to cut the throats of their fellow-creatures? Certainly not that on which the sovereignty and laws are founded. The laws, as I have said before, are only the sum of the smallest portions of the private liberty of each individual, and represent the general will, which is the aggregate of that of each individual. Did any one ever give to others the right of taking away his life?[1] Is it possible, that in the smallest portions of the liberty of each, sacrificed to the good of the public, can be obtained the greatest of all good, life? If it were so, how shall it be reconciled to the maxim which tells us that a man has no right to kill himself? Which he certainly must have, if he could give it away to another.

But the punishment of death is not authorized by any right; for I have demonstrated that no such right exists. It is therefore a war of a whole nation against a citizen, whose destruction they consider as necessary or useful to the general good. But if I can further demonstrate that it is neither necessary nor useful, I shall have gained the cause of humanity.

The death of a citizen cannot be necessary but in one case. When, though deprived of his liberty, he has such power and

---

[1] For a contrary view, see Rousseau's *Contrat social*, Bk. II, chap. 5.

connections as may endanger the security of the nation; when his existence may produce a dangerous revolution in the established form of government. But even in this case, it can only be necessary when a nation is on the verge of recovering or losing its liberty; or in times of absolute anarchy, when the disorders themselves hold the place of laws. But in a reign of tranquillity; in a form of government approved by the united wishes of the nation; in a state fortified from enemies without, and supported by strength within, and opinion, perhaps more efficacious; where all power is lodged in the hands of the true sovereign; where riches can purchase pleasures and not authority, there can be no necessity for taking away the life of a subject. . . .

A punishment, to be just, should have only that degree of severity which is sufficient to deter others. Now there is no man, who, upon the least reflection, would put in competition the total and perpetual loss of his liberty with the greatest advantages he could possibly obtain in consequence of a crime. Perpetual slavery, then, has in it all that is necessary to deter the most hardened and determined, as much as the punishment of death. I say, it has more. There are many who can look upon death with intrepidity and firmness; some through fanaticism, and others through vanity, which attends us even to the grave; others from a desperate resolution, either to get rid of their misery, or cease to live: but fanaticism and vanity forsake the criminal in slavery, in chains and fetters, in an iron cage; and despair seems rather the beginning than the end of their misery. The mind, by collecting itself and uniting all its force, can, for a moment, repel assailling grief; but its most vigorous efforts are insufficient to resist perpetual wretchedness.

. . . Let us, for a moment, attend to the reasoning of a robber or assassin, who is deterred from violating the laws by the gibbet or the wheel. I am sensible, that to develop the sentiments of one's own heart is an art which education only can teach; but although a villain may not be able to give a clear account of his principles, they nevertheless influence his conduct. He reasons thus: "What are these laws that I am bound to respect, which make so great a difference between me and the rich man? He refuses me the farthing I ask of him, and excuses himself by bidding me have recourse to labour, with which he is unacquainted. Who made these laws? The rich and the great, who never deigned to visit the miserable hut of the poor; who have never seen him dividing a piece of mouldy bread, amidst the cries of his famished children, and the tears of his wife. Let us break those ties, fatal to the greatest part of mankind, and only useful to a few indolent tyrants. Let us attack injustice at its source. I will return to my natural state of independence. I shall live free and happy on the fruits of my courage and industry. A day of pain and repentance may come, but it will be short; and for an hour of grief, I shall enjoy years of pleasure and liberty. King of a small number, as determined as myself, I will correct the mistakes of fortune; and shall see those tyrants grow pale and tremble at the sight of him, whom, with insulting pride, they would not suffer to rank with dogs and horses. . . ."

The punishment of death is pernicious to society, from the example of barbarity it affords. If the passions, or necessity of war, have taught men to shed the blood of their fellow creatures, the laws which are intended to moderate the ferocity of mankind, should not increase it by examples of barbarity, the more horrible, as this punishment is usually attended with formal pageantry. Is it not absurd, that the laws, which detect and punish homicide, should, in order to prevent murder, publicly commit murder themselves? . . .

VII

Progress

PROGRESS WAS the "faith of reason" in the Age of Enlightenment. The advances of sciences in the seventeenth century brought the question to the fore; it was debated in the Quarrel of the Ancients and the Moderns. As the belief spread that scientific methodology and inquiry could be applied to social, political, and moral problems and that laws could be discovered in those domains, and as the Lockean psychology was extended to a theory of the malleability of behavior, the idea of progress became stronger and bolder, especially toward the end of the century. Yet many voices of caution and distrust were heard.[1] Progress, said the doubters, has limits, even in science. Men do not change, and the societies they make reflect their viciousness: the book of history is evidence for that. Some thought that progress and regress follow each other in cycles; others, that the sum of good and evil and the happiness of the species remains a constant. Despite these warnings, the majority of thinkers held not only that the material and intellectual condition of mankind could be considerably enhanced, but that society itself could be improved. In the conditions of a good society—or, some affirmed, in response to intensive pressures of government and education—behavior, at least, could be controlled.

Diderot had an abiding faith in progress. It infuses his great work, the *Encyclopédie* (1751-65). Nevertheless, he thought that even science had its limits, as the first selection, from his *De l'Interprétation de la nature* (1753), makes plain. His *"Encyclopédie"* was one of the key articles in the famous *Encyclopédie*. It is imbued with a consciousness of his mission. Diderot maintains the rights and the power of reason but also (in a passage not included) indicates that there are limits to what can be accomplished. His dedication transcends national confines and, true to the cosmopolitan spirit of the age, includes all mankind.

The brief letter from Benjamin Franklin to Priestley bears witness to the spread of the Enlightenment to the new American nation. Franklin's well-known interest in science, his boundless intellectual curiosity are

---

[1] See H. Vyverberg, *Historical Pessimism in the French Enlightenment* (Cambridge, Mass.: Harvard University Press, 1958).

accompanied by an extreme optimism concerning the future that antici-
pates Condorcet's utopian vision.

Edward Gibbon, like Diderot and Franklin, was a cosmopolitan spirit
whose *Decline and Fall of the Roman Empire* (1776–88) is one of the
two greatest historical creations of the eighteenth century. His view of
the future rises hopefully above national boundaries and interests to embrace all men. His reading of history is not unlike Voltaire's in the latter's *Essai sur les moeurs et l'esprit des nations* (1756), which is the
other outstanding historical work of the century. History is the record
of man's crimes and follies and yet, despite them, the line of progress
across the centuries is clear. Gibbon, however, was rather more hope-
ful for the future than Voltaire. Some of the lessons in the passage
included here are applicable in our own times.

Immanuel Kant (1724–1804) was unable to dissociate himself from
his roots in the Enlightenment, even though an important motive of his
work was to react against it, especially in ethics. He held man to be a
being inherently moral, yet inherently evil. In the *Project for a Perpetual Peace* his optimism is striking. Kant is too realistic to believe that
the nations of the world will ever unite under one government. He does
believe it possible for them to form an "alliance for peace" and to observe such a treaty, even though there are no means of compulsion to
enforce it. When he wonders that a nation has not yet thrown off the
pretense of "right" and defied the world with naked force, he foreshadows the later history of his own country.

The limits of optimism were reached by Condorcet (1743–1794), a
noble figure who perished a victim of the Revolution he had helped to
guide in its earlier stages. His *Esquisse d'un tableau historique des
progrès de l'esprit humain*, written shortly before his death, was published between 1801 and 1804. It is dominated by his faith in science, in
the applicability of predictive laws to human history, and in the unlimited reach of future progress, which would be assured by universal
education and the cumulative character of knowledge. All nations will
become equally civilized; discrimination against the colored races will
disappear. Disease will be conquered and life extended "indefinitely."
Even more: man himself, through education (whose effects Condorcet
apparently believed to be hereditary) and eugenic breeding, will develop into a being far superior to the creature we know now.

Condorcet was answered by Malthus. In *An Essay on the Principle of
Population* (1798), he argues that all the evidence refutes the visionary
notion that human life does not have a maximum possible length. Above
all, he advances his famous theory that food production will be outstripped by population, with disastrous effects. This idea, though previously adumbrated in England, was revolutionary in countering the accepted principle that underpopulation was the danger to the strength of
nations and of the species. In a later edition (1803), Malthus was somewhat less gloomy and admitted the possibility of limiting reproduction
by moral restraint and the influence of education.

44. *Diderot, On the Interpretation of Nature*

VI

WHEN WE compare the infinite multiplicity of natural phenomena with the limitations of our understanding and the weakness of our powers of perception and when we consider how slowly our work progresses, forever hampered by long and frequent interruptions and by the scarcity of creative geniuses, can we ever expect anything from it but a few broken and isolated fragments of the great chain that links all things together? . . .

Then what is our goal? The execution of a work that can never be completed and that would be far beyond the comprehension of human intelligence if it ever were completed. Are we not madder than those first inhabitants of the plain of Sennar? We know that the distance separating the earth from the sky is infinite, and yet we do not stop building our tower. But is it to be presumed that a time will never come when our disheartened pride will abandon the operations? . . . Besides, utility sets bounds to everything. It is utility that in a few more centuries will call a halt to experimental science, just as it is on the point of doing with geometry. I grant the former study a few more centuries because its sphere of usefulness is infinitely greater in extent than that of any abstract science and because it is, beyond dispute, the basis of all our genuine knowledge.

XLV

Just as, in mathematics, all the properties of a curve turn out upon examination to be all the same property, but seen from different aspects, so in nature, when experimental science is more advanced,

SOURCE: Translated by Derek Coltman in *Diderot's Selected Writings*, ed. L. G. Crocker (New York: The Macmillan Company, 1966), pp. 71–72, 76–77. Reprinted by permission of the publishers.

we shall come to see that all phenomena, whether of weight, elasticity, attraction, magnetism, or electricity, are all merely aspects of a single state. But how many intermediary phenomena still remain to be discovered, between the known phenomena already attributed to one of these causes, before we can form the links, fill in the lacunae, and so produce proof of this ultimate identity? That is what we are unable to determine. There perhaps exists a central phenomenon that would throw light not only on the others we already know but also on those that time will reveal in the future, and that would unite them all into a complete system. But without this central point of reference, they will always remain isolated. All the future discoveries of experimental science, though they may decrease the gaps between phenomena, can never unite them into a whole; and even were they to succeed in that task, it would only be by forming them into a closed circle in which we should be unable to distinguish which was the first and which the last. This singular situation, in which experimental science, by dint of sheer hard work, would have created a labyrinth in which the rational investigation of nature, confused and lost, would merely turn in an endless circle, is not impossible in the natural sciences as it is in mathematics. In mathematics, one can always find, either by synthesis or by analysis, the intermediary propositions that separate the fundamental property of a curve from even the remotest subproperty deriving from it.

45. The Encyclopedia

Philosophy

ENCYCLOPEDIA, f.n. (philosophy). This word means the interrelation of all knowledge; it is made up of the Greek prefix en, in, and the nouns kyklos, circle, and paideia, instruction, science, knowledge. In truth, the aim of an encyclopedia is to collect all the

SOURCE: Translated by Stephen J. Gendzier in *Denis Diderot's The Encyclopedia* (New York: Harper & Row, Inc., 1967), pp. 92–95. Reprinted by permission of the publishers.

knowledge scattered over the face of the earth, to present its general outlines and structure to the men with whom we live, and to transmit this to those who will come after us, so that the work of past centuries may be useful to the following centuries, that our children, by becoming more educated, may at the same time become more virtuous and happier, and that we may not die without having deserved well of the human race. . . .

We have seen that our Encyclopedia could only have been the endeavor of a philosophical century; that this age has dawned, and that fame, while raising to immortality the names of those who will perfect man's knowledge in the future, will perhaps not disdain to remember our own names. We have been heartened by the ever so consoling and agreeable idea that people may speak to one another about us, too, when we shall no longer be alive; we have been encouraged by hearing from the mouths of a few of our contemporaries a certain voluptuous murmur that suggests what may be said of us by those happy and educated men in whose interests we have sacrificed ourselves, whom we esteem and whom we love, even though they have not yet been born. We have felt within ourselves the development of those seeds of emulation which have moved us to renounce the better part of ourselves to accomplish our task, and which have ravished away into the void the few moments of our existence of which we are genuinely proud. Indeed, man reveals himself to his contemporaries and is seen by them for what he is: a peculiar mixture of sublime attributes and shameful weaknesses. But our weaknesses follow our mortal remains into the tomb and disappear with them; the same earth covers them both, and there remains only the total result of our attributes immortalized in the monuments we raise to ourselves or in the memorials that we owe to public respect and gratitude— honors which a proper awareness of our own deserts enables us to enjoy in anticipation, an enjoyment that is as pure, as great, and as real as any other pleasure and in which there is nothing imaginary except, perhaps, the titles on which we base our pretensions. Our own claims are deposited in the pages of this work, and posterity will judge them.

I have said that it could only belong to a philosophical age to attempt an encyclopedia; and I have said this because such a work constantly demands more intellectual daring than is commonly found in ages of pusillanimous taste. All things must be examined, debated, investigated without exception and without regard for anyone's feelings. . . . We must ride roughshod over all these ancient puerilities, overturn the barriers that reason never erected, give back to the arts and sciences the liberty that is so precious to them. . . . We have for quite some time needed a reasoning age when men would no longer seek the rules in classical authors but in nature, when men would be conscious of what is false and true about so many arbitrary treatises on aesthetics: and I take the term treatise on aesthetics in its most general meaning, that of a system of given rules to which it is claimed that one must conform in any genre whatsoever in order to succeed.

It would be desirable for the government to authorize people to go into the factories and shops, to see the craftsmen at their work, to question them, to draw the tools, the machines, and even the premises.

There are special circumstances when craftsmen are so secretive about their techniques that the shortest way of learning about them would be to apprentice oneself to a master or to have some trustworthy person do this. There would be few secrets that one would fail to bring to light by this method, and all these secrets would have to be divulged without any exception.

I know that this feeling is not shared by everyone. These are narrow minds, deformed souls, who are indifferent to the fate of the human race and who are so enclosed in their little group that they see nothing beyond its special interest. These men insist on being called good citizens, and I consent to this, provided that they permit me to call them bad men. To listen to them talk, one would say that a successful encyclopedia, that a general history of the mechanical arts, should only take the form of an enormous manuscript that would be carefully locked up in the king's library, inaccessible to all other eyes but his, an official document of the state, not meant to be consulted by the people. What is the good of divulging the knowledge a nation possesses, its private transactions, its inventions, its industrial processes, its resources, its trade secrets, its enlightenment, its arts, and all its wisdom? Are not these the things to which it owes a part of its superiority over the rival nations that surround it? This is what they say; and this is what they might add: would it not be desirable if, instead of enlightening the foreigner, we could spread darkness over him or even plunge all the rest of the world into barbarism so that we could dominate more securely over everyone? These people do not realize that they occupy only a single point on our globe and that they will endure only a moment in its existence. To this point and to this moment they would sacrifice the happiness of future ages and that of the entire human race.

They know as well as anyone that the average duration of empires is not more than two thousand years and that in less time, perhaps, the name Frenchman, a name that will endure forever in history, will be sought after in vain over the surface of the earth. These considerations do not broaden their point of view; for it seems that the word humanity is for them a word without meaning. All the same, they should be consistent! For they also fulminate against the impenetrability of the Egyptian sanctuaries; they deplore the loss of the knowledge of the ancients; they accuse the writers of the past for having been silent or negligent in writing so badly on an infinite number of important subjects; and these illogical critics do not see that they demand of the writers of earlier ages something they call a crime when it is committed by a contemporary, that they are blaming others for having done what they think it honorable to do.

These good citizens are the most dangerous enemies that we have had. In general we have tried to profit from just criticism without defending ourselves, while we have simply ignored all unfounded attacks. Is it not a rather pleasant prospect for those who have persisted stubbornly in blackening paper with their censure of us that if ten years from now the Encyclopedia has retained the reputation it enjoys today, no one will read or even remember their opinions; and if by chance our work is forgotten, their abusive remarks will fall into total oblivion!

I have heard it said that M. de Fontenelle's rooms were not large enough to hold all the works that had been published against him. Who knows the title of a single one of them? Montesquieu's *Spirit of Laws* and Buffon's *Natural History* have only just appeared, and the harsh criticism against them has been entirely forgotten. We have already remarked that among those who have set themselves up as censors of the Encyclopedia there is hardly a single one who had enough talent to enrich it by even one good article. I do not think I would be exaggerating if I should add that it is a work the greater part of which is about subjects that these people have yet to study. It has been composed with a philosophical spirit, and in this respect most of those who pass adverse judgment on us fall far short of the level of their own century. I call their works in evidence. It is for this reason that they will not endure and that we venture to say that our Encyclopedia will be more widely read and more highly appreciated in a few years' time than it is today. It would not be difficult to cite other authors who have had, and will have, a similar fate. Some (as we have already said) were once praised to the skies because they wrote for the multitude, followed the prevailing ideas, and accommodated their standards to those of the average reader, but they have lost their reputations in proportion as the human mind has made progress, and they have finally been forgotten altogether. Others, by contrast, too daring for the times in which their works appeared, have been little read, hardly understood, not appreciated, and have long remained in obscurity, until the day when the age they had outstripped had passed away and another century, to which they really belonged in spirit, overtook them at last and finally gave them the justice their merits deserved.

[Diderot]

46.   Franklin, Letter to Joseph Priestley

True Science and Its Progress.—Inconveniences Attend
All Situations in Life

Passy, 8 February, 1780

DEAR SIR,
   Your kind letter of September 27th came to hand but very lately, the bearer having stayed long in Holland. I always rejoice to hear of your being still employed in experimental researches into nature, and the success you meet with. The rapid progress true science now makes, occasions my regretting sometimes that I was born so soon. It is impossible to imagine the height to which may be carried, in a thousand years, the power of man over matter. We

SOURCE: J. Bigelow (ed.), *The Works of Benjamin Franklin* (New York: G. E. Putnam's Sons, 1904), vol. VIII.

may perhaps learn to deprive large masses of their gravity, and give them absolute levity, for the sake of easy transport. Agriculture may diminish its labor and double its produce; all diseases may by sure means be prevented or cured, not excepting even that of old age and our lives lengthened at pleasure even beyond the antediluvian standard. O that moral science were in as fair a way of improvement, that men would cease to be wolves to one another, and that human beings would at length learn what they now improperly call humanity!

I am glad my little paper on the Aurora Borealis pleased. If it should occasion further inquiry, and so produce a better hypothesis, it will not be wholly useless. I am ever, with the greatest and most sincere esteem, dear Sir, &c.

B. FRANKLIN

47. Gibbon, The Decline and Fall of the Roman Empire

As THE happiness of a *future* life is the great object of religion, we may hear without surprise or scandal, that the introduction, or at least the abuse of Christianity, had some influence on the decline and fall of the Roman empire. The clergy successfully preached the doctrines of patience and pusillanimity; the active virtues of society were discouraged; and the last remains of military spirit were buried in the cloister: a large portion of public and private wealth was consecrated to the specious demands of charity and devotion; and the soldiers' pay was lavished on the useless multitudes of both sexes, who could only plead the merits of abstinence and chastity. Faith, zeal, curiosity, and the more earthly passions of malice and ambition, kindled the flame of theological discord; the church, and even the state, were distracted by religious factions, whose conflicts were sometimes bloody, and always implacable; the attention of the emperors was diverted from camps to synods; the Roman world was oppressed by a new species of tyranny;

SOURCE: Edward Gibbon, *The Decline and Fall of the Roman Empire* (New York: The Heritage Press, 1946), pp. 1220–25.

and the persecuted sects became the secret enemies of their country. Yet party-spirit, however pernicious or absurd, is a principle of union as well as of dissension. The bishops, from eighteen hundred pulpits, inculcated the duty of passive obedience to a lawful and orthodox sovereign; their frequent assemblies, and perpetual correspondence, maintained the communion of distant churches; and the benevolent temper of the Gospel was strengthened, though confined, by the spiritual alliance of the Catholics. The sacred indolence of the monks was devoutly embraced by a servile and effeminate age; but if superstition had not afforded a decent retreat, the same vices would have tempted the unworthy Romans to desert, from baser motives, the standard of the republic. Religious precepts are easily obeyed, which indulge and sanctify the natural inclinations of their votaries; but the pure and genuine influence of Christianity may be traced in its beneficial, though imperfect, effects on the Barbarian proselytes of the North. If the decline of the Roman empire was hastened by the conversion of Constantine, his victorious religion broke the violence of the fall, and mollified the ferocious temper of the conquerors.

This awful revolution may be usefully applied to the instruction of the present age. It is the duty of a patriot to prefer and promote the exclusive interest and glory of his native country: but a philosopher may be permitted to enlarge his views, and to consider Europe as one great republic, whose various inhabitants have attained almost the same level of politeness and cultivation. The balance of power will continue to fluctuate, and the prosperity of our own, or the neighbouring kingdoms, may be alternately exalted or depressed; but these partial events cannot essentially injure our general state of happiness, the system of arts, and laws, and manners, which so advantageously distinguish, above the rest of mankind, the Europeans and their colonies. The savage nations of the globe are the common enemies of civilised society; and we may inquire, with anxious curiosity, whether Europe is still threatened with a repetition of those calamities, which formerly oppressed the arms and institutions of Rome. Perhaps the same reflections will illustrate the fall of that mighty empire, and explain the probable causes of our actual security.

The Romans were ignorant of the extent of their danger, and the number of their enemies. Beyond the Rhine and Danube, the Northern countries of Europe and Asia were filled with innumer-

able tribes of hunters and shepherds, poor, voracious, and turbulent; bold in arms, and impatient to ravish the fruits of industry.
The Barbarian world was agitated by the rapid impulse of war; and
the peace of Gaul or Italy was shaken by the distant revolutions of
China. The Huns, who fled before a victorious enemy, directed
their march towards the West; and the torrent was swelled by the
gradual accession of captives and allies. The flying tribes who
yielded to the Huns assumed in *their* turn the spirit of conquest;
the endless column of Barbarians pressed on the Roman empire
with accumulated weight; and, if the foremost were destroyed, the
vacant space was instantly replenished by new assailants. Such
formidable emigrations can no longer issue from the North; and
the long repose, which has been imputed to the decrease of population, is the happy consequence of the progress of arts and agriculture. Instead of some rude villages, thinly scattered among its
woods and morasses, Germany now produces a list of two thousand three hundred walled towns: the Christian kingdoms of
Denmark, Sweden, and Poland, have been successively established;
and the Hanse merchants, with the Teutonic knights, have extended their colonies along the coast of the Baltic, as far as the Gulf
of Finland. From the Gulf of Finland to the Eastern Ocean, Russia
now assumes the form of a powerful and civilised empire. The
plough, the loom, and the forge, are introduced on the banks of the
Volga, the Oby, and the Lena; and the fiercest of the Tartar
hordes have been taught to tremble and obey. The reign of
independent Barbarism is now contracted to a narrow span; and
the remnant of Calmucks or Uzbecks, whose forces may be almost
numbered, cannot seriously excite the apprehensions of the great
republic of Europe. Yet this apparent security should not tempt us
to forget, that new enemies, and unknown dangers, may *possibly*
arise from some obscure people, scarcely visible in the map of the
world. The Arabs or Saracens, who spread their conquests from
India to Spain, had languished in poverty and contempt, till Mahomet breathed into those savage bodies the soul of enthusiasm.

The empire of Rome was firmly established by the singular and
perfect coalition of its members. The subject nations, resigning the
hope, and even the wish, of independence, embraced the character
of Roman citizens; and the provinces of the West were reluctantly
torn by the Barbarians from the bosom of their mother country.
But this union was purchased by the loss of national freedom and

military spirit; and the servile provinces, destitute of life and motion, expected their safety from the mercenary troops and governors, who were directed by the orders of a distant court. The
happiness of an hundred millions depended on the personal merit of
one or two men, perhaps children, whose minds were corrupted by
education, luxury, and despotic power. The deepest wounds were
inflicted on the empire during the minorities of the sons and
grandsons of Theodosius; and, after those incapable princes seemed
to attain the age of manhood, they abandoned the church to the
bishops, the state to the eunuchs, and the provinces to the Barbarians. Europe is now divided into twelve powerful, though
unequal kingdoms, three respectable commonwealths, and a variety
of smaller, though independent, states: the chances of royal and
ministerial talents are multiplied, at least, with the number of its
rulers; and a Julian, or Semiramis, may reign in the North, while
Arcadius and Honorius again slumber on the thrones of the
South. The abuses of tyranny are restrained by the mutual influence of fear and shame; republics have acquired order and stability;
monarchies have imbibed the principles of freedom, or, at least, of
moderation; and some sense of honour and justice is introduced
into the most defective constitutions by the general manners of the
times. In peace, the progress of knowledge and industry is accelerated by the emulation of so many active rivals: in war, the
European forces are exercised by temperate and undecisive con-
tests. If a savage conqueror should issue from the deserts of
Tartary, he must repeatedly vanquish the robust peasants of Russia, the numerous armies of Germany, the gallant nobles of France,
and the intrepid freemen of Britain; who, perhaps, might confed-
erate for their common defence. Should the victorious Barbarians
carry slavery and desolation as far as the Atlantic Ocean, ten
thousand vessels would transport beyond their pursuit the remains
of civilised society; and Europe would revive and flourish in the
American world, which is already filled with her colonies and
institutions.

Cold, poverty, and a life of danger and fatigue, fortify the
strength and courage of Barbarians. In every age they have oppressed the polite and peaceful nations of China, India, and Persia,
who neglected, and still neglect, to counterbalance these natural
powers by the resources of military art. The warlike states of
antiquity, Greece, Macedonia, and Rome, educated a race of sol-

diers; exercised their bodies, disciplined their courage, multiplied their forces by regular evolutions, and converted the iron, which they possessed, into strong and serviceable weapons. But this superiority insensibly declined with their laws and manners; and the feeble policy of Constantine and his successors armed and instructed, for the ruin of the empire, the rude valour of the Barbarian mercenaries. The military art has been changed by the invention of gunpowder; which enables man to command the two most powerful agents of nature, air and fire. Mathematics, chemistry, mechanics, architecture, have been applied to the service of war; and the adverse parties oppose to each other the most elaborate modes of attack and of defence. Historians may indignantly observe, that the preparations of a siege would found and maintain a flourishing colony; yet we cannot be displeased, that the subversion of a city should be a work of cost and difficulty; or that an industrious people should be protected by those arts, which survive and supply the decay of military virtue. Cannon and fortifications now form an impregnable barrier against the Tartar horse; and Europe is secure from any future irruption of Barbarians; since, before they can conquer, they must cease to be barbarous. Their gradual advances in the science of war would always be accompanied, as we may learn from the example of Russia, with a proportionable improvement in the arts of peace and civil policy; and they themselves must deserve a place among the polished nations whom they subdue.

Should these speculations be found doubtful or fallacious, there still remains a more humble source of comfort and hope. The discoveries of ancient and modern navigators, and the domestic history, or tradition, of the most enlightened nations, represent the *human savage*, naked both in mind and body, and destitute of laws, of arts, of ideas, and almost of language. From this abject condition, perhaps the primitive and universal state of man, he has gradually arisen to command the animals, to fertilise the earth, to traverse the ocean, and to measure the heavens. His progress in the improvement and exercise of his mental and corporeal faculties has been irregular and various: infinitely slow in the beginning, and increasing by degrees with redoubled velocity: ages of laborious ascent have been followed by a moment of rapid downfall; and the several climates of the globe have felt the vicissitudes of light and darkness. Yet the experience of four thousand years should enlarge our hopes, and diminish our apprehensions: we cannot determine to what height the human species may aspire in their advances towards perfection; but it may safely be presumed, that no people, unless the face of nature is changed, will relapse into their original barbarism. The improvements of society may be viewed under a threefold aspect. 1. The poet or philosopher illustrates his age and country by the efforts of a *single* mind; but these superior powers of reason or fancy are rare and spontaneous productions; and the genius of Homer, or Cicero, or Newton, would excite less admiration, if they could be created by the will of a prince, or the lessons of a preceptor. 2. The benefits of law and policy, of trade and manufactures, or arts and sciences, are more solid and permanent; and *many* individuals may be qualified, by education and discipline, to promote, in their respective stations, the interest of the community. But this general order is the effect of skill and labour; and the complex machinery may be decayed by time, or injured by violence. 3. Fortunately for mankind, the more useful, or, at least, more necessary arts, can be performed without superior talents, or national subordination; without the powers of *one*, or the union of *many*. Each village, each family, each individual, must always possess both ability and inclination, to perpetuate the use of fire and of metals; the propagation and service of domestic animals; the methods of hunting and fishing; the rudiments of navigation; the imperfect cultivation of corn, or other nutritive grain; and the simple practice of the mechanic trades. Private genius and public industry may be extirpated; but these hardy plants survive the tempest, and strike an everlasting root into the most unfavourable soil. The splendid days of Augustus and Trajan were eclipsed by a cloud of ignorance; and the Barbarians subverted the laws and palaces of Rome. But the scythe, the invention or emblem of Saturn, still continued annually to mow the harvests of Italy; and the human feasts of the Læstrigons have never been renewed on the coast of Campania.

Since the first discovery of the arts, war, commerce, and religious zeal have diffused, among the savages of the Old and New World, these inestimable gifts: they have been successively propagated; they can never be lost. We may therefore acquiesce in the pleasing conclusion, that every age of the world has increased, and still increases, the real wealth, the happiness, the knowledge, and perhaps the virtue, of the human race.

48. Kant, Project for a Perpetual Peace

THE PUBLIC right ought to be founded upon a federation of free states.

Nations, as states, like individuals, if they live in a state of nature and without laws, by their vicinity alone commit an act of lesion. One may, in order to secure its own safety, require of another to establish within it a constitution which should guarantee to all their rights. This would be a federation of nations, without the people however forming one and the same state, the idea of a state supposing the relation of a sovereign to the people, of a superior to his inferior. Now several nations, united into one state, would no longer form but one; which contradicts the supposition, the question here being of the reciprocal rights of nations, inasmuch as they compose a multitude of different states, which ought not to be incorporated into one and the same state.

But when we see savages in their anarchy prefer the perpetual combats of licentious liberty to a reasonable liberty, founded upon constitutional order, can we refrain to look down with the most profound contempt on this animal degradation of humanity? Must we not blush at the contempt to which the want of civilization reduces men? And would one not rather be led to think that civilized nations, each of which form a constituted state, would hasten to extricate themselves from an order of things so ignominious? But what, on the contrary, do we behold? Every state placing its majesty (for it is absurd to talk of the majesty of the people) precisely in this independence of every constraint of any external legislation whatever.

The sovereign places his glory in the power of disposing at his pleasure (without much exposing himself) of many millions of men, ever ready to sacrifice themselves for an object that does not concern them. The only difference between the savages of

SOURCE: Immanuel Kant, *Perpetual Peace* (Los Angeles: U.S. Library Association, Inc., 1932), pp. 30–38. The text is that of an anonymous eighteenth-century translation.

America and those of Europe, is, that the former have eaten up many a hostile tribe, whereas the latter have known how to make a better use of their enemies; they preserve them to augment the number of their subjects, that is to say, of instruments destined to more extensive conquests. When we consider the perverseness of human nature, which shews itself unveiled and unrestrained in the relations of nations with each other, where it is not checked, as in a state of civilization, by the coercive power of the law, one may well be astonished that the word right has not yet been totally abolished from war-politics as a pedantic word, and that a state has not yet been found bold enough openly to profess this doctrine. For hitherto Grotius, Puffendorf, Vattel, and other useless and impotent defenders of the rights of nations, have been constantly cited in justification of war; though their code, purely philosophic or diplomatic, has never had the force of law, and cannot obtain it; states not being as yet subjected to any coercive power. There is no instance where their reasonings, supported by such respectable authorities, have induced a state to desist from its pretentions. However this homage which all states render to the principle of right, if even consisting only in words, is a proof of a moral disposition, which, though still slumbering, tends nevertheless vigorously to subdue in man that evil principle, of which he cannot entirely divest himself. For otherwise states would never pronounce the word right, when going to war with each other; it were then ironically, as a Gallic prince interpreted it. "It is," said he, "the prerogative nature has given to the stronger, to make himself obeyed by the weaker."

However, the field of battle is the only tribunal before which states plead their cause; but victory, by gaining the suit, does not decide in favour of their cause. Though the treaty of peace puts an end to the present war, it does not abolish a state of war (a state where continually new pretences for war are found); which one cannot affirm to be unjust, since being their own judges, they have no other means of terminating their differences. The law of nations cannot even force them, as the law of nature obliges individuals to get free from this state of war, since having already a legal constitution, as states, they are secure against every foreign compulsion, which might tend to establish among them a more extended constitutional order.

Since, however, from her highest tribunal of moral legislation, reason without exception condemns war as a mean of right, and makes a state of peace an absolute duty; and since this peace cannot be effected or be guaranteed without a compact among nations, they must form an alliance of a peculiar kind, which might be called a pacific alliance different from a treaty of peace inasmuch as it would for ever terminate all wars, whereas the latter only finishes one. This alliance does not tend to any dominion over a state, but solely to the certain maintenance of the liberty of each particular state partaking of this association, without being therefore obliged to submit, like men in a state of nature, to the legal constraint of public force. It can be proved, that the idea of a federation, which into a republic (a government which in its nature inclines to a perpetual peace, may be realized. For if fortune should so direct, that a people as powerful as enlightened, should constitute itself into a republic (a government which in its nature inclines to a perpetual peace) from that time there would be a centre for this federative association; other states might adhere thereto, in order to guarantee their liberty according to the principles of public right; and this alliance might insensibly be extended.

That a people should say, "There shall not be war among us: we will form ourselves into a state; that is to say, we will ourselves establish a legislative, executive, and judiciary power, to decide our differences,"—can be conceived.

But if this state should say, "There shall not be war between us and other states, although we do not acknowledge a supreme power, that guarantees our reciprocal rights;" upon what then can this confidence in one's rights be founded, except it is upon this free federation, this supplement of the social compact, which reason necessarily associates with the idea of public right.

The expression of public right, taken in a sense of right of war, presents properly no idea to the mind; since thereby is understood a power of deciding right, not according to universal laws, which restrain within the same limits all individuals, but according to partial maxims, namely, by force. Except one would wish to insinuate by this expression, that it is right, that men who admit such principles should destroy each other, and thus find perpetual peace only in the vast grave that swallows them and their iniquities.

At the tribunal of reason, there is but one means of extricating states from this turbulent situation, in which they are constantly menaced with war; namely, to renounce, like individuals, the anarchic liberty of savages, in order to submit themselves to coercive laws, and thus form a society of nations (*civitas gentium*) which would insensibly embrace all the nations of the earth. But as the ideas which they have of public right, absolutely prevent the realization of this plan, and make them reject in practice what is true in theory, there can only be substituted, to the positive idea of an universal republic (if all is not to be lost) the negative supplement of a permanent alliance, which prevents war, insensibly spreads, and stops the torrent of those unjust and inhuman passions, which always threaten to break down this fence.

49. Condorcet, Sketch of a Historic Tableau of the Progress of the Human Mind

---

On the Future Progress of Mankind

IF MAN can predict, almost with certainty, those appearances of which he understands the laws; if, even when the laws are unknown to him, experience or the past enables him to foresee, with considerable probability, future appearances; why should we suppose it a chimerical undertaking to delineate, with some degree of truth, the picture of the future destiny of mankind from the results of its history? The only foundation of faith in the natural sciences is the principle, that the general laws, known or unknown, which regulate the phenomena of the universe, are regular and constant; and why should this principle, applicable to the other operations of nature, be less true when applied to the development of the intellectual and moral faculties of man? In short, as opinions formed from experience, relative to the same class of objects, are the only rule by which men of soundest understanding are governed in their conduct, why should the philosopher be proscribed from supporting his conjectures upon a similar basis, provided he attribute to

SOURCE: Condorcet, *Esquisse d'un Tableau historique des progrès de l'esprit humain* (Paris, 1822). The version here reprinted is from an anonymous eighteenth-century translation.

them no greater certainty than the number, the consistency, and the accuracy of actual observations shall authorise?

Our hopes, as to the future condition of the human species, may be reduced to three points: the destruction of inequality between different nations; the progress of equality in one and the same nation; and lastly, the real improvement of man.

Will not every nation one day arrive at the state of civilization attained by those people who are most enlightened, most free, most exempt from prejudices, as the French, for instance, and the Anglo-Americans? Will not slavery of countries subjected to kings, the barbarity of African tribes, and the ignorance of savages gradually vanish? Is there upon the face of the globe a single spot the inhabitants of which are condemned by nature never to enjoy liberty, never to exercise their reason?

Does the difference of knowledge, of means, and of wealth, observable hitherto in all civilized nations, between the classes into which the people constituting those nations are divided; does that inequality which the earliest progress of society has augmented, or, to speak more properly, produced, belong to civilization itself, or to the imperfections of the social order? Must it not continually weaken, in order to give place to that actual equality, the chief end of the social art, which diminishing even the effects of the natural difference of the faculties, leaves no other inequality subsisting but what is useful to the interest of all, because it will favour civilization, instruction, and industry, without drawing after it either dependence, humiliation or poverty? In a word, will not men be continually verging towards that state, in which all will possess the requisite knowledge for conducting themselves in the common affairs of life by their own reason, and of maintaining that reason uncontaminated by prejudices; in which they will understand their rights, and exercise them according to their opinion and their conscience; in which all will be able, by the development of their faculties, to procure the certain means of providing for their wants; lastly, in which folly and wretchedness will be accidents, happening only now and then, and not the habitual lot of a considerable portion of society?

In fine, may it not be expected that the human race will be meliorated by new discoveries in the sciences and the arts, and, as an unavoidable consequence, in the means of individual and general prosperity; by farther progress in the principles of conduct, and in moral practice; and lastly, by the real improvement of our faculties, moral, intellectual and physical, which may be the result either of the improvement of the instruments which increase the power and direct the exercise of those faculties, or of the improvement of our natural organization itself?

In examining the three questions we have enumerated, we shall find the strongest reasons to believe, from past experience, from observation of the progress which the sciences and civilization have hitherto made, and from the analysis of the march of the human understanding, and the development of its faculties, that nature has fixed no limits to our hopes.

If we take a survey of the existing state of the globe, we shall perceive, in the first place, that in Europe the principles of the French constitution are those of every enlightened mind. We shall perceive that they are too widely disseminated, and too openly professed, for the efforts of tyrants and priests to prevent them from penetrating by degrees into the miserable cottages of their slaves, where they will soon revive those embers of good sense, and rouse that silent indignation which the habit of suffering and terror have failed totally to extinguish in the minds of the oppressed.

If we next look at the different nations, we shall observe in each, particular obstacles opposing, or certain dispositions favouring this revolution. We shall distinguish some in which it will be effected, perhaps slowly, by the wisdom of the respective governments; and others in which, rendered violent by resistance, the governments themselves will necessarily be involved in its terrible and rapid motions.

Can it be supposed that either the wisdom or the senseless feuds of European nations, co-operating with the slow but certain effects of the progress of their colonies, will not shortly produce the independence of the entire new world; and that then, European population, lending its aid, will fail to civilize or cause to disappear, even without conquest, those savage nations still occupying there immense tracts of country?

Run through the history of our projects and establishments in Africa or in Asia, and you will see our monopolies, our treachery, our sanguinary contempt for men of a different complexion or different creed, and the proselyting fury or the intrigues of our priests, destroying that sentiment of respect and benevolence which the superiority of our information and the advantages of our commerce had at first obtained.

But the period is doubtless approaching, when, no longer exhibiting to the view of these people corruptors only or tyrants, we shall become to them instruments of benefit, and the generous champions of their redemption from bondage.

The progress of the sciences secures the progress of the art of instruction, which again accelerates in its turn that of the sciences; and this reciprocal influence, the action of which is incessantly increased, must be ranked in the number of the most prolific and powerful causes of the improvement of the human race. At present, a young man, upon finishing his studies and quitting our schools, may know more of the principles of mathematics than Newton acquired by profound study, or discovered by the force of his genius, and may exercise the instrument of calculation with a readiness which at that period was unknown. The same observation, with certain restrictions, may be applied to all the sciences. In proportion as each shall advance, the means of compressing, within a smaller circle, the proofs of a greater number of truths, and of facilitating their comprehension, will equally advance. Thus, notwithstanding future degrees of progress, not only will men of equal genius find themselves, at the same period of life, upon a level with the actual state of science, but, respecting every generation, what may be acquired in a given space of time, by the same strength of intellect and the same degree of attention, will necessarily increase, and the elementary part of each science, that part which every man may attain, becoming more and more extended, will include, in a manner more complete, the knowledge necessary for the direction of every man in the common occurrences of life, and for the free and independent exercise of his reason.

In the political sciences there is a description of truths, which particularly in free countries (that is, in all countries in certain generations), can only be useful when generally known and avowed. Thus, the influence of these sciences upon the freedom and prosperity of nations, must, in some sort, be measured by the number of those truths that, in consequence of elementary instruction, shall pervade the general mind; and thus, as the growing progress of this elementary instruction is connected with the necessary progress of the sciences, we may expect a melioration in the doctrines of the human race which may be regarded as indefinite, since it can have no other limits than those of the two species of progress on which it depends.

We have still two other means of general application to consider, and which must influence at once both the improvement of the art of instruction and that of the sciences. One is a more extensive and more perfect adoption of what may be called technical methods; the other, the institution of an universal language.

It might be shown that the formation of such a language, if confined to the expressing of simple and precise propositions, like those which form the system of a science, or the practice of an art, would be the reverse of chimerical; that its execution, even at present, would be extremely practicable as to a great number of objects; and that the chief obstacle that would stand in the way of extending it to others, would be the humiliating necessity of acknowledging how few precise ideas, and accurately defined notions, understood exactly in the same sense by every mind, we really possess.

It might be shown that this language, improving every day, acquiring incessantly greater extent, would be the means of giving to every object that comes within the reach of human intelligence, a rigour, and precision, that would facilitate the knowledge of truth, and render error almost impossible. Then would the march of every science be as infallible as that of the mathematics, and the propositions of every system acquire, as far as nature will admit, geometrical demonstration and certainty.

All the causes which contribute to the improvement of the human species, all the means we have enumerated that insure its progress, must, from their very nature, exercise an influence always active, and acquire an extent for ever increasing. The proofs of this have been exhibited, and from their development in the work itself they will derive additional force: accordingly we may already conclude, that the perfectibility of man is indefinite. Meanwhile we have hitherto considered him as possessing only the same natural faculties, as endowed with the same organization. How much greater would be the certainty, how much wider the compass of our hopes, could we prove that these natural faculties themselves, that this very organization, are also susceptible of melioration? And this is the last question we shall examine.

The organic perfectibility or deterioration of the classes of the vegetable, or species of the animal kingdom, may be regarded as one of the general laws of nature.

This law extends itself to the human race; and it cannot be doubted that the progress of the sanative art, that the use of more wholesome food and more comfortable habitations, that a mode of life which shall develope the physical powers by exercise, without at the same time impairing them by excess; in fine, that the destruction of the two most active causes of deterioration, penury and wretchedness on the one hand, and enormous wealth on the other, must necessarily tend to prolong the common duration of man's existence, and secure him a more constant health and a more robust constitution. It is manifest that the improvement of the practice of medicine, become more efficacious in consequence of the progress of reason and the social order, must in the end put a period to transmissible or contagious disorders, as well to those general maladies resulting from climate, ailments, and the nature of certain occupations. Nor would it be difficult to prove that this hope might be extended to almost every other malady, of which it is probable we shall hereafter discover the most remote causes. Would it even be absurd to suppose this quality of melioration in the human species as susceptible of an indefinite advancement; to suppose that a period must one day arrive when death will be nothing more than the effect either of extraordinary accidents, or of the slow and gradual decay of the vital powers; and that the duration of the middle space, of the interval between the birth of man and this decay, will itself have no assignable limit? Certainly man will not become immortal; but may not the distance between the moment in which he draws his first breath, and the common term when, in the course of nature, without malady or accident, he finds it impossible any longer to exist, be necessarily protracted? As we are now speaking of a progress that is capable of being represented with precision, by numerical quantities or by lines, we shall embrace the opportunity of explaining the two meanings that may be affixed to the word *indefinite*.

In reality, this middle term of life, which in proportion as men advance upon the ocean of futurity, we have supposed incessantly to increase, may receive additions either in conformity to a law by which, though approaching continually an illimitable extent, it could never possibly arrive at it; or a law by which, in the im-

mensity of ages, it may acquire a greater extent than any determinate quantity whatever that may be assigned as its limit. In the
latter case, this duration of life is indefinite in the strictest sense of
the word, since there exist no bounds on this side of which it must
necessarily stop. And in the former, it is equally indefinite to us; if
we cannot fix the term, it may for ever approach, but can never
surpass; particularly if, knowing only that it can never stop, we are
ignorant in which of the two senses the term indefinite is applicable
to it: and this is precisely the state of the knowledge we have as yet
acquired relative to the perfectibility of the species.

Thus, in the instance we are considering, we are bound to
believe that the mean duration of human life will for ever increase,
unless its increase be prevented by the physical revolutions of the
system; but we cannot tell what is the bound which the duration of
human life can never exceed; we cannot even tell, whether there be
any circumstance in the laws of nature which has determined and
laid down its limit.

But may not our physical faculties, the force, the sagacity, the
acuteness of the senses, be numbered among the qualities, the individual improvement of which it will be practicable to transmit? An
attention to the different breeds of domestic animals must lead us to
adopt the affirmative of this question, and a direct observation of
the human species itself will be found to strengthen the opinion.

Lastly, may we not include in the same circle the intellectual and
moral faculties? May not our parents, who transmit to us the
advantages or defects of their conformation, and from whom we
receive our features and shape, as well as our propensities to certain
physical affections, transmit to us also that part of organization
upon which intellect, strength of understanding, energy of soul or
moral sensibility depend? Is it not probable that education, by
improving these qualities, will at the same time have an influence
upon, will modify and improve this organization itself? Analogy,
an investigation of the human faculties, and even some facts, appear
to authorise these conjectures, and thereby to enlarge the boun-
dary of our hopes.

Such are the questions with which we shall terminate the last
division of our work. And how admirably calculated is this view of
the human race, emancipated from its chains, released alike from
the dominion of chance, as well as from that of the enemies of its
progress, and advancing with a firm and indeviate step in the paths

of truth, to console the philosopher lamenting the errors, the flagrant acts of injustice, the crimes with which the earth is still polluted? It is the contemplation of this prospect that rewards him for all his efforts to assist the progress of reason and the establishment of liberty. He dares to regard these efforts as a part of the eternal chain of the destiny of mankind; and in this persuasion he finds the true delight of virtue, the pleasure of having performed a durable service, which no vicissitude will ever destroy in a fatal operation calculated to restore the reign of prejudice and slavery. This sentiment is the asylum into which he retires, and to which the memory of his persecutors cannot follow him; he unites himself in imagination with man restored to his rights, delivered from oppression, and proceeding with rapid strides in the path of happiness; he forgets his own misfortunes while his thoughts are thus employed; he lives no longer to adversity, calumny and malice, but becomes the associate of these wiser and more fortunate beings whose enviable condition he so earnestly contributed to produce.

50.   Malthus, *An Essay on the Principle of Population*

Chapter I

THE GREAT and unlooked for discoveries that have taken place of late years in natural philosophy, the increasing diffusion of general knowledge from the extension of the art of printing, the ardent and unshackled spirit on inquiry that prevails throughout the lettered and even unlettered world, the new and extraordinary lights that have been thrown on political subjects which dazzle and astonish the understanding, and particularly that tremendous phenomenon in the political horizon, the French revolution, which, like a blazing comet, seems destined either to inspire with fresh life and vigor, or to scorch up and destroy the shrinking inhabitants of the earth, have all concurred to lead able men into the opinion that we were touching on a period big with the most important changes, changes

SOURCE: Thomas Robert Malthus, *An Essay on the Principles of Population* (London, 1878).

that could in same measure be decisive of the future fate of mankind.

It has been said that the great question is now at issue, whether man shall henceforth start forwards with accelerated velocity towards illimitable, and hitherto unconceived improvement, or be condemned to a perpetual oscillation between happiness and misery, and after every effort remain still at an immeasurable distance from the wished-for goal.

Yet, anxiously as every friend of mankind must look forwards to the termination of this painful suspense, and eagerly as the inquiring mind would hail every ray of light that might assist its view into futurity, it is much to be lamented that the writers on each side of this momentous question still keep aloof from each other. Their mutual arguments do not meet with a candid examination. The question is not brought to rest on fewer points, and even in theory scarcely seems to be approaching to a decision.

The advocate for the present order of things is apt to treat the sect of speculative philosophers either as a set of artful and designing knaves who preach up ardent benevolence and draw captivating pictures of a happier state of society only the better to enable them to destroy the present establishments and to forward their own deep-laid schemes of ambition, or as wild and mad-headed enthusiasts whose silly speculations and absurd paradoxes are not worthy of the attention of any reasonable man.

The advocate for the perfectibility of man, and of society, retorts on the defender of establishments a more than equal contempt. He brands him as the slave of the most miserable and narrow prejudices; or, as the defender of the abuses of civil society, only because he profits by them. He paints him either as a character who prostitutes his understanding to his interest, or as one whose powers of mind are not of a size to grasp any thing great and noble, who cannot see above five yards before him, and who must therefore be utterly unable to take in the views of the enlightened benefactor of mankind.

In this unamicable contest the cause of truth cannot but suffer. The really good arguments on each side of the question are not allowed to have their proper weight. Each pursues his own theory, little solicitous to correct or improve it by an attention to what is advanced by his opponents.

The friend of the present order of things condemns all political speculations in the gross. He will not even condescend to examine the grounds from which the perfectibility of society is inferred. Much less will he give himself the trouble in a fair and candid manner to attempt an exposition of their fallacy.

The speculative philosopher equally offends against the cause of truth. With eyes fixed on a happier state of society, the blessings of which he paints in the most captivating colors, he allows himself to indulge in the most bitter invectives against every present establishment, without applying his talents to consider the best and safest means of removing abuses and without seeming to be aware of the tremendous obstacles that threaten, even in theory, to oppose the progress of man towards perfection.

It is an acknowledged truth in philosophy that a just theory will always be confirmed by experiment. Yet so much friction, and so many minute circumstances occur in practice, which it is next to impossible for the most enlarged and penetrating mind to foresee, that on few subjects can any theory be pronounced just, that has not stood the test of experience. But an untried theory cannot fairly be advanced as probable, much less as just, till all the arguments against it have been maturely weighed and clearly and consistently refuted.

I have read some of the speculations on the perfectibility of man and of society with great pleasure. I have been warmed and delighted with the enchanting picture which they hold forth. I ardently wish for such happy improvements. But I see great, and, to my understanding, unconquerable difficulties in the way to them. These difficulties it is my present purpose to state, declaring, at the same time, that so far from exulting in them, as a cause of triumph over the friends of innovation, nothing would give me greater pleasure than to see them completely removed.

The most important argument that I shall adduce is certainly not new. The principles on which it depends have been explained in part by Hume, and more at large by Dr. Adam Smith. It has been advanced and applied to the present subject, though not with its proper weight, or in the most forcible point of view, by Mr. Wallace, and it may probably have been stated by many writers that I have never met with. I should certainly therefore not think of advancing it again, though I mean to place it in a point of view in some degree different from any that I have hitherto seen, if it had ever been fairly and satisfactorily answered.

The cause of this neglect on the part of the advocates for the perfectibility of mankind is not easily accounted for. I cannot doubt the talents of such men as Godwin and Condorcet. I am unwilling to doubt their candor. To my understanding, and probably to that of most others, the difficulty appears insurmountable. Yet these men of acknowledged ability and penetration scarcely deign to notice it, and hold on their course in such speculations, with unabated ardor and undiminished confidence. I have certainly no right to say that they purposely shut their eyes to such arguments. I ought rather to doubt the validity of them, when neglected by such men, however forcibly their truth may strike my own mind. Yet in this respect it must be acknowledged that we are all of us too prone to err. If I saw a glass of wine repeatedly presented to a man, and he took no notice of it, I should be apt to think that he was blind or uncivil. A juster philosophy might teach me rather to think that my eyes deceived me and that the offer was not really what I conceived it to be.

In entering upon the argument I must premise that I put out of the question, at present, all mere conjectures, that is, all suppositions, the probable realization of which cannot be inferred upon any just philosophical grounds. A writer may tell me that he thinks man will ultimately become an ostrich, I cannot properly contradict him. But before he can expect to bring any reasonable person over to his opinion, he ought to show, that the necks of mankind have been gradually elongating, that the lips have grown harder and more prominent, that the legs and feet are daily altering their shape, and that the hair is beginning to change into stubs of feathers. And till the probability of so wonderful a conversion can be shown, it is surely lost time and lost eloquence to expatiate on the happiness of man in such a state; to describe his powers, both of running and flying, to paint him in a condition where all narrow luxuries would be condemned, where he would be employed only in collecting the necessaries of life, and where, consequently, each man's share of labor would be light, and his portion of leisure ample.

I think I may fairly make two postulata.

First, That food is necessary to the existence of man.

Secondly, That the passion between the sexes is necessary and will remain nearly in its present state.

These two laws, ever since we have had any knowledge of

mankind, appear to have been fixed laws of our nature, and, as we have not hitherto seen any alteration in them, we have no right to conclude that they will ever cease to be what they now are, without an immediate act of power in that Being who first arranged the system of the universe, and for the advantage of his creatures, still executes, according to fixed laws, all its various operations. . . .

Assuming then, my postulata as granted, I say, that the power of population is indefinitely greater than the power in the earth to produce subsistence for man.

Population, when unchecked, increases in a geometrical ratio. Subsistence increases only in an arithmetical ratio. A slight acquaintance with numbers will show the immensity of the first power in comparison of the second.

By that law of our nature which makes food necessary to the life of man, the effects of these two unequal powers must be kept equal.

This implies a strong and constantly operating check on population from the difficulty of subsistence. This difficulty must fall somewhere and must necessarily be severely felt by a large portion of mankind.

Through the animal and vegetable kingdoms, nature has scattered the seeds of life abroad with the most profuse and liberal hand. She has been comparatively sparing in the room and the nourishment necessary to rear them. The germs of existence contained in this spot of earth, with ample food, and ample room to expand in, would fill millions of worlds in the course of a few thousand years. Necessity, that imperious all pervading law of nature, restrains them within the prescribed bounds. The race of plants, and the race of animals shrink under this great restrictive law. And the race of man cannot, by any efforts of reason, escape from it. Among plants and animals its effects are waste of seed, sickness, and premature death. Among mankind, misery and vice. The former, misery, is an absolutely necessary consequence of it. Vice is a highly probable consequence, and we therefore see it abundantly prevail, but it ought not, perhaps, to be called an absolutely necessary consequence. The ordeal of virtue is to resist all temptation to evil.

This natural inequality of the two powers of population and of production in the earth and that great law of our nature which

must constantly keep their effects equal form the great difficulty
that to me appears insurmountable in the way to the perfectibility
of society. All other arguments are of slight and subordinate
consideration in comparison of this. I see no way by which man
can escape from the weight of this law which pervades all animated
nature. No fancied equality, no agrarian regulations in their utmost
extent, could remove the pressure of it even for a single century.
And it appears, therefore, to be decisive against the possible existence of a society, all the members of which should live in ease,
happiness, and comparative leisure; and feel no anxiety about
providing the means of subsistence for themselves and families.

Consequently, if the premises are just, the argument is conclusive
against the perfectibility of the mass of mankind.

I have thus sketched the general outline of the argument, but I
will examine it more particularly, and I think it will be found that
experience, the true source and foundation of all knowledge,
invariably confirms its truth.

Chapter IX

The last question which Mr. Condorcet proposes for examination is the organic perfectibility of man. He observes that if the
proofs which have been already given and which, in their development will receive greater force in the work itself, are sufficient to
establish the indefinite perfectibility of man upon the supposition
of the same natural faculties and the same organization which he
has at present, what will be the certainty, what the extent of our
hope, if this organization, these natural faculties themselves, are
susceptible of amelioration?

From the improvement of medicine, from the use of more
wholesome food and habitations, from a manner of living which
will improve the strength of the body by exercise without impairing it by excess, from the destruction of the two great causes of the
degradation of man, misery, and too great riches, from the gradual
removal of transmissible and contagious disorders by the improvement of physical knowledge, rendered more efficacious by the
progress of reason and of social order, he infers that though man
will not absolutely become immortal, yet that the duration between his birth and natural death will increase without ceasing, will
have no assignable term, and may properly be expressed by the
word indefinite. He then defines this word to mean either a

constant approach to an unlimited extent, without ever reaching it, or an increase in the immensity of ages to an extent greater than any assignable quantity.

But surely the application of this term in either of these senses to the duration of human life is in the highest degree unphilosophical and totally unwarranted by any appearances in the laws of nature. Variations from different causes are essentially distinct from a regular and unretrograde increase. The average duration of human life will to a certain degree vary from healthy or unhealthy climates, from wholesome or unwholesome food, from virtuous or vicious manners, and other causes, but it may be fairly doubted, whether there is really the smallest perceptible advance in the natural duration of human life since first we have had any authentic history of man. The prejudices of all ages have indeed been directly contrary to this supposition, and though I would not lay much stress upon these prejudices, they will in some measure tend to prove that there has been no marked advance in an opposite direction.

It may perhaps be said that the world is yet so young, so completely in its infancy, that it ought not to be expected that any difference should appear so soon.

If this be the case, there is at once an end of all human science. The whole train of reasonings from effects to causes will be destroyed. We may shut our eyes to the book of nature, as it will no longer be of any use to read it. The wildest and most improbable conjectures may be advanced with as much certainty as the most just and sublime theories, founded on careful and reiterated experiments. We may return again to the old mode of philosophizing and make facts bend to systems, instead of establishing systems upon facts. The grand and consistent theory of Newton will be placed upon the same footing as the wild and eccentric hypotheses of Descartes. In short, if the laws of nature are thus fickle and inconstant, if it can be affirmed and be believed that they will change, when for ages and ages they have appeared immutable, the human mind will no longer have any incitements to inquiry, but must remain fixed in inactive torpor, or amuse itself only in bewildering dreams and extravagant fancies.

The constancy of the laws of nature and of effects and causes is the foundation of all human knowledge, though far be it from me to say that the same power which framed and executes the laws of nature, may not change them all "in a moment, in the twinkling of an eye." Such a change may undoubtedly happen. All that I mean to say is that it is impossible to infer it from reasoning. If without any previous observable symptoms or indications of a change, we can infer that a change will take place, we may as well make any assertion whatever and think it as unreasonable to be contradicted in affirming that the moon will come in contact with the earth to-morrow, as in saying that the sun will rise at its usual time.

With regard to the duration of human life, there does not appear to have existed from the earliest ages of the world to the present moment the smallest permanent symptom of indication of increasing prolongation.[1] The observable effects of climate, habit, diet, and other causes, on length of life have furnished the pretext for asserting its indefinite extension; and the sandy foundation on which the argument rests, is that because the limit of human life is

[1] Many, I doubt not, will think that the attempting gravely to controvert so absurd a paradox as the immortality of man on earth, or indeed, even the perfectibility of man and society, is a waste of time and words, and that such unfounded conjectures are best answered by neglect. I profess, however, to be of a different opinion. When paradoxes of this kind are advanced by ingenious and able men, neglect has no tendency to convince them of their mistakes. Priding themselves on what they conceive to be a mark of the reach and size of their own understandings, of the extent and comprehensiveness of their views; they will look upon this neglect merely as an indication of poverty, and narrowness, in the mental exertions of their contemporaries; and only think, that the world is not yet prepared to receive their sublime truths.

On the contrary, a candid investigation of these subjects, accompanied with a perfect readiness to adopt any theory warranted by sound philosophy, may have a tendency to convince them that in forming improbable and unfounded hypotheses, so far from enlarging the bounds of human science, they are contracting it, so far from promoting the improvement of the human mind, they are obstructing it; they are throwing us back again almost into the infancy of knowledge and weakening the foundations of that mode of philosophizing, under the auspices of which, science has of late made such rapid advances. The present rage for wide and unrestrained speculation seems to be a kind of mental intoxication, arising, perhaps, from the great and unexpected discoveries which have been made of late years, in various branches of science. To men elate and giddy with such successes, everything appeared to be within the grasp of human powers; and, under this illusion, they confounded subjects where no real progress could be proved, with those, where the progress had been marked, certain, and acknowledged. Could they be persuaded to sober themselves with a little severe and chastised thinking, they would see, that the cause of truth, and of sound philosophy, cannot but suffer by substituting wild flights and unsupported assertions, for patient investigation, and well authenticated proofs.

undefined; because you cannot mark its precise term, and say so far exactly shall it go and no further; that therefore its extent may increase forever, and be properly termed, indefinite or unlimited. But the fallacy and the absurdity of this argument will sufficiently appear from a slight examination of what Mr. Condorcet calls the organic perfectibility, or degeneration, of the race of plants and animals, which he says may be regarded as one of the general laws of nature.

I am told that it is a maxim among the improvers of cattle that you may breed to any degree of nicety you please, and they found this maxim upon another, which is that some of the offspring will possess the desirable qualities of the parents in a greater degree. In the famous Leicestershire breed of sheep, the object is to procure them with small heads and small legs. Proceeding upon these breeding maxims, it is evident that we might go on till the heads and legs were evanescent quantities, but this is so palpable an absurdity that we may be quite sure that the premises are not just and that there really is a limit, though we cannot see it or say exactly where it is. In this case, the point of the greatest degree of improvement, or the smallest size of the head and legs, may be said to be undefined, but this is very different from unlimited, or from indefinite, in Mr. Condorcet's acceptation of the term. Though I may not be able in the present instance to mark the limit at which further improvement will stop, I can very easily mention a point at which it will not arrive. I should not scruple to assert that were the breeding to continue forever, the head and legs of these sheep would never be so small as the head and legs of a rat.

It cannot be true, therefore, that among animals, some of the offspring will possess the desirable qualities of the parents in a greater degree, or that animals are indefinitely perfectible. . . . The whole affair in all these cases, in plants, animals, and in the human race, is an affair of experience, and I only conclude that man is mortal because the invariable experience of all ages has proved the mortality of those materials of which his visible body is made.

What can we reason but from what we know

Sound philosophy will not authorize me to alter this opinion of the mortality of man on earth, till it can be clearly proved that the human race has made, and is making, a decided progress towards an illimitable extent of life. And the chief reason why I adduced the particular instances from animals was to expose and illustrate, if I could, the fallacy of that argument which infers an unlimited progress, merely because some partial improvement has taken place, and that the limit of this improvement cannot be precisely ascertained. . . .

Chronology

1685	Revocation of Edict of Nantes
	Death of Charles II
	James II, king of England (1685–88)
	Birth of J. S. Bach (1685–1750)
1686	Fontenelle, *Entretiens sur la pluralité des mondes*
1688	War of the League of Augsburg (1688–97)
	"Glorious Revolution" (England)
1689	William III, king of England (1689–1702)
	Bill of Rights and Toleration Act
	Locke, *First Letter on Toleration*
1690	Locke, *Essay concerning Human Understanding* and *Two Treatises on Civil Government*
1694	Birth of Voltaire (1694–1778)
1701	War of the Spanish Succession (1701–13)
1702	Anne, queen of England (1702–14)
1704	Newton, *Optics*
1708	Pope dissolves Jansenist Port-Royal des Champs
1710	Leibniz, *Theodicy*
1711	Shaftesbury, *Characteristics of Men, Manners, Opinions, Times*
1713	Bull *Unigenitus* condemns Quesnel's *Jansenist Reflections*
1714	George I, king of England, 1714–27
1715	Death of Louis XIV
1715–23	Regency of Philippe d'Orléans
1717	Watteau's "Embarquement pour Cythère"
1721	Montesquieu, *Lettres persanes*
1723	Louis XV ascends throne
1723–26	Ministry of Duc de Bourbon
1725	Vico, *Scienza nuova*
1726–43	Ministry of Cardinal Fleury
1727	George II, king of England (1727–60)
1732–34	Pope, *Essay on Man*
1733–35	War of the Polish Succession

1734   Voltaire, *Lettres philosophiques* and (unpublished) *Traité de métaphysique*
1738   Voltaire introduces Newton's ideas into France
1739–40   Hume, *Treatise of Human Nature*
1740   Frederick the Great, king of Prussia (1740–86)
           Richardson, *Pamela*
1740–48   War of the Austrian Succession
1745   Maupertius, *Vénus physique*
1745–64   Ascendancy of Mme. de Pompadour
1747   La Mettrie, *L'Homme machine*
1748   Montesquieu, *De l'Esprit des lois*
           Richardson, *Clarissa*
1749   Buffon, *Histoire naturelle*, vols I to III
           Diderot, *Lettre sur les aveugles*
           Fielding, *Tom Jones*
1750   Rousseau, *Discours sur les sciences et les arts*
1751–72   The *Encyclopédie*
1753–56   Voltaire, *Essai sur les moeurs*
1754   Condillac, *Traité des sensations*
1755   Rousseau, *Discours sur l'origine de l'inégalité*
           Morelly, *Code de la nature*
1756–63   The Seven Years' War
1756   Voltaire, *Poème sur le désastre de Lisbonne*
           Birth of Mozart (1756–91)
           Burke, *Philosophical Enquiry into the Origin of Our Ideas of the Sublime and Beautiful*
1757   *Encyclopédie* banned by Parlement
1758–70   Ministry of Choiseul
1758   Helvétius, *De l'Esprit*
           Quesnay, *Tableau économique*
1759   Voltaire, *Candide*
           Johnson, *Rasselas*
           Adam Smith, *Theory of Moral Sentiments*
1760   George III, king of England (1760–1820)
           Macpherson publishes Ossian's poems
1761   Greuze, "L'Accordée de village"
           Gainsborough first exhibits in London
           Rousseau, *La Nouvelle Héloïse*
1762   Rousseau, *Le Contrat social* and *Emile*
           Diderot, *Le Neveu de Rameau*
           Catherine the Great, empress of Russia (1762–96)
           Jean Calas, Huguenot, executed at Toulouse
           Glück, *Orfeo*

1764   Voltaire, *Dictionnaire philosophique*
          Stanislaw Poniatowski, king of Poland (1764–95)
          Walpole, *Castle of Otranto*
          Beccaria, *Crimes and Punishments*
          Winckelmann, *History of the Art of Antiquity*
1765   Watt's steam engine
1766   Cavendish discovers hydrogen
1766   Lessing, *Laocoön*
1767   Lessing, *Minna von Barnhelm*
1768   Royal Academy founded in London
1769–74 Ascendancy of Mme. du Barry
          Birth of Napoleon Bonaparte (1769–1821)
1770   d'Holbach, *Système de la nature*
1772   First partition of Poland
          Rutherford describes nitrogen
1774   Death of Louis XV. Louis XVI becomes king of France
          Priestley discovers oxygen
          Goethe, *Sorrows of Werther*
1775–83 American Revolution
1776   American Declaration of Independence
          Adam Smith, *The Wealth of Nations*
          Thomas Paine, *Common Sense*
1777   Franklin in Paris
1778   Lavoisier discredits phlogiston theory
1779   Lessing, *Nathan the Wise*
1781   Kant, *Critique of Pure Reason*
          Rousseau, *Confessions*
1784   Beaumarchais, *Le Mariage de Figaro*
          Cavendish explodes hydrogen and oxygen into water
1785   Kant, *Fundamental Principles of the Metaphysic of Morals*
1787   First Assembly of Notables in France
          Edict of Toleration for Protestants
          Schiller, *Don Carlos*
1788   Regency in England
          Impeachment of Warren Hastings
          Kant, *Critique of Practical Reason*
          Lagrange, *Mécanique analytique*
          Mozart, *Jupiter Symphony*
1789   Estates-General meet in May
          Fall of the Bastille, July 14
          American Constitution inaugurated
          Washington first President
          Abolition of Manorial régime, August 4

Declaration of Rights of Man, August 26
Blake, *Songs of Innocence*
Lavoisier, *Traité élémentaire de chimie*
Galvani and Volta experiment with electricity
1793   Louis XVI guillotined

General Works on the Age of Enlightenment

In English

Cassirer, Ernst. *The Philosophy of the Enlightenment*, Princeton, N.J.: Princeton University Press, 1951.

Crocker, L. G. *An Age of Crisis, Man and World in Eighteenth Century Thought*, Baltimore, Johns Hopkins University Press, 1959.

——. *Nature and Culture. Ethical Thought in the French Enlightenment*, Baltimore, The Johns Hopkins Press, 1963.

Frankel, Charles. *The Faith of Reason.* New York: King's Crown Press, 1948.

Gay, Peter. *The Enlightenment. An Interpretation*, vol. 1, *The Rise of Modern Paganism*, New York: Knopf, 1966.

Havens, George R. *The Age of Ideas*, New York: Holt, 1955.

Hampson, Norman. *A Cultural History of the Enlightenment*, New York: Pantheon Books, 1969.

Martin, Kingsley. *French Liberal Thought in the Eighteenth Century*, 3rd edn., New York: Harper, 1963.

Palmer, R. R. *Catholics and Unbelievers in Eighteenth Century France*, Princeton, N.J.: Princeton University Press, 1939.

Sampson, R. V. *Progress in the Age of Reason*, London: Heinemann, 1956.

In French

Ehrard, Jacques. *L'Idée de nature en France, dans la première moitié du XVIIIᵉ siècle*, Paris: S.E.V.P.E.N., 1963.

Hazard, Paul. *La Crise de la conscience européenne*, 3 vols. Paris: Boivin, 1935.

——. *La Pensée européenne au XVIIIᵉ siècle*, 3 vols. Paris: Boivin, 1946.

Mauzi, Robert. *L'Idée de bonheur au XVIIIᵉ siècle*, Paris: Colin, 1960.

Mornet, Daniel. *La Pensée française au XVIIIᵉ siècle*, Paris: Colin, 1929.

——. *Les origines intellectuelles de la Révolution française*, Paris: Colin, 1933.

Index

DOCUMENTARY HISTORY OF WESTERN CIVILIZATION
Edited by Eugene C. Black and Leonard W. Levy

ANCIENT AND MEDIEVAL HISTORY OF THE WEST

Morton Smith: ANCIENT GREECE

A. H. M. Jones: A HISTORY OF ROME THROUGH THE FIFTH CENTURY
Vol. I: The Republic
Vol. II: The Empire

Deno Geanakoplos: BYZANTINE EMPIRE

Marshall W. Baldwin: CHRISTIANITY THROUGH THE CRUSADES

Bernard Lewis: ISLAM THROUGH SULEIMAN THE MAGNIFICENT

David Herlihy: HISTORY OF FEUDALISM

William M. Bowsky: RISE OF COMMERCE AND TOWNS

David Herlihy: MEDIEVAL CULTURE AND SOCIETY

EARLY MODERN HISTORY

Hanna H. Gray: CULTURAL HISTORY OF THE RENAISSANCE

Florence Edler de Roover: MONEY, BANKING,
AND COMMERCE, THIRTEENTH THROUGH SIXTEENTH CENTURIES

V. J. Parry: THE OTTOMAN EMPIRE

Ralph E. Giesey: EVOLUTION OF THE DYNASTIC STATE

J. H. Parry: THE EUROPEAN RECONNAISSANCE: *Selected Documents*

Hans J. Hillerbrand: THE PROTESTANT REFORMATION

John C. Olin: THE CATHOLIC COUNTER-REFORMATION

Orest Ranum: THE CENTURY OF LOUIS XIV

Thomas Hegarty: RUSSIAN HISTORY THROUGH PETER THE GREAT

Marie Boas Hall: NATURE AND NATURE'S LAWS

Barry E. Supple: HISTORY OF MERCANTILISM

Arthur J. Slavin: IMPERIALISM, WAR, AND DIPLOMACY, 1550-1763

Herbert H. Rowen: THE LOW COUNTRIES

C. A. Macartney: THE HABSBURG AND HOHENZOLLERN DYNASTIES
IN THE SEVENTEENTH AND EIGHTEENTH CENTURIES

Lester G. Crocker: THE AGE OF ENLIGHTENMENT

Robert and Elborg Forster: EUROPEAN SOCIETY IN THE EIGHTEENTH CENTURY